BOURDAIN

ALSO BY LAURIE WOOLEVER

World Travel: An Irreverent Guide
(with Anthony Bourdain, 2021)

Appetites: A Cookbook
(with Anthony Bourdain, 2016)

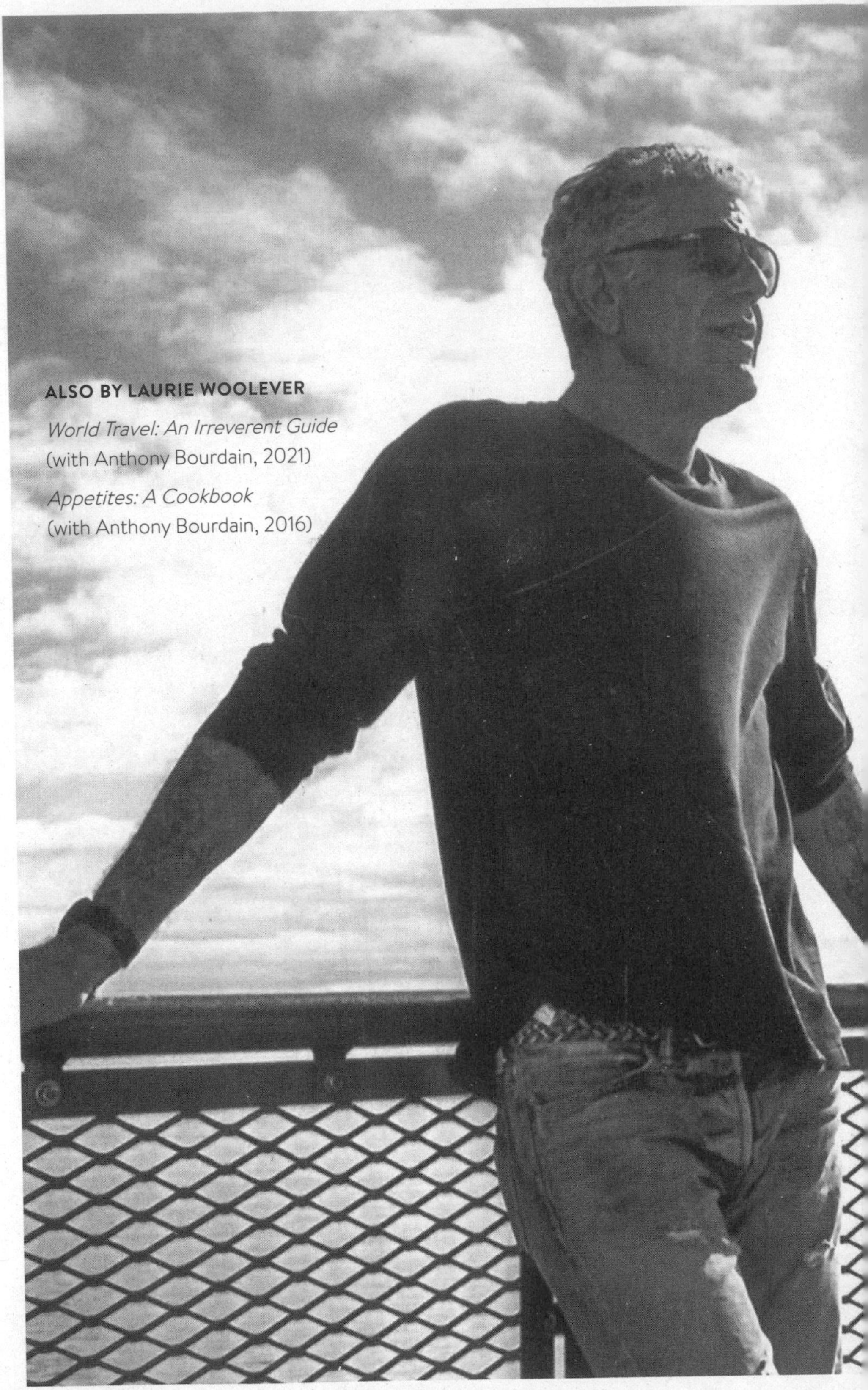

BOURDAIN

THE DEFINITIVE ORAL BIOGRAPHY

LAURIE WOOLEVER

An Imprint of HarperCollinsPublishers

HarperCollins books may be purchased for educational, business, or sales promotional use. For information, please email the Special Markets Department at SPsales@ harpercollins.com.

Ecco® and HarperCollins® are trademarks of HarperCollins Publishers.

Excerpt from Karen Rinaldi's *(It's Great to) Suck at Something* (New York: Atria, 2019) reprinted with permission.

Frontispiece courtesy of CNN.

Epigraph photograph courtesy of Helen Lang.

All other photographs are from the collection of Christopher Bourdain unless otherwise noted.

FIRST EDITION

DESIGNED BY RENATA DE OLIVEIRA

Library of Congress Cataloging-in-Publication Data has been applied for.

ISBN 978-0-06-290910-7

21 22 23 24 25 LSC 10 9 8 7 6 5 4 3 2 1

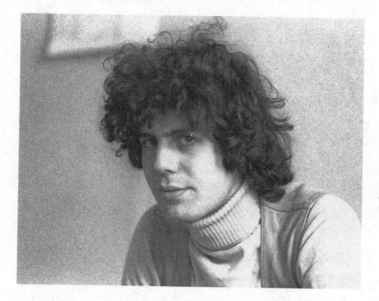

An ounce of sauce covers a multitude of sins.

—ANTHONY BOURDAIN, *KITCHEN CONFIDENTIAL*

CONTENTS

CAST OF CHARACTERS

(IN ORDER OF FIRST APPEARANCE)

Note: Nearly everyone in the list that follows, with the exception of family members and those few with strictly business relationships (such as journalists), considered Tony a friend. Therefore, the designation is reserved here for school friends and those who otherwise had no professional association with him. It is generally understood that Tony befriended his coworkers in the realm of restaurants, television, publishing, and elsewhere. "TV sidekick" refers to those who appeared alongside Tony on his various televised endeavors.

CHRISTOPHER BOURDAIN, brother.

GLADYS BOURDAIN, mother (born 1934, died 2020).

NANCY BOURDAIN, wife (married 1985–2005).

SAM GOLDMAN, childhood friend; kitchen colleague in Provincetown and New York.

JEFF FORMOSA, childhood friend.

HELEN LANG, college friend.

ALEX GETMANOV (A.K.A. "DIMITRI" IN *KITCHEN CONFIDENTIAL*), kitchen colleague in Provincetown and New York.

ROBERT VUOLO, kitchen colleague in New York.

HILLARY SNYDER, kitchen colleague in New York.

JAMES GRAHAM, kitchen colleague in New York.

LENNY MOSSE, kitchen colleague in New York.

JOEL ROSE, frequent writing collaborator.

PATRICK RADDEN KEEFE, writer, profiled Tony for *The New Yorker* ("Anthony Bourdain's Moveable Feast") in 2017.

SCOTT BRYAN, fellow New York chef.

STEVEN TEMPEL, kitchen colleague in New York.

PATTI JACKSON, kitchen colleague in New York.

MATT WALSH, TV fixer and translator.

BETH ARETSKY (A.K.A. "GRILL BITCH"), kitchen colleague in New York; former assistant.

DAVID ROSENTHAL, editor and publisher of *Bone in the Throat* and *Gone Bamboo*.

ROB STONE, would-be writing and publishing partner in the nineties.

WEB STONE, would-be writing and publishing partner in the nineties.

KAREN RINALDI, former editor and publisher at Bloomsbury USA, now at HarperCollins.

PHILIPPE LAJAUNIE, Les Halles restaurant owner; coauthor of *Anthony Bourdain's Les Halles Cookbook*; TV sidekick.

SAM SIFTON, former *New York Press* editor, now a *New York Times* editor.

KIMBERLY WITHERSPOON, longtime literary and business agent.

PANIO GIANOPOULOS, writer; former book editor at Bloomsbury USA.

BILL BUFORD, former *New Yorker* fiction editor; author (*Among the Thugs*, *Heat*, *Dirt*); TV sidekick.

DAVE MCMILLAN, chef-restaurateur; TV sidekick.

FRED MORIN, chef-restaurateur; TV sidekick.

JOSÉ ANDRÉS, chef-restaurateur; TV sidekick; published a book (*We Fed an Island*) through Tony's imprint.

DANIEL HALPERN, poet; Tony's longtime editor and publishing partner at Ecco.

NIGELLA LAWSON, writer and television host in the United Kingdom; costar on *The Taste*.

CHRISTIANE AMANPOUR, CNN reporter and anchor.

ERIC RIPERT, chef-restaurateur; frequent collaborator on various TV, speaking, and publishing endeavors.

MICHAEL RUHLMAN, writer; TV sidekick.

ANDERSON COOPER, CNN anchor.

LYDIA TENAGLIA, cofounder and executive producer of Zero Point Zero Production.

EILEEN OPATUT, former executive VP of programming, Food Network.

CHRIS COLLINS, cofounder and executive producer of Zero Point Zero Production.

PAT YOUNGE, former president, Travel Channel.

MUSTAFA BHAGAT, editor for Zero Point Zero Production.

RENNIK SOHOLT, producer-director for Zero Point Zero Production.

ASHA GILL, former TV host.

MIKE RUFFINO, composer for Zero Point Zero Production; published a book (*Adios, Motherfucker*) through Tony's imprint.

PAULA FROELICH, writer and travel journalist.

OTTAVIA BUSIA-BOURDAIN, wife (married 2007–2018).

DIANE SCHUTZ, producer for Zero Point Zero Production.

TODD LIEBLER, cinematographer for Zero Point Zero Production.

ALEX LOWRY, director for Zero Point Zero Production.

HELEN CHO, producer-director for Zero Point Zero Production.

DAVE CHANG, chef-restaurateur; frequent TV and publishing collaborator.

NATHAN THORNBURGH, editor-writer; partner in *Roads & Kingdoms*.

ADAM EPSTEIN, lecture tour producer.

JOSH HOMME, musician (Queens of the Stone Age, Eagles of Death Metal); TV sidekick.

DEAN FERTITA, musician (Queens of the Stone Age); TV sidekick.

PETER MEEHAN, journalist; TV sidekick; frequent publishing collaborator.

ARIANE BUSIA-BOURDAIN, daughter (born 2007).

TOM VITALE, producer-director for Zero Point Zero Production.

NARI KYE, producer-director for Zero Point Zero Production; co-director of *Wasted!* documentary.

JARED ANDRUKANIS, producer for Zero Point Zero Production.

SALLY FREEMAN, director for Zero Point Zero Production.

JOSH FERRELL, producer for Zero Point Zero Production.

MICHAEL STEED, director for Zero Point Zero Production.

MORGAN FALLON, director-cinematographer for Zero Point Zero Production.

SANDY ZWEIG, series producer for Zero Point Zero Production.

ROY CHOI, chef-restaurateur; TV sidekick; published a book (*L.A. Son*) through Tony's imprint.

NATASHA PHAN, Roy Choi's business partner and coauthor.

BONNIE MCFARLANE, comic; published a book (*You're Better Than Me*) through Tony's imprint.

YEGANEH REZAIAN, journalist; TV sidekick.

JASON REZAIAN, journalist; TV sidekick; published a book (*Prisoner*) through Tony's imprint.

DAVID SIMON, cocreator, *Treme*.

LOLIS ELIE, journalist; writing colleague on *Treme*; TV sidekick.

ERIC OVERMYER, cocreator, *Treme*.

LAURIE BARNETT, lecture agent.

DAVID CHOE, artist; TV sidekick.

MATT GOULDING, editor-writer; partner in *Roads & Kingdoms*.

ALISON MOSSHART, musician (the Kills, the Dead Weather); TV sidekick.

JEFF ALLEN, producer for Zero Point Zero Production.

MARIA BUSTILLOS, journalist ("Bourdain Confidential," on *Popula*, and "Searching for the Real Anthony Bourdain," on *Eater*).

NICK BRIGDEN, director-cinematographer-editor for Zero Point Zero Production.

AMY ENTELIS, executive vice president for talent and content development, CNN Worldwide.

JEFF ZUCKER, president of CNN Worldwide.

LIZZIE FOX, former vice president of CNN Original Series, now senior vice president of nonfiction programming at HBO Max.

SHANT PETROSSIAN, TV producer, formerly at CNN.

ROBIN STANDEFER, production designer, Roman and Williams.

DARREN ARONOFSKY, film director; TV sidekick.

BEN SELKOW, director for Zero Point Zero Production.

WHITNEY WARD, friend.

JOE COLEMAN, artist; TV sidekick.

JOHN LURIE, artist and musician; TV sidekick.

W. KAMAU BELL, CNN colleague, host of *United Shades of America*; TV sidekick.

INTRODUCTION

I met Tony Bourdain in 2002, when he hired me to help with a cookbook he'd just begun writing, in the wake of *Kitchen Confidential*'s life-upending success. We got together in person once or twice during the whole process, conducting most business by email. Toward the end, we had a long sit-down editing session at his apartment, and he handed me a big bonus check.

That was a signature Tony move. He wasn't constantly handing out money, but when he did, it was always a generous amount, beyond what he owed, meant to signify gratitude for a job well done. It indicated an awareness that his luck had recently changed. It also signaled, I think, his desire to be a tide, lifting helpful boats.

Tony wrote a hyperbolic paragraph about me in the book's acknowledgments. This was another signature Tony move: outsize public praise, almost more than one could really live up to, as a sly form of appreciation, which I think was far easier for him than expressing his thanks and admiration face-to-face.

Anthony Bourdain's Les Halles Cookbook was published in 2004, Tony's television career really took off, and I went to work as a magazine editor.

In 2007, he hired me to pinch-hit at a cooking and speaking gig in Montana, as his assistant was then pregnant and unavailable to travel. Tony was newly married with a six-month-old baby at home, full of optimism and ecstatic about the unexpected turn his life had taken. We prepared a lavish dinner at the home of the local college football coach, using the Les Halles cookbook for our menu. I remember how happy he was to make a super-rich lobster bisque, using double the usual number of lobsters, which, he said conspiratorially, wasn't something you could get away with in a restaurant and still expect to stay within the food-cost margins.

A few years later, I had a baby and was looking for a flexible part-time job. I emailed a few dozen people, just kind of putting it out there, and one of them was Tony. He wrote back right away—another signature Tony move.

He said, "My assistant's leaving; would you want that job? Here's what it entails. What would it cost?"

I suggested what I thought was a reasonable number, and he actually raised it a bit. I started working for him then, and in some ways, I haven't yet stopped.

Tony's unexpected death in June 2018 meant the end of anything new from him; all that he had ever written, drawn, recorded, or filmed in the world was done, a complete body of work.

Tony's death also marked the beginning of a yearslong process of discovery, in which I interviewed ninety-one people who'd known him, to hear their stories and learn more about him than what he'd already shared in the pages of *Kitchen Confidential*, his subsequent works of nonfiction, and on television. This book is the result of that process.

As his assistant and occasional coauthor, I thought I'd already gotten to know Tony quite well. I knew where he was nearly every minute of every day, whom he was with, what he was planning to do, and why. I was steeped in his work, deeply familiar with his voice and all the beats of his highly public origin story. However, in talking with the people who knew him in his youth, as a wayward college student, fledgling cook, dedicated beach bum, thrill-seeking drug addict, journeyman chef, ambitious young writer, semireluctant television star, steadfast spouse and father, supportive friend and collaborator, I came to realize that I'd really known only a fraction of who Tony was, what motivated him, his ambivalence, his vulnerability, his blind spots, and his brilliance.

Need it be said that memory is fallible? That two or more people may remember the same event in very different ways? That we're each always the protagonist of our own stories, even when those stories are centered on an extremely charismatic and well-known public figure?

In reading this book, you'll come across the occasional contradiction, the varying recollection or interpretation of events between two or more parties, and this calls to mind Tony's own well-known habit of sometimes sanding down or finely sharpening the edges of an anecdote, in order to make it a highly repeatable story.

Though filled with words of love, admiration, respect, and gratitude, this book is not a hagiography. Tony was extraordinary, but mortal. He did great things, and made a lot of people very happy, and he made some bad choices, and he hurt some people. As he insisted in the introduction to our 2016 cookbook, *Appetites*, again with a touch of that characteristic hyperbole, "I am a monster of self-regard."

I would guess that it's hard *not* to be vain, when one is constantly the center of attention, at work and at rest. At times, it seemed that Tony's responses and contributions were the barometer in every conversation, at every meeting, wherever he went. Well-meaning people would approach him on what they assumed was his level, making crass jokes they hoped he'd find funny, or otherwise parroting their interpretation of his oratory back at him.

As he said to his friend Patti Jackson, once he became famous, "You'll never know the consequences of getting what you want until you get what you want."

When I agreed to be Tony's assistant, I'd been juggling "real" writing and paycheck-type work for many years, and there were times when I grew frustrated with the more mundane aspects of the job, especially as I aged out of the socially acceptable range for such endeavors. But: if I was going to do the work, I knew there was no one better than Tony to do it for.

And I now feel compelled to add that I'd gladly trade this life of being a "real writer" to resume the privileged burden of making his hotel reservations and scheduling his dishwasher maintenance, if it meant that Tony could still be here among us. Barring that, I'll settle for having helped the people he loved tell the following version of his story.

—LW

BOURDAIN

1

"I ABSOLUTELY ALWAYS SAW A TALENT IN HIM"

EARLY LIFE

CHRISTOPHER BOURDAIN, BROTHER: Our parents were very politically aware. Our dad [Pierre Bourdain; born 1930, died 1987] went to an amazingly globalist school, the Birch Wathen School, when he was a kid, in Manhattan. It was founded by these two very progressive individuals who were all into the obligation of the citizenry to be informed in a proper democracy. Our dad spoke French with his parents, at home, growing up.

And our mother [Gladys Bourdain; born 1934, died 2020] grew up in a very middle-class Jewish neighborhood in the Bronx, surrounded by a lot of very progressive and hypereducated people.

When we were kids, we did not know that our mother was Jewish. I mean, in the fifties, if you were Jewish and came from New

York City and you wanted to live in a proper suburb, there was a lot of prejudice and redlining, and you were not welcome in a lot of places. So, I know other people whose parents also kind of glossed over the fact they were Jewish to real estate agents, or changed their name to something more WASPy sounding, so that it wouldn't cause any questions when they were moving out of the city. I know plenty of people who went that route, but then, once they got their house and were all settled, they asked, "Where is a synagogue near here? Let's go."

Our mom buried it completely. She swore our dad to secrecy. She swore old friends, who might have known her when, to secrecy. Her maiden name was Sacksman, but she told us, growing up, that it was *Saxon*, like "Anglo-Saxon." I would see her filling out applications for shit, and she would type in her typewriter, S-A-X-O-N, Saxon. She never wanted to talk about it, ever. I don't think Tony and I found out until late in high school. We found some piece of paper that had her maiden name spelled the way it actually was spelled. One of us said, "That sounds kind of Jewish. Was your family Jewish?" And she went blank and said, "No, no, of course not," or maybe, "No comment."

And just to give you an idea of how absurd it got, our parents had a wedding picture up on their dresser in the bedroom that we grew up seeing, this wedding photo. It was just always there, and after they separated, my mom lived alone, she still had that photo around.

So, our mom died in January 2020, and I'm digging through all her old papers, and bugger all, I did not know that that photo we'd seen our entire lives, which looked like a happy couple standing on the steps of a church, it was the steps of a synagogue, on the Grand Concourse. I did not find that out until after she'd died.

It was about wanting to fit in with the "right people." Our mom created a whole thing. First off, she's marrying this up-and-coming, dashing French American who seemed to be going someplace, and was working in the classical records business, and loved opera just like her, and actually took her to the opera, which her parents never did. She was going places, and she had, now, a French last name, Bourdain, so she could bury anything that spoke of a less-distinguished upbringing in a Jewish neighborhood in the Bronx.

We also were never quite told that she grew up in the Bronx. She always said, "I grew up on the Upper West Side." Not really. From what I can tell, she was actually born in her parents' apartment in the west seventies, but after her brother died—she had an older brother who died when she was about four years old—her parents apparently couldn't stand being around that place anymore, so they moved to University Heights, which was a perfectly middle-class Jewish neighborhood in those days. There are a lot of famous Jewish New Yorkers who come from that area—but I don't think we found out until well into high school or college that she spent part of her childhood in the Bronx.

She also told us, "I went to Hunter College for two years." Now, we all know a Hunter College on Lexington Avenue in the sixties [in Manhattan], so I always assumed it was that, and she never said anything to refute that. I found out, only many years later, that what's now Lehman College in the Bronx, it used to be called Hunter College in the Bronx. So she went to Hunter College near where she lived; she walked there.

She really loved both her parents, especially her mom, and she would always say that they were very close. They died when she was pregnant with Tony, both of them. She had the theory that because Tony always seemed somehow anxious, always had a sort of dark view of things, she blamed it on the fact that she had that double tragedy when she was pregnant with him.

The only grandparent we ever knew was our father's mother,

who was old and infirm when we knew her. We would go visit her, near Columbia University, on Sundays. She had very bad arthritis and could barely move, so she would sit there on the couch and our dad would chat with her. I can't remember a single conversation I had with this woman.

Our parents were both very into film, including foreign films. We had books about Fellini, and Bergman, and Truffaut, and Kurosawa sitting around in the living room. We all read them. We all watched the occasional Bergman rerun week on channel eleven, and Japanese films.

They were both totally plugged into politics. They were anti-McCarthyism, and they were pro–civil rights, they were anti–Vietnam War, they were pro rights of workers, all those things. Not in a flaming radical way, more just what's fair, and what's just.

That was the backdrop we grew up in. That was the backdrop Tony was a young adult in, and I think you can certainly see in his shows, where he would go to troubled spots, places that had had a civil war of some kind, earthquakes and famine—he was just continuing to inform himself, and us, about all of these things that we kind of grew up hearing about.

Our parents had their friends who, of course, had the same views, and they'd all be grumbling, "Oh, can you believe Nixon?" or whatever, the same way we all do now. We would certainly talk about Vietnam. And we still had the draft. I remember Tony was definitely worried.

We went to public school in Leonia, New Jersey, to grammar school. Some kid was verbally and emotionally tormenting Tony in his early grade school years. I don't know all the details, but he was just a mean bastard. And also, Tony was way ahead of the class. He was reading fifth- and sixth-grade stuff in second grade, and he was bored to tears. And then he had this kid tormenting him.

I'm not sure the order of events, but some of the teachers at the public school said to our parents, "You know what, if you have a chance, there's the private school in the next town, and we think Tony would do better there."

Around that same time, our grandmother did us the economic favor of dying. She left our dad a bunch of money, and so they thought they could afford private school for a long time, and they sent Tony, starting in fifth grade. And they sent me the following year.

GLADYS BOURDAIN (1934–2020), MOTHER: Tony always had a fabulous vocabulary, and he read early. I absolutely always saw a talent in him, for writing. In fact, when he was in second grade, his teacher recommended that we send him to private school, because while all the other kids were *learning* to read, he was in the corner, reading a book. Part of the reason he got into the private school was that he did a long composition about some French voyager who discovered the western part of France. I forget the name.

He was a wonderful writer, always. When he was, I think, nine, he wrote a long composition about his younger brother, which was quite fabulous, and I wish to hell I still had it.

And he was a gifted illustrator. He actually won prizes at school for some of the art that he did. I remember one particular thing— each child in his class was given a large piece of drawing paper with the first letter of his or her last name. And so, his was a *B*, a vertical *B*, and whereas everyone else took that letter and tried to make a picture out of it, he turned the picture sideways, and that *B* became a pair of ski goggles and he drew the person and the skis and everything.

My husband came from a French family, and so we stayed with my husband's aunt and uncle in the southwest of France for a while, and one of their neighbors was an oyster fisherman. We went out on the boat with them one day . . . oysters were very precious, but they gave their foreign visitors, us, a taste of oysters. I remember hating mine—I hate raw things like that—but Tony was just delighted with it. Tony always said that his first taste of vichyssoise, and then the oyster, sort of changed his life.

CHRISTOPHER BOURDAIN: Our parents never had enough money, really. Our dad inherited a bunch of money when his mother died. She was one of these people who saved every penny for forty years, so she had a decent amount. We had two wonderful trips to France. We bought a ridiculously goofy British car while in France and had it shipped back to New Jersey. We were sent to private school. But, actually, our parents kind of ran out of money after three or four years, and then were struggling for the next, well, *forever*, to pay for private school. I honestly don't know how they did it. Once in a while, bill collectors would show up, or there would be obvious things in the mail, that bills had been unpaid. But, meanwhile, they kept it all looking OK, you know; they never let on.

2

"SUPER SMART, SUPER FUNNY"

THE TEENAGE YEARS

CHRISTOPHER BOURDAIN: Tony and I really just didn't hang out together as teenagers. We were into very different things. He hung out with a mostly older pack of friends, so already in ninth grade, he was in with friends in eleventh, twelfth grade, and he was gone a lot. But we got along well, and I think we always had, in our house, especially my dad and Tony and me, we had a very similar sense of humor. We were very much into the foibles and weaknesses of society, and people in general. And we respected each other, I think.

We were a typical sixties household, you know: Dad went to work every day on the bus, Mom cooked dinner. Our mom, being a well-read person, very into culture, and who had married a guy whose mom was French, she was very interested in learning French cooking, and trying to impress with her French cooking. And it was right around that time, of course, when Julia Child first came along, and like so many women in this country, our mom got fully on board.

When we had guests, she'd break out the Julia Child cookbook and make some nice stuff. I would have said, "Oh, Mom's a good cook," but what she was missing was, she had no spontaneity at all. It was formulaic. She could follow a recipe well, but she had no creativity. If you just gave her some ingredients and said, "Make a nice thing," I think she would have fallen apart. She'd have no idea.

Our dad got into the game when we were teenagers, because our mom, I think, was just starting to get tired of being the housewife doing all the cooking. It was around the time when Chinese cookbooks started showing up, and Szechuan food appeared. When we were really young, the only kind of Chinese food you could have was Cantonese, and then suddenly Szechuan food became the rage, in the seventies. We were one of the first families we knew with a wok. Our dad got the book *An Encyclopedia of Chinese Food and Cooking*; it was one of the early biggies.

NANCY BOURDAIN, WIFE (1985–2005): When did I meet Tony? I don't really remember. We did go to high school together. Back then, it was the Englewood School for Boys and the Dwight School for Girls. Everybody knew each other. Of course, I was in love, like you are in high school, with somebody else.

SAM GOLDMAN, FRIEND: Nancy and I were high school sweethearts.

JEFF FORMOSA, FRIEND: I met Tony in 1969, at the Englewood School for Boys, and we became fast friends. When I first met him, he was little; he was a shrimp.

SAM GOLDMAN: He was tiny. He and [his brother] Chris, they were little kids, and then they had growing spurts. I remember we used to jam him up in the luggage racks of long-distance buses, because he was that small.

NANCY BOURDAIN: He was shorter than I was. I think I must have been fifteen, so he must have been fourteen. He was a little kid, and he could tuck and roll really well. But he was very funny. And we had this big wall in the soccer field, and he would tell upperclassmen, "I'll go jump. I'll fall off that wall for a couple of bucks." He would get money for falling off a wall. One summer, he completely grew. It was incredible, like a kitten or something, you know?

SAM GOLDMAN: He was super smart, super funny. He was new to the school, and he needed to get into a clique, so he weaseled his way into ours, which wasn't very hard. We were New Jersey teenagers; we never really went anywhere, but we drove around and smoked hash and hung out and ate.

JEFF FORMOSA: We were inseparable. We'd ride bicycles behind my house, in front of his house. His mom would drive us to Bruce Lee movies. Gladys had a very good nose, and she always knew what we were up to.

CHRISTOPHER BOURDAIN: I did wonder for a time, *Why does Tony always seem to be in trouble?* I was aware that he was using some drugs. I didn't know to what extent. I mean, nobody had a major problem, even then, with weed. I think he was trying just about anything and everything that came along in those days.

GLADYS BOURDAIN: He was a difficult teenager, not a great student. He wasn't the kind of teenager who ran away. He just wanted to be everywhere, but he was home for dinner every night. When Woodstock happened, I know he wished he could be there, but he wasn't. He was too young. I think he must have been fourteen.

CHRISTOPHER BOURDAIN: There was a lot of conflict between Tony and our parents, especially our mom. Our dad hated conflict, and he usually ran from arguments, because he just wanted everybody to be happy, like, "Why can't we all just get along, and listen to our music, and have a nice meal?"

Our mom was always more argumentative and frustrated with her lot in life. When people weren't doing what she thought was right, she would initiate arguments. Tony was into a lot of stuff that she disliked. I mean, he was into drugs, and he was hanging out with the "wrong" people. He wasn't doing terrible things, but he wasn't doing as well as she would have liked, and he seemed to disrespect the system. So they argued a lot.

Sometimes our mom would sort of drag our dad to the table, so he'd sit there and do the bobblehead thing and say, "Yes, dear. Tony, listen to what your mother's saying." He would be kind of forced uncomfortably to sit in the same room, and to agree with my mom. But I don't even know if he did, honestly.

JEFF FORMOSA: You know, Tony's speech, it all came from comic books. And it was infectious the way he spoke, his attitude. At school, you didn't get your ass kicked, you'd "eat shoe."

That was his talent: he made everything sound better than it really was. He made you want to be there. When we hung out at each other's houses, Tony would sit around and draw. I'd play the drums. We'd listen to music, try to get drugs, whatever we could get our hands on. A friend came back from boarding school and we took our first hit of acid and went to a swimming party.

Tony had an endless stream of records, from when his dad worked in the music business. His dad is where he got his zaniness from. His mom is where he got his sneer.

CHRISTOPHER BOURDAIN: Our dad was never particularly career successful. He lost his job several times, in our childhood and teenage years. I never really quite got the story there, but I suspect he was so not into corporate politics and weaseling your way up the corporate ladder. He just liked his classical music, and he liked reading biographies and history books, and knowing immense amounts of interesting shit, and never ever wanted to kowtow.

The only two big company jobs he had, one was at a company that's no longer around, called London Records. And he worked at Columbia Records, which later became CBS Records, and then later Sony Music. But he worked at a record store, and he worked at a stereo store, and was unemployed for quite long periods, and didn't seem to feel a burning urgency. So we never had the money that those around us had.

It was compounded, optically, by the fact that we were going to this private school, and were surrounded with people so much wealthier than us. Several of them had a second house somewhere. They would go to Florida on spring vacation; they would go to Europe a lot. I mean, we had been super lucky and had gone there as kids twice, but, you know, these other families got to travel a lot.

In the brief couple of years where they had money, our parents did a huge house upgrade, a really nice kitchen, two nice new bathrooms upstairs. They turned the attic into a master bedroom suite. So they got that done, but then they kind of ran out of money, and the front hall, where all our guests came into the house, was never finished. It had this chandelier, but they had never quite hooked the wires up right, so it had this dangling-wire thing. And the steps were unfinished wood that had been painted years and years before—black, scuffed wooden steps with a broken banister. That was what our guests saw, you know, coming into the house, and then you turned left, and you saw this really nice, brand-new kitchen. It was weird.

They both spent stupid money they didn't have. And honestly, I think she was worse at it than him, but he was no good. Five thousand dollars would come into their hands, and somehow they would spend ten. *We have money for one nice vacation, so let's take two.* They would be going out to the opera and dinner, when my school was saying, "You're four months late with the tuition."

That was our story, and I'm sure Tony felt that to a degree. I know I felt it a lot. I don't think Tony ever had the delightful experience, at age fourteen, of opening the door after school, and there was a debt collector, delivering some collection notice related to my orthodontist. I don't know how conscious Tony was of the gory details like that. He knew there was a sham going on, and that they never had as much money as they portrayed. But I don't know if he ever got down in the weeds that way.

If you lived in a suburb in those days, you could knock on people's doors and offer to mow their lawn, you know, for a dollar. Tony did a paper route, mowed some lawns, babysat for people around the block, people who knew us. And then he got this job as a bicycle messenger in Manhattan.

Back then, advertising agencies on Madison Avenue had cans of film that needed to be physically developed, in a vat of chemicals somewhere, usually over near Twelfth Avenue or in Tribeca. So there were all of these messengers bringing stuff around Manhattan on bicycles—legal documents, film for the ad agencies, and it paid well, and you'd have these crazy kids like Tony, who was seventeen, bicycling around Midtown traffic in the middle of the day, trying to rush a can of film from Madison Avenue to Twelfth Avenue. And he would tell these stories of grabbing on to the back of a bus, kind of getting a ride for a few blocks, stuff that would completely freak our mom out.

SAM GOLDMAN: I was at Boston University; Nancy and Tony were still back in high school. Jeff [Formosa] called me and said, "I got bad news for you: your best girl and your best friend are—" and I just started laughing, because I was in bed with [another girl] at the time, so I got over that really fast. It never was a thing with Tony.

NANCY BOURDAIN: We did start dating in high school. I look back and I think, none of us had it that bad, OK? None of us kids had it bad. But, of course, it was, "We gotta get out of this place." In your senior year, once you had the [college acceptance] letter, you could take your last trimester off, if you learned something. So that was Tony's thing. Like, "I just want to get out of here, too."

CHRISTOPHER BOURDAIN: Tony graduated from high school one year earlier than normal. He took some summer classes, managed to scrape up enough credits, got himself out after eleventh grade. And mainly the agenda was, he wanted to be with Nancy, who had gone to Vassar, so he went to Vassar.

SAM GOLDMAN: Tony was a couple of years behind me, but somehow, he managed to graduate from prep school a year early. I think they wanted to get rid of him.

CHRISTOPHER BOURDAIN: The French trips, the childhood trips, those are the ones Tony mostly talked about; he would have been ten and then eleven, and I was seven and eight. But I think, for both of us, the more memorable trip was the one we did in 1973, after our father's aunt died and did the unfortunate favor of leaving her house to our family. Our parents realized pretty quick they had to sell it. The inheritance tax in those days was 65 percent of the estate. They had to get it ready for sale, so Tony and my mom and I went over for pretty much the entire summer. I was thirteen or fourteen, and Tony therefore would have been seventeen.

We would occasionally dodge out and do stuff together. We got into a couple of the same books. We didn't have a big supply, and once you ran out of your English-language books, you couldn't find many around in this place. We had brought this big, fat book, which I still have at home, *The Complete Sherlock Holmes*, and we both read it. And we were doing work, we were painting the house, and we put in a full indoor bathroom, just to get it ready to sell.

And it was also memorable, because I think it was the first time we realized—we were alone with our mom for six weeks, and Tony was at the peak of his "I want out of here" phase, and our mom was heading into her "I'm unhappy with my life" years, and so she was acting out a lot that summer, and would get mad about wacky stuff. It was the first time when Tony and I realized, *Oh my god, there is something wrong with this woman. I mean, she is really, really unhappy, and she's maybe gonna go off the deep end.*

It was really the first time that we'd seen it in such intense doses, at close hand, because we were all together, all day for six weeks, for the first time in a long time. And we would talk with each other, out of hearing from her, and we were not particularly kind with some of the things we said that summer.

We were very happy when our dad finally showed up, and we could start to get a little pressure relieved, and do some fun things as a family.

Our dad was the type of person, he wasn't a saint, but he was the type of person who liked quirky people. He liked people who had something unusual about them, and he liked people who were into unusual things. He had a couple of friends—one of them was a guy who worked for a very high-end loudspeaker company, and the guy collected fire engines. He lived in Katonah, New York, and he had a big property, and he always had three or four fire engines, just sitting around on his lawn, and fire engine parts, and firehouse equipment on shelves in the house. Dad loved people like that. It was like, *Whatever you're into, as long as you're into something.*

He was just a very special man. I had the constant impression that somehow our dad knew everything about everything. He just knew so much, but he was never in your face about it, he was never show-offy, ever. I was into trains for a while, and Tony was really, really into art and drawing, growing up, and took a lot of art classes, and our dad loved that.

He had a hysterical sense of humor. Tony's sense of humor came from our dad, but got sharper. Our dad never had a nasty edge to his sense of humor; it was always satiric, spoofing, but gentle. He was just *nice*. He never hurt anybody, he was never mean to anybody. And we just thought he was great. He was never a particular success, never made a lot of money, but we really just loved him a lot.

And our mom was much more the other way. She didn't like quirky and odd, and didn't like most friends of our dad's, and she was much more judgmental, and always made very, very clear what her judgment was. Just very, very different personalities. I mean, they loved a lot of the same things, they loved movies, they loved music, they loved kind of the same kinds of restaurants, they loved travel, so many things in common, but then they had this fundamental difference in life attitude, and approaching disagreements.

3

"A LOT OF FUN TO BE AROUND"

YOUNG ADULTHOOD

GLADYS BOURDAIN: I certainly hoped that Tony would go through college and graduate, and have some sort of degree, and proceed from there.

HELEN LANG, FRIEND: I met Tony in 1973, at Vassar. He was a very striking person, his height, and his whole demeanor. He was firmly ensconced in the bad-boy persona. There were a lot of drugs at Vassar; when I was a freshman, Vassar made the front page of the *New York Times* for the number of quaaludes available on campus. I was in that whole drug scene, and Tony was obviously drawn to that as well. We hit it off immediately; we became fast friends, drinking buddies, drugging buddies, et cetera. He had a wicked sense of humor and was a lot of fun to be around.

NANCY BOURDAIN: Tony always seemed to make friends pretty easily. Back at school, a lot of people I got friendly with, I knew through Tony, like Gordon [Howard] and Helen Lang.

HELEN LANG: I was pretty good friends with Nancy. There was a fourth person whom I became involved with later on, Gordon Howard; he and Tony were really close.*

NANCY BOURDAIN: Tony was really bad at Vassar. He didn't work. [He did] terrible things that even I, who had no shame basically, would be embarrassed [of]. He'd be hungry in the middle of the night, after a night of drinking or after taking drugs, and he would show up with a couple of eggs and a fresh green pepper. He'd just go into somebody else's—they had these town houses and tourist apartments; nobody locked their door—he'd just go rob somebody else's refrigerator. And I didn't realize. You can be willfully blind for only so long. I felt bad about it, but I ate the eggs. I cooked 'em. I was complicit. We had a lot of fun.

HELEN LANG: As far as Tony was concerned, there were no boundaries. At that time, there was a lot of sexual freedom. Everybody whom I knew at the time had multiple partners, and we were all very casual. Very casual drug use, especially the major drugs that we used to do, which were LSD and quaaludes and cocaine.

We would break into the gym at night and go skinny-dipping in the pool. We were just having a good time. We didn't do anything seriously criminal, with the exception of breaking every drug law on the books. But other than that, we were pretty well behaved.

---

* *Gordon Howard, now deceased, would, more than two decades later, become Tony's de facto first literary agent.*

I mean, Tony was somebody whom I considered 100 percent trustworthy. He would never betray a friend. He would never hurt another person. He had a very keen sense of right and wrong, in the way that matters. Not, *Oh, I can't break that rule*, but *Be a decent human being*. I never saw him hurt anyone with his words or his actions. He could be very cutting, but he would never pick on someone who was vulnerable.

GLADYS BOURDAIN: He and a group of his friends, including his then girlfriend [Nancy], went to Provincetown for a summer and they all found jobs. And he was a dishwasher and decided he liked it.

NANCY BOURDAIN: My sister was going to Cape Cod for the summer with a friend of hers. [My parents] were going to send me there to straighten me up. They sent me to Provincetown. Tony came up to visit us and, I'll be honest, he wasn't looking for a job, but we had a wonderful roommate who said, "You can't keep staying here and not contribute. We all work, you know. You gotta do something." He started dishwashing, I think, at the Flagship.

ALEX GETMANOV, CHEF (IDENTIFIED IN *KITCHEN CONFIDENTIAL* AS "DIMITRI"): Siro, of Siro's Italian restaurant fame (or infamy), in Provincetown, for whom I had worked for a lot of years by then—he bought a place across the street, called the Flagship ["The Dreadnaught" in *Kitchen Confidential*], which was a steak, chop, and fried seafood place. Tony, this brash and somewhat shy, tall, skinny drink of water shows up in our kitchen and wants a job.

He didn't impress, in the beginning. He didn't know anything, and he had this attitude that he could do anything, which doesn't get you far in a working kitchen. But we hired him. He resented our attitude toward him so much that he claimed that's why he went to the Culinary Institute of America [CIA]: he was gonna show us.

What a salesman! Oh my god, he could sell snow to the Eskimos. Getting waiters to push a special, or talking his way into catering gigs in Provincetown.

The second year he was in Provincetown, we started this silly little catering company called Moonlight Menus, because we were moonlighting on Siro, and we were using his kitchens for the prep, and maybe a very few of his ingredients. We were drugged out, crazed, drunk. Siro gave an annual garden party for charity. Tony and I catered it together, and that was really an insanity.

We spent eighteen hours, with hardly a break, in the basement of the Flagship. Certain people who shall remain nameless came in and charitably fed us large quantities of white powders of the cocaine type. Somewhere in the wee hours, we just couldn't deal with it anymore, and mostly it was done, so we crawled off onto a couple of banquettes in the back. The next morning, somebody came in and found us passed out, covered with flies, because we were all sticky with aspic.

We bit off a lot more than we could chew, but we usually came through. We catered a number of staff parties for different establishments in town, and one absolutely disastrous wedding in a bar and restaurant. They wanted a steamship roast. We'd never done anything of that sort before. Tony talked to a couple of people, and I talked to a few people, and everybody said something different. So we had this forty- to fifty-pound leg of beef, and we cooked it to death. Then we had a fight afterward about who was gonna be out there in the monkey suit, carving, and we settled it that I would do the first half, and he would do the second half. And the working line for the victims was, "Oh, I'm sorry, sir, we haven't gotten to the rare portion yet," and then when Tony came on it was, "Oh, you just missed it."

There was a lot of food left over. The wife of the owner of the restaurant was like a vulture over it; she scooped it all up, and then they sold it the next day. It's a rotten business.

NANCY BOURDAIN: We had a lot of family meals. But when I look back—'cause I'm a pretty good cook now—I was not even a *commis*; I was the prep girl. I cleaned the pots, I did all the chopping, and soup making. I'd say, "What about the fish or the meat?" He'd say, "Oh, I don't want you to screw it up. That's the really important thing." It's kind of the easiest part, but I didn't find that out till later.

GLADYS BOURDAIN: At the end of the summer, I think it was me who suggested that since he wasn't showing any interest in college, and he did seem to be interested in that summer's work, I said, "Why don't you think about continuing on this path?"

CHRISTOPHER BOURDAIN: I don't know who chose to pull the plug on Vassar. I mean, Tony had never done particularly well there in his own right. He had gotten As on a lot of people's papers that he had ghostwritten for them, but never did particularly well with his own grades, as far as I heard from my parents. One time we went to pick him up. We were driving home, and we stopped for dinner at a restaurant on Route 22, somewhere near Patterson, New York. I still remember that night of screaming argument at the table. My parents were saying, "Why are we spending all this money, and you're wasting it?!"

GLADYS BOURDAIN: Thanks to a friend of mine whose father was the co-owner of '21' Club, Tony was able to get ahead of some on the waiting list for the Culinary Institute [of America], and managed to get in.

NANCY BOURDAIN: He was [at Vassar] for about two years. I wasn't really disappointed when he left, because he clearly didn't want to be there, and he was going to CIA. He kind of buckled down. He'd said that this was something that he wanted to do. Before that, I think Tony always wanted to be a writer. I know he did, so I was surprised how serious he was about the cooking.

SAM GOLDMAN: Tony was at CIA; I was twenty-four, and I was executive chef at a restaurant in New York. I made him my weekend omelet guy; he used to come down from CIA and make omelets. He was notorious for leaving the kitchen a complete fucking mess.

CHRISTOPHER BOURDAIN: I attended Tony's graduation from the CIA. The capstone of it was a dinner where the graduating class had made a very formal, French-style high-end dinner, and not only were they cooking, but they were also serving it to the guests. I can't remember what we ate, but I remember the room. They had it all decked out with nice drapes and flags and stuff, and made a very nice show of it.

I think Tony was pleased to show off a little bit, because he hadn't been given that many opportunities in high school to show off about anything, and our parents always had some criticism of things he was doing or should have been doing. I definitely think he was proud. I think he was pretty happy about it right then.

"IT WAS WHAT THE COOL KIDS WERE DOING"

THE EARLY NEW YORK YEARS

CHRISTOPHER BOURDAIN: Tony and Nancy lived together in her sister's apartment on Riverside Drive at first, a two-bedroom apartment. And then, later, around 1979, they got their own apartment in that same building, which was a great location—near the subway, near Columbia, with affordable, student-oriented dining available up the street, because obviously, they didn't have boatloads of money. They had a super view of the Hudson River.

Those first couple of years, we couldn't see Tony that often, but we enjoyed seeing them at Easter, because they always had an Easter brunch at their place. And that's when Nancy's parents would come over, and they'd have this elaborate pretext that Tony was living elsewhere, because they were not married, and she was a proper

Roman Catholic. They eventually got married in September 1985, if I remember right, in one of the chapels at Saint Patrick's Cathedral [in Manhattan], which is pretty funny, because—I mean, I got married in a church, too, but Tony and I were lifelong atheists and skeptics, and somehow we both ended up getting married in churches. They had a reception on the Upper East Side, which was not huge, but it was nice. And then they could finally actually live together, as far as Nancy's parents were concerned. It gave them legitimacy, so they didn't have to play that stupid game anymore.

And we'd see them at Christmas, sometimes. Tony and I had separated parents at that point, so Christmas in the early eighties was already getting complicated.

Our parents separated probably around 1979, 1980-ish, and then, a couple of years later, our dad moved in with another woman, and I think was perfectly happy. She was nice to him. Our mom had been kind of mean to him the last couple of years, and so I think he was very happy to be with somebody who was nice to him.

It was fun being with Tony and Nancy. In those days, Tony liked talking about the Kennedy assassination. Probably, to this day, he was one of the foremost scholars in the United States on the Kennedy assassination. Unheralded and unhailed, or whatever, but I think he knew more about it than many. And he was very into anything to do with double agents, between the Soviet Union and the United States, and turned agents from MI6, and things like that. He knew all their stories. My wife was a Russian studies major in college, so he found a ready audience, and she was, to a degree, interested in hearing him expound on this. He knew so damn much. He was always reading.

SAM GOLDMAN: When he finished CIA, I got another executive job [at WPA, in New York], and I was in way over my head. I brought Tony and Alex on board, and they basically made me look really good.

JEFF FORMOSA: When he was cooking at WPA, he talked about wanting to do a TV show, with chefs sitting around in the kitchen, talking about food, telling their stories. He was always thinking about that stuff.

SAM GOLDMAN: We really thought we were hotshots, and it turns out we were horrible and had no understanding of the business end of the restaurant business. We were just young and dumb, you know?

ROBERT VUOLO, KITCHEN COLLEAGUE: I met Tony and Alex and Sam at WPA. These guys, they became my mentors, took me under their wings. I was nineteen. Tony was only four years older than me, but four years, at that age, was significant. I was the kid. They taught me how to cook, and I became part of their social circle as well. They took me to my first sushi dinner ever, at a place called Chin-Ya.

SAM GOLDMAN: Tony came back from a trip to France in the winter of 1979 or 1980, and we're sitting around—me, him, and Alex—and Tony goes, "You won't fucking believe it; over there, chefs are like athletes, rock stars." And then he made us each cough up $200 and have these amazing photographs done. In that particular moment, he was a visionary.

HELEN LANG: He told me, "Come over to WPA and I'll make you something to eat." I rode my bicycle over there; it was this little restaurant, and the kitchen was in the basement, so I went through those doors that they have in New York that lead to the basement from the outside. He was so happy to see me. He put a napkin down on one of the stools in the kitchen, and he made me a filet mignon with truffles.

ROBERT VUOLO: There was a certain amount of cocaine and marijuana, and to some degree, heroin. Heroin is not altogether compatible for working the line; it's an after-hours drug—but cocaine, absolutely. There was an enormous amount of cocaine that got used, and none of us were thinking about any long-term health issues that might arise from it. And marijuana was like an endless— There was a shaft-way that you could stand in at the base of the steps at WPA; you could look up to the sky but it was completely enclosed, and cooks could go in there at night and smoke marijuana, completely unseen by anyone inside the kitchen area, so that upped the dramatics of being able to do this in plain sight.

ALEX GETMANOV: In early eighties New York, Tony and Sam [Goldman] and I did a lot of bad things together. Freebase—the three of us would kill an ounce of coke in a weekend, and drank I don't know how many quarts of Rémy or Martell, just to taper down, and eat a bunch of valium.

SAM GOLDMAN: Everything that Tony said about what he learned as a dishwasher was true. He was a show-up guy. He wasn't a genius cook. Like myself, he was a proficient mechanical cook. He knew the drill. It didn't matter if we were fucked up on acid. I remember after this one weekend at WPA, we woke up Monday morning like, "What happened the last few days?" It turns out that we had been really busy and we'd done a good job. That was being a chef in those days, with that flavor of recreational drugs: as long as you showed up and did the job, nobody fucking cared.

I remember driving around with Tony in the East Village, in this little red Rabbit I had, before we were doing heroin, trying to find it. It was what the cool kids were doing, and Johnny Thunders was doing it, and we all kind of idolized Lou Reed's life, and you know Lou

Reed has done it. It was a natural progression of drug addiction. We did a lot of junk together.

ROBERT VUOLO: Tony, his addiction was always odd to me. I'm gonna be somewhat frank here: it felt often part of the persona that he wanted to portray of himself. He sort of constructed this image of himself that he wanted to perpetuate, and it involved this streety, kind of on the edge of the law—I wouldn't say *gangster*, but he romanticized that kind of lifestyle. Tony was always playing with how he looked to other people; he was very conscious of it. There was a little bit of a distance between the things he did and who he was.

SAM GOLDMAN: I never had a fight with Tony. Well, that's not entirely true. We had one really big fight, and it was about which version of "Sweet Jane" was the best version. And once we fought about how much cheese should go into a Mornay sauce.

HILLARY SNYDER, KITCHEN COLLEAGUE: They thought the Escoffier cookbook was the bible, you know, and they always referred to it. And I think Tony was especially proud of it because of his French heritage.

ROBERT VUOLO: Tony was very well spoken and smart, and he knew his stuff, and worked very hard in many respects.

ALEX GETMANOV: He'd really picked up the classic French idea of "the job must get done" no matter what, no matter how you feel or what's going on. There was this famous story of Vatel, chef and steward from the time of Louis XIV. He was a perfectionist, and he would do these stunning banquets and parties for the king's court. He was very unpopular with a lot of people; they hated him. Somebody screwed him over for a major party. The main fish ingredients for his dish failed to arrive, so he fell on his sword and killed himself. Tony used to laugh about this guy, but you could tell was admiring him all the same.

JAMES GRAHAM, KITCHEN COLLEAGUE: Tony and I met working at WPA. I was eighteen, and he was twenty-two or twenty-three. A few years later he got his first chef job, at Chuck Howard's, and I worked with him there a little bit, and then he recruited me to work at Nikki & Kelly. I was part of a codependent, dysfunctional team.

LENNY MOSSE, KITCHEN COLLEAGUE: I was working at Nikki & Kelly, on Seventy-Seventh and Columbus. I was the sous chef there. This was 1983. The owners had just fired the chef, who had locked himself in the office with a mountain of coke. They hired Tony, and he brought in Sam [Goldman] and Alex [Getmanov].

JAMES GRAHAM: I put a lot of faith in mentors like Tony and Sam, who were really not qualified for mentorship. But [at Nikki & Kelly] Tony gave me license to run a kitchen staff of fifteen, and he couldn't be happier, because that meant he didn't have to cook.

He didn't mind if I fucked things up; he was so elastic. If things went bad, he would just patch that over right away with a smile and charm.

One day, everything had gone to hell in a handbasket. Tony had disappeared to go tanning. That was a thing; his nickname at the time was Zonker, after the character from the *Doonesbury* cartoon strip, Zonker Harris, who was a professional tanner. He would tan, I think, largely to hide the pallor of heroin. He would play hooky, to go to the beach with Lenny, and tan aggressively. He looked like a Versace bag.

NANCY BOURDAIN: We used to joke about George Hamilton, and it was a joke, but he did like to have a healthy tan. I didn't know about tanning places till Tony turned me on to them.

CHRISTOPHER BOURDAIN: He definitely liked being tanned, definitely. I remember him joking that he would be competing in the George Hamilton Tanning Olympics. He liked sprawling out in the sun, like a seal on the beach, and just getting tanned. I mean, for him, a great day was tan for four, five hours, swim a little bit, have some beers and some beachy fried food.

ROBERT VUOLO: Summer of 1983, we were all working at Nikki & Kelly, and there was an effort, on Tony's part, to kind of relive what his Provincetown lifestyle was about. All of us, and a handful of waitresses, would get up early and go to Long Beach on the train, go to the beach and have a bunch of food and smoke a lot of marijuana and sun ourselves. There was a little bit of a tanning competition that summer, primarily between Lenny and Tony. Somewhere in the early afternoon, around two, we would catch the train back into Manhattan, and go to the Upper West Side and work, then party all night, and do the same thing the next day.

JAMES GRAHAM: So, the kitchen went to shit one day; three people didn't show up, I was trying to keep it together, and it was just a disaster. Tony showed up at 4:45, five minutes before dinner service, and within ten minutes, he had everybody charmed and laughing and at ease, and everything was fine. My prep cook turned to me and said, "You can't stay mad at this guy, he's magic!" All day long we were cursing his name, but five minutes in, we were all good. He just put everybody at ease; he was that charismatic, and that charming.

NANCY BOURDAIN: At one point, I was selling advertising. I said to Tony, "You should do this; you'd make a million dollars." People just listened to him. If he believed, he could sell anything.

ROBERT VUOLO: He was such a charmer. Tony's ability to get wherever he needed to get was very much because of his persona and his ability to talk and charm. It was a little dangerous, it was seductive, and very exciting. What he was always able to do was make everyone excited about the thing that we were all involved in.

HILLARY SNYDER: Tony was always way more knowledgeable than skillful, in terms of his cooking. I mean, Tony was a brilliant guy, very smart, so he had a lot of nerdy knowledge about food that was always appreciated. He might have been arrogant, but he did not live in a world without mirrors. He was aware. He had an idea of, ultimately, how his skill set ranked, you know?

A lot of us had that bullshit public persona back then, because it was—the punk rock thing was happening, and it was a defensiveness. There was a bit of an arrogant attitude. Sometimes it was more on the paper-tiger end of the scale, and then there were some people who could really back it up. I always thought Tony was somebody who could back it up.

LENNY MOSSE: Tony was never afraid to be an asshole. He was never afraid to say what he was thinking, the unpopular opinion, his truth. Tony was this gangly, kind of goofy guy. He was manic, and he had a lot of energy. He was impulsive. I mean, no one decides to become a heroin addict after long, careful consideration.

JAMES GRAHAM: The money, and the attention, and the glamour of Nikki & Kelly—he was extremely happy there, because he was getting all this attention, from women especially. He liked that it was a well-oiled machine; we were all cooking, and he was in the dining room, flirting with movie stars. He loved that.

ROBERT VUOLO: It was a real coming-of-age, my association with Tony, Sam, and Alex. During the course of the next seven or eight years, I worked with some combination of those three in various restaurants around New York. An average job length was somewhere around six months, which seemed like an enormously long period of time, but looking back, it was extraordinarily brief.

HILLARY SNYDER: I worked for Sam [Goldman] for years and years, just following him around from restaurant to restaurant. So that's how I got to know Tony, through Sam, and we also had another mutual friend in common: heroin, which was a great relationship for a while.

We used together a lot, but we did not cop together a lot. He was copping while I was cooking. We were all knucklehead drug users back then; he was kind of an absentee chef, like, MIA. Which, look, if you're an executive chef, you don't have to be on the line, necessarily, but the truth of the matter is, a lot of the times, Tony and Sam were just out on the street, copping.

LENNY MOSSE: Sam and Tony were junkies, but they had kind of a "nothing stops me" mentality at work. On the line, they would turn their heads and throw up into garbage cans. Sometimes Tony would leave the kitchen to score [heroin].

CHRISTOPHER BOURDAIN: I did not realize that Tony was going through heroin addiction. I didn't know that. Other than being scarecrow skinny, he hid it very well. I mean, I knew he was into weed; he'd smoke that in front of me. I didn't give a shit. I remember being kind of horrified when I found out about the heroin. You have an image in your head of somebody who's strung out and is completely useless; somebody who is holding up grocery stores to feed his habit. Tony went to work every day, though I did learn later that he had been desperate at points, and was basically selling his books on Broadway to get a few dollars to go find more heroin. But, as far as I know, I don't think he robbed any bodegas or anything like that.

ROBERT VUOLO: It really became apparent to me that he was struggling with heroin when we were working at Nikki & Kelly. That was probably his biggest chef job at that point. It was a very high-volume restaurant, and he put together a remarkable kitchen crew.

He had an odd idea that it was OK to run out of food by Sunday afternoon or evening, because I think he loved the idea of getting rid of all of that food and starting anew on Monday. The problem was that it created this kind of chaos, because brunches were really busy there. He just would disappear on Sundays, and call in mid-afternoon.

One afternoon I picked up the phone and he said, "How are things going in there?" and I was like, "Oh my god, it's kinda crazy, I gotta tell you, we're running out of this, we're running out of that, the place is packed, I'm not sure what we're gonna do," and he said, "OK great! I'll check in with you a little later," and got off the phone.

It was apparent that he heard nothing of the urgency in that message; he just kind of heard what he wanted to hear. That was the point where I was thinking, *OK, he is separating on some level? Is he not taking this job as seriously as those of us who are on the front lines?* There was a certain amount of antipathy that started to evolve at that point.

That restaurant, I think it was a high-stress situation for him, and that's when he started to do heroin on a more regular basis. We all started to notice it. One busy night I went down into the dry goods area to get something, and walking past the linen area, there were these enormous bags of linens and Tony was passed out on them.

The owners of Nikki & Kelly were crazy scumbags with way too much money, and it was sort of chaotic and very, very busy; one of the busiest places on the strip at that point. I can't tell exactly what prompted the owners to do this, but they brought in a consultant—I don't know what his credentials were—but he spent a few weeks in the kitchen and around the restaurant, and by the end of it, we were all fired. The consultant suddenly took over as chef, and brought in his own crew, and we were all gone.

JAMES GRAHAM: When we moved into Gianni's, it was a huge pay boost, and a huge facility, all this equipment.[*] He just moved right into that and charmed everybody. Morale was phenomenal.

The kitchen was so big that it took an expeditor to run service, and Tony loved that, because then he could just do his cartoon voices and his narration. He loved making fun of food writers, so every dish that we would put out, instead of just saying, "Take this to table nineteen," he would put on some voice and be like, "One overdecorated horror after another," making everyone laugh. He was so good at that, and so spontaneous. Everyone believed that he was going to be a professional cartoonist or a comedian.

He was always doing caricatures of people—he would do them right on the walls. The bathroom of Gianni's was just a gallery of portraits of the staff, because Tony would go into the bathroom, to get high, probably, and do a cartoon of me, spilling soup.

----

[*] *Tony took James Graham with him when he was hired to run a large Italian restaurant called Gianni's, at the South Street Seaport. In* Kitchen Confidential *he refers to it as "Gino's."*

He put all of his energy into cartooning. It wasn't until after that time, when we were working at La Dolce Vita, on Thirteenth Street, and Alex was the head chef—at that time, Tony was starting to lose faith in his cartooning. We would look at *Tintin* comics together. I remember I found a book of [Tintin creator] Hergé's work, and I brought it in and we looked at it together, and Tony said, "Yeah, this is why I'll never make it as a cartoonist. I'm just not this good. I can't compete with this."

It was when we were at Gianni's that Tony started shooting up regularly.

ROBERT VUOLO: The drug-work stuff started to get heavier; both Tony and Sam battled their way through it.

HILLARY SNYDER: He just became more and more unemployable, and, you know, once you get to a certain echelon, your reputation will catch up with you. If you're doing fine dining, haute cuisine, those circles are tighter. So if you rip off a place or burn a kitchen down, people are gonna find out about it.

I think he might have been involved with some thievery at some point. But aside from that, the one thing I know for sure is his absenteeism was really bad.

CHRISTOPHER BOURDAIN: I would always try to go to the restaurants he worked at. I always wanted to sort of show the flag. I don't know if it was important to him. I have no idea whether he cared. I like to imagine he cared and thought it was nice, but he never would have said the words "It means a lot to me that you're here." Never.

He had a couple of bouts where he would go for a little bit of time here and there without a job. I don't remember any of them being really long, but, you know, there would be times. I did wonder at times, *Does he think I'm being patronizing by showing up; am I looking down on him in some way?* You know, me with my office job and blah, blah, blah. There were a couple of his jobs where I kind of shrugged and said, in my heart of hearts, "Couldn't you do better than this?" I didn't voice that to him, but I knew that our mother would say it, probably, at some point. That would be exactly the kind of comment that she would verbalize, and she probably would think that she was being helpful in some way.

Our mother had this miraculous knack for asking things in a way where you just kind of knew that there was a disappointment there.

ROBERT VUOLO: I remember running into him in the early nineties. He was working the wet bar at a restaurant called Formerly Joe's, which was behind the Riviera, on West Tenth and West Fourth Street. He had this whole thing: "I'm gonna write this book." He was always a very talented guy; he was one of these guys who you felt like could do almost anything. He was a good writer, he was a good illustrator, and he was brilliant, smart, and well spoken. I remember reading some of his shorter pieces, and they were all sort of kitchen related, but there was a point where you could tell that he was struggling a little bit, and it wasn't totally clear to me when he said, "I'm working on this book," that it was actually something that he was really working on.

JAMES GRAHAM: Tony was the guy who made me want to be a chef, and ten years later, he was the guy who made me want to get out of the business. I saw him being miserable and unhappy, not able to do what he wanted, and being hostage to these big jobs that were really a servant's job; there was no prestige.

CHRISTOPHER BOURDAIN: Early on, I thought he was happy enough. I guess I first started understanding that this wasn't really what he wanted to do, longer term, around the time our dad died. That was when he started to say, "I don't wanna do this anymore. This isn't how I want it to be. The long hours, and the low pay, and no health insurance, and no prospects, and constant—restaurants close, a new one opens, a new one closes, the turmoil"—the many things he wrote about in *Kitchen Confidential*, in terms of egos and consequent failure among restaurant owners. He was getting a bit tired of that.

ROBERT VUOLO: We had a thing at Nikki & Kelly: someone got a bunch of those bandannas that the Japanese pilots wore during World War II, before they were about to kamikaze into the side of a warship, and that was so much part of that persona we were all sucked up into. Actually, you needed something around your forehead to keep from sweating all over your food, so it just added to the dramatics. And we were all into movies together. We had a tape of the soundtrack of *Apocalypse Now* going on in the kitchen for months.

HILLARY SNYDER: I think a lot of us, as cooks, identified with Martin Sheen, who was the army assassin who was sent to kill Marlon Brando's character because he had gone insane. And then the insane person, you know, the Marlon Brando character, was almost always the restaurant owner, you know what I mean? And also just being fascinated with how absurd it all was; and, you know, that was another thing I think we all heavily identified with, the absurdity, the irony, that you don't really know your ass from your elbow as a cook unless you've been doing it for five years. It's a pretty intense skill set, and to be able to do your job properly, you're wearing a lot of different hats, right? And you gotta have a lot of different sets of knowledge, including scientific stuff. I mean, the properties of an egg would just astound people, you know?

And then there's floor staff. So here you are, right, dedicating your life to the craft, and then there's the floor staff, these waiters and waitresses who would rather be doing something else with their lives, who are making two and three times what you're making in a night—the absurdity of that was always a big deal, and still is. He just felt so much injustice that there was not—the cooking profession was not given the weight that it deserved. I was so proud of Tony, later, for making this such a public issue, that not only are kitchen staffs heavily immigrant in fine dining, I mean, they cook everything really fucking well, and they don't complain about shit, and they bust their asses, but wages have not changed since, I don't know, the late seventies, early eighties? Cooks still make the same damn money. I was really proud he made that such an issue.

After about 1986, I would say, I never saw Tony again. I think he did get, um, grouchier, shall we say? I think there was more alcohol involved at some point, but we were all so self-centered and self-serving back then. It was, from my perspective, just a case of drifting apart. We were more interested in getting high than keeping hold of relationships, friendships, you know; that's just the way it was.

It wasn't exactly clear when I first met Tony, but it did become clear, from hanging out with him, that he was so much more multi-dimensional than just your average chef. He was just so much broader than that. He had his interest in literature, and culture, and life in general. I mean, he struck me as a quintessential New Yorker, and he wasn't from New York, but he just embodied that global-citizen thing, before he had all his stamps on his passport, way before he kind of had that going on.

I really did look up to Tony in a lot of ways. He was this brilliant guy, doing stuff, young, creative, and very intelligent. In the short amount of time that I knew him, he made a really big impression on me, and that was at a time before he was famous, and there wasn't that Pavlovian response that people give to celebrities, you know?

LENNY MOSSE: I still use things in the kitchen that I learned from those guys. Tony was one of my formative mentors in New York kitchens. I learned a lot about the finer aspects of cooking, the restaurant business, cutting out the bullshit. I learned how to create a team, a cohesive fighting unit.

5

"HE JUST WANTED TO BE A WRITER IN THE WORST WAY"

MEETING JOEL ROSE

JOEL ROSE, WRITING COLLABORATOR: I had this little literary magazine called *Between C & D*. I had some friends write for it—Patrick McGrath, [my ex-wife] Catherine [Texier]. I wrote for it, a bunch of people wrote for it, and I brought it to Saint Mark's Bookshop and East Side Books. I did all the covers by hand, because it was the old days, you couldn't do anything on a computer, really. It was all dot matrix, Courier print, but they were beautiful.

One day after the first issue was out, in 1983 or 1984, I got a submission; it was a comic book. It was from somebody I didn't know—Anthony Bourdain. Nobody knew him. And I wrote back that it was "interesting." I said, "Your drawings sort of suck, but your writing doesn't." And the next thing I knew, somebody was ringing the buzzer downstairs. I went down, and it was Bourdain, in his chef whites. He had run over to Second Street to score [heroin] and he was high and he came over. The address was on the magazine. And he stayed for like two or three hours.

PATRICK RADDEN KEEFE, *NEW YORKER* WRITER WHO PROFILED TONY IN 2017: When Tony talked about his early days as a writer—one of the really big questions in my mind was, you hear the story that Tony has told a million times: all he ever wanted to be is a chef. He works his way through kitchens. He's got a crew that kind of collects around him; they're total badasses. Their biggest ambition is to work one perfect brunch shift. He really made it sound as though he wasn't hustling all that time to get out of the kitchen. I didn't buy it, instinctively. What I was wondering was, "Were you a frustrated writer all that time?" And he basically said he wasn't, and then I went to NYU to find the archives of *Between C & D*, the downtown zine that he wrote for.

There's all these letters from young Tony to Joel Rose, where he's so fucking hungry . . . I've gotten these emails from people. I used to write these emails myself. It's the young writer who is trying to sound brash and casual, but actually is super needy and wants affirmation. Playing it cool, but hitting the jokes a little too hard. And it's all those things that I didn't associate with Tony, but he *was* that guy.

JOEL ROSE: Tony and I just hit it off right from the start. We just became really close friends. He didn't know any writers. He always said it: "You're the only writer I know." He just wanted to be a writer in the worst way, and I thought he was a terrific writer.

Aside from that first time, and maybe a few more times, I didn't really see him strung out or anything like that. Truthfully, when we were together, we talked about writing.

We stayed real close. I followed him from every shithole restaurant he worked in, you know, just every place. I think I was in every kitchen he ever worked in.

I don't want to say he looked up to me, but he trusted me. He talked a lot about his insecurities as a writer. "Can I do this? Do I have anything to say?"

He was always so brilliant. His mind was so sharp. He was a catalog of stuff that was astonishing. He would just entertain me. And as much as I was a mentor to him, he was a mentor to me. He turned me on to so much stuff.

While he had insecurities about his writing, he was a good writer, right from the start. He had a voice that he could access.

JOEL ROSE: I was so adamantly against him taking that course with Gordon Lish.* I thought he had nothing to teach him and could only hurt him in his writing. I thought Tony was a natural writer, a dedicated writer. He knew not where he was going—he couldn't possibly—but he was willing to figure it out. He was already good, and I was afraid that someone as ego driven as Lish would confuse his own egocentric feelings and pollute Tony's work.

JAMES GRAHAM: As soon as he took Gordon Lish's class, it was like someone joining a cult. He started dressing differently, he started getting his hair done differently, he changed the kind of cigarettes he smoked. He became very aloof and referred to himself as a writer. He was a bit insufferable at times. It's hard for me to say then what his poison was; there was quite a lot of cocaine going around back then.

---

* *In 1985, Tony enrolled in a creative writing course with the renowned literary editor and writer Gordon Lish.*

JOEL ROSE: I don't think anybody had any influence on Tony except for Tony. For all his insecurities, I felt that the backbone was very strong. That's what I was trying to tell him. "Wherever you're going, whatever trip you're on, just go there." Because I knew he was on a very special track right from the start. I was always cheering him on.

I think he dreamed of being a crime novelist. He thought that was an incredible place to be, if he could ever achieve that. And he really did.

NANCY BOURDAIN: Tony always wanted to be with the in-crowd, and he usually found it, even in Saint Maarten. We used to stay at a lovely hotel, only twenty rooms. The Oyster Pond Hotel. It was very small, and at night—it used to be quite something in its heyday, but by then it was a quite staid place, a lot of old people, and we were young then. And at night we'd hear laughter and partying and fun from across the inlet, and finally we got on the scooter and tracked it down.

There were two wrong bars first, and one of them really was like *Star Wars*—there were all these really weird creatures, nobody looked alike, and they looked like they'd been there since the stone age. And then we found the Dinghy Dock, which was right across from us. He used to write there, and that became a big hangout.

6

"THEY GOT SOME MONEY, AND IT JUST WENT INTO THEIR VEINS"

HEROIN

CHRISTOPHER BOURDAIN: We were having lunch with my dad, shortly after [my wife] Jennifer's grandmother died. She had lived most of her life in DC but wanted to be buried in Queens. So we were with my dad, having a nice lunch or something, and—he had a nice, very resonating kind of voice. He would have been a very good classical radio announcer. Jennifer asked, "How do they get a body from Washington to New York?" Our dad looked at her, and said, in this very serious tone, "Well, first thing they do is they need to dress it completely in a clown costume." That was him to a T, totally.

Our dad never took care of himself. He was never hugely overweight, but he was always overweight. He never got exercise, and
he smoked. There were always people who smoked more, but he
smoked. Anyway, he dropped dead at two in the morning one night,
in 1987. We got a call from his partner, and Tony and I ran to his
apartment, you know; it was too late.

He was penniless when he died. He had zero assets, and in fact,
I think he owed the IRS like $15,000, but his aunt had been one
of those people who squirreled away money for fifty years, from the
Depression on, and had left a trust fund. My dad was the beneficiary
of the trust fund while he was alive, and then after he died, Tony
and I each got a chunk of money, about a quarter-million dollars for
each of us. I mean, this was not money to sneeze at. I ended up using
mine to buy my first house.

NANCY BOURDAIN: Tony was bad with money. When his dad died
[in 1987], he inherited a little bit of money, and it was annoying to
me, because we were married then, and he would just spend money
like—it was stuff for us, a TV or something, but not practical. You
want to be in on big decisions, but once he made up his mind, he was
gonna do it anyway, if you were on board or you weren't.

CHRISTOPHER BOURDAIN: Tony and Nancy were talking about buying
a little casita, a little two-room house in a project under construc-
tion in Saint Maarten that was mostly for tourists who wanted to
buy a pied-à-terre down there. He said, "Yeah, we're just gonna go
live there, and I'll be able to go to the beach every day, and sprawl
out, and tan, and find some kind of a job in a restaurant down
there, if need be." He was really, really on that for a few months. I
mean, he had this whole offering document from this sponsor and
everything.

He let himself be talked out of the idea by our mom. She was definitely down on it. I remember her saying, "That's a crazy idea." And I remember him saying, "I should've never let her talk me down from that idea." He was very, very angry with her for quite a while after that. I think they went through a time where he didn't want to talk to her, because she'd talked him out of his dream. I can't remember how long it went on. I mean, they would periodically go for anywhere from three months to a year without talking.

JEFF FORMOSA: When [Tony and Nancy] were really junkies, they wouldn't answer the phone. When Tony's dad died, they got some money, and it just went into their veins. They were reclusive, they would just cop dope, and they went on vacations, and then they were destitute again.

SCOTT BRYAN, NEW YORK CHEF: I knew that Tony went to CIA and was classically trained, but he always went for the money. He never went through the rigors that I did. I worked at fucking Gotham. I worked at Bouley. I worked with Gray Kunz at Lepinasse. I worked with Tom Colicchio at Mondrian. I worked at Le Bernardin, with Eric [Ripert]. Tony never went through that sort of hardship. He would work in the West Village for that guy Bigfoot [Andy Menschel], who would pay him $700 cash a week, while I worked like an idiot, making $400 for eighty hours a week. I think Tony saw himself as more of a writer than a chef.

SAM GOLDMAN: It didn't matter how much money any of us made; it just didn't matter. If you're a dope fiend, it's gone.

NANCY BOURDAIN: Tony was always generous, with our house, with our apartment. We had a friend at the Supper Club, when he worked there, who got very sick. He went to the hospital. When he got out, whoever was taking care of his apartment had lost his apartment, had never paid rent for three months, and he had no place to go, so he came to live with us. It was kind of a fait accompli. I knew the guy. It worked out very well. I was very fond of him. But we did that a lot. You know, people would need help, he'd help them.

LENNY MOSSE: When I had a fire at my apartment building and we had no heat, Tony let me stay with him.

NANCY BOURDAIN: There was another guy who had come [to Supper Club] on work release, and we were going to the islands. We needed someone to water the plants or watch the cat or whatever, and Tony let this guy Clarence do it. I think a week, that's all he knew him, but he was willing to gamble on that.

He never said anything to me that this guy had been work-released, but he said, "You better take care of all your jewelry." I didn't have a lot, but what I had, I liked. Tony had a gold pocket watch that had either been his grandfather's or his father's, which Clarence did steal. I think he was an addict, and the temptation was too strong. Tony mentioned it to him, and he admitted what he had done, but it was too late to get it back.

I don't think that was the end of trusting people in that way. Tony helped people out, and we had a few bad experiences. There was one guy we put up for a while who didn't steal or anything, but he was just kind of a pig, and he started a fire on the mattress he was sleeping on.

ALEX GETMANOV: There was one year when I needed a place to stay in New York, in the summer. Gladys [Bourdain] was in Paris, and Tony

sublet her apartment on West Sixty-Eighth to me. It was across the
street from a firehouse, and my god, the alarm would go off every
three minutes. I never got used to it, couldn't stand it anymore, so I
moved out.

As I was walking out, I had a suitcase, and as I was opening the
front door, guess who's standing there? Gladys. She didn't know I'd
been subletting her apartment, and she never saw a penny of the
money, as far as I know. This was at a point when Tony had started
his heroin hobby, and he wasn't the most reliable person at that point.
He and I drifted apart because of his heavy heroin use; I couldn't
deal with it anymore.

SAM GOLDMAN: Tony and Nancy rolled out of heroin and into the
crack thing; they weren't great company then. They were the first
people I knew to get into treatment through methadone, and to
this day I think without methadone he wouldn't be alive. Or rather,
he would've died a lot sooner.

By the time he got off dope and was doing crack, the quality of
restaurant jobs he could get was not great, but for some reason, in
the restaurant business, especially in New York, you can't get blackballed. You can always get another job. I'd get fired and go work for
him. He'd get fired and go work for me. We'd both get fired and go
work somewhere else together.

LENNY MOSSE: Between Sam, Alex, and Tony, there was never a
time— When you were unemployed, if you didn't want to be, they'd
say, "I need a body," which meant it was an unskilled job, or, "I need a
pair of hands," which meant they were looking to fill a slightly more
skilled role. Later, I actually gave Tony a few gigs, after he had fallen
on hard times. I fed him one Thanksgiving, right before I left New
York. I had to get away from all that.

SAM GOLDMAN: The three of us stayed really tight, until it became impossible to be in my company, because he cleaned up way before I did. I thought it would be a good idea to start drinking, instead of doing heroin, and I became intolerable.

Before I [got sober], I really saw a lot of people turn their back on me. What happens is, it's too fucking painful to watch us kill ourselves. I remember, with great clarity, when Tony just threw his hands up in the air and said, "I can't take you anymore."

When I eventually went to prison, he was just lifesaving. He was encouraging me to write, to read books; it was a time in my life when I had run out of friends, and he and Nancy were the only ones who took my call.

7

"I'M TONY MOTHERFUCKING BOURDAIN— YOU GOT A PROBLEM?"

NEW YORK IN THE NINETIES

JOEL ROSE: He loved the kitchen, and hated it. It was so taxing on him. He loved his staff, just loved them, and counted on them, and talked about them a lot, but he was worried about being on the line when he got older, that he would physically not be able to do it. He worried about him and Nancy just paying the bills. He had nothing, and was frightened. And he just dreamed of [living] that life he later wrote about in *Gone Bamboo*. That was his dream, one day, to be able to just lie on the beach and have a cocktail in some shack in the sand.

STEVEN TEMPEL, NEW YORK KITCHEN COLLEAGUE: I met Tony in 1993, at the Supper Club, and became his sous chef. I brought my friend Adam [from *Kitchen Confidential*, "Adam Real Last Name Unknown"] in. Tony hated us. He was always begging [executive chef] John [Tesar] to fire both of us. We'd be in the middle of a rush, and I'd lean over and whip a tomato at the line and hit Adam in the side of the head. I was twenty-three years old.

I come in and do my work and don't listen to you, but you can't complain because I'm getting it done well. Eventually Tony stopped hating me. During service, he would just look at me, and I knew what he meant, what he wanted me to do. We would go out every single night after work and party, but then it would be one a.m., and he would go home, and I'd stay out all night.

When we were together, he always let me know that I was doing a good job. He bought me knives. I was thinking about buying myself a Global [knife], and the next morning, there's an $80 Global sitting on my workstation. That was a lot of money at the time.

PATTI JACKSON, NEW YORK KITCHEN COLLEAGUE: Tony was such a raconteur, such a great storyteller. And he was super friendly. I mean, you know, you couldn't *not* start talking to him. We'd hang out, and drink beers, and tell stories. And when Coco Pazzo Teatro opened, it was great. Tony's office, the chef's office, was right off the pastry kitchen, and we'd all hang out in there. It was tiny. I mean, you could have one chair, maybe, and he'd open the file drawer, and put a six-pack in it, and somebody would sit on his desk, and somebody would squat in the door, and he would just tell stories. He had the best stories. He knew where all the shittiest bars were. We went to Siberia, when it was in the Fiftieth Street train station. We used to go to Desmond's, on Park Avenue. At the time, it was still a serious Irish Republican [Army] bar, a little weird and dangerous, you know, 'cause there weren't many of those left. We used to go to McManus every once in a while, across the street. He just really liked a divey bar.

SCOTT BRYAN: When I met Tony, he was nobody. He had no money, he lived in a rent-stabilized apartment with his first wife. On the weekend they'd smoke bones, I think, and he'd cook for her, you know, and he was just a laid-back— No one knew who Tony Bourdain was. And he was just a happy-go-lucky guy, an easygoing guy.

STEVEN TEMPEL: He was not shy. He was not anxious. He was not depressed. He used to walk around going, "I'm Tony Motherfucking Bourdain—you got a problem?"

MATT WALSH, TV FIXER AND TRANSLATOR: He was a New York archetype that I was very familiar with. I think a lot of people around the rest of America, and perhaps around the world, found Tony's voice to be like nothing they'd ever heard. His persona. And, to a certain extent, that's true. Tony was very talented in that regard. But there's also something about that unique voice that I found familiar. The type of expressions that he used, his view of life, I knew a hundred guys in New York just like that. It's very well informed, very articulate, but also bad boy, not part of an intelligentsia crowd, standing around art galleries, stroking their chin. It was just so familiar. I think a lot of people ascribe to that being Tony's. I think that the cultural milieu that is New York has a claim on Tony Bourdain's vibe.

BETH ARETSKY, NEW YORK KITCHEN COLLEAGUE AND FORMER ASSISTANT: I met Tony about '94 or '95, when I was working at One Fifth Avenue [restaurant in Manhattan]; I think it was called Vince and Linda's at the time. The chef had quit, and a bunch of staff walked out with him, except for me and a couple others. Tony came in, with

Steven Tempel. He liked me enough to keep me, so I stayed, because I needed a job.

As a boss, he was very cool. He was an asshole only to the waiters, and not even really an asshole, just snarky, you know, with his sharp tongue, calling them bed-wetting shit stains. That was probably the most commonly used phrase: "You incompetent, bed-wetting shit stain." Right to their face.

Back then, there was no HR, no nothing. Lots of drugs prevalent in the kitchen. Smoking was allowed on the line. Tony was always smoking in his office. He had a little desk in the kitchen, so he'd always be sitting there, smoking.

We would go to the Stoned Crow [bar] on Washington Place after work. Tony was always telling stories about Provincetown, and all kinds of kitchens, before anyone knew he was writing anything. He was always the center of attention, the best at telling stories.

I left One Fifth Avenue to open up Butterfield 81 with my dad [restaurateur Ken Aretsky], then Tony became unemployed and came to me, looking for a job. I said, "There's no way I can hire you, Tony, you're my chef. That would be awkward, and you're way too tall for the line. You'll hit your head on the exhaust."

He totally understood. Later, I went with him to Coco Pazzo Teatro. Then I became the chef at Carola's, on Sixtieth between Park and Lex. He was still the chef at Coco Pazzo Teatro. We both got reviewed in the *New York Post* on the same day; we both got two stars.

I never felt competitive with him. We were friends, and I was never attracted to him. From the first time he walked in the door, I thought, *He's really tall, he's really skinny, and he's got a long head. He's not my type.*

PATTI JACKSON: You know, working in a kitchen with a bunch of guys, like— Tony was always really respectful of the girls. He never had that— I don't know whether it's an insecurity thing, or an ego thing, or whatever makes men be absolute pigs—he didn't have that.

BETH ARETSKY: I ended up with him over at Sullivan's. It was a very lax kitchen, I'll put it that way. Whoever was smoking was smoking on the line. If someone wanted a steak well done, we always took the steak that had the most sinew in it, made it as well done as possible, sent it out, and if it came back saying it wasn't well done enough, Tony would tell me to drop it in the fryer, burn it into a shoe.

PATTI JACKSON: Years later, watching him become the piece of art he became, watching him doing interviews and on TV, people would say to me, "Oh my god, I read *Kitchen Confidential*. What's Tony Bourdain like?" And I'd say, "What you see is what he's like. He loves a good story. He loves a good meal. He loves to smoke a Lark."

8

"SUCH WAS MY LUST TO SEE MY NAME IN PRINT"

HELEN LANG: All the energy he'd put into trying to destroy himself, he put that into building himself back up. All that negative energy became something else. He became so serious, and so driven and focused. He worked really hard.

It takes a lot of determination to wake up early in the morning and write, and then go to a job in the kitchen, and come home at god knows what hour, and get up the next morning and do it again. He was a fiend. One time, he said about his disciplined writing regimen, "Such was my lust to see my name in print." He threw himself into his work in a manner that I found astonishing.

DAVID ROSENTHAL, BOOK PUBLISHER: I was at what we called "the old Random House," the pre-Bertelsmann Random House, when it was owned by the Newhouse family. I had made a deal to do a distribution of *The Old Farmer's Almanac* and some spin-off books. The person who repped *The Old Farmer's Almanac* was one Gordon Howard; he was a licensing guy.

HELEN LANG: Gordon gave Tony some money to just go somewhere and write, and I think Gordon was very invested in the whole thing.

DAVID ROSENTHAL: I remember Gordon telling me, "I know this guy who's written a novel, and it's really good. I was his college roommate," and I'm thinking, *Oh, shit*, because there's nothing worse than getting books from civilians. People don't go through life thinking they can be a neurosurgeon, but they all think they can be an author. It's a real problem sometimes. But I said, "Sure," and within a relatively short period, I read it, and the big surprise was, I liked it. It was very fresh, funny, and I thought, *This could be a continuing character*. There wasn't all that much work to do [on the manuscript], not too many structural things; just some beginner's mistakes.

I remember calling Gordon, saying I wanted to buy it, and his reaction was, "Really?" He brought Tony down to the office. I only vaguely knew that Tony was an actual chef.

I had an amateur's interest in cooking; I remember getting into an argument with Tony about how, in his manuscript, he had the hero making a beurre blanc, and adding cream to it, and I said, "That's not how you make a beurre blanc." The attitude I got was, he didn't give a shit. He made it clear that he had some experience in, shall we say, low-rent Italian kitchens, and that they were obviously a nasty place to be, and all sorts of shit went down.

So *Bone in the Throat* comes out [in 1995]. A few people at Random House liked it, but to be honest, the sales force was not behind it, which is always a liability. I remember doing a lot of mailings and calling, but I couldn't really get the bookstores to take a bite. They bought it, of course—in those days, if you were Random House, you always were guaranteed a certain number of copies going out, but I was disappointed with the sales, because I thought we had, not a *breakout* with this book, but [good enough] to get up to a certain level.

The sense I got was that Tony wasn't nearly as disappointed as I was. He was optimistic about the whole process; he really wanted to do it, and the money I was paying him was tiny; it had to be less than $15,000 for each book, which in those days was a going rate for a debut novelist writing something that was not really gonna [sell] a hundred thousand copies.

HELEN LANG: I went to Tony's first book party. I hadn't seen Gordon for many, many years. We sat in his car and talked for a little while, and he was very excited about the success of the book.

My impression, when I spoke to Tony that night, was that he didn't want to be tethered by Gordon, that he was more ambitious than that, and he had bigger plans. I don't remember exactly what he said, but I felt that he was maybe ready to kick Gordon to the curb. That's a little harsh, but Gordon was just a person; he didn't have connections, as far as I know. He was just kind of a good friend. I think Tony was ready for bigger things.

"APPALLING STORIES OF REMORSELESS CRIMINALITY"

THE STONE BROTHERS

In 1995, following the publication of Bone in the Throat, *Tony made the acquaintance of Rob and Web Stone, Harvard-educated brothers who worked together in book and film development.*

ROB STONE, WRITING AND PUBLISHING PARTNER: We had an overall deal at the Walt Disney Company. Jane Rosenthal, who runs Robert De Niro's company, invited us to take an office, practically for nothing, at the Tribeca Film Center, in order to help them develop a couple of projects that they had in mind. And they wanted us to help develop nonfiction books.

We were sort of book producers, who developed nonfiction books. We would acquire the rights to a story, a nonfiction subject, and then

Web and I would write the proposal and sample chapters, and then hire a writer with whom we would sell the book to a publisher, for a book advance.

The first project that Tribeca Productions wanted out of us was, they had an extremely corrupt cop, a detective first grade who'd spent a couple of decades on the job, whom De Niro believed would make an amazing movie subject, and they wanted us to develop a nonfiction book out of his story, which they would use as a launchpad for a movie.

For that book, Tony was the first call we made. Web read a review of *Bone in the Throat* in the *New York Times*, and Tony sounded like the kind of guy who was clearly able to capture the voice of New Yorkers, and this cop was a quintessential New Yorker.

We felt pretty important, having an office at the Tribeca Film Center, and attracting a hot up-and-coming writer, so we wanted to have a meeting there, with Tony and Jane Rosenthal and De Niro and the cop. We would record this session to find out, in an introductory meeting, what the cop's story was.

Tony arrived early—he was pretty punctual, but most important, he wanted to get to the bar at the Tribeca Grill, to have a drink or two and a couple of smokes before going into the meeting. So, we're at the bar, and this guy walks up wearing, I'd say, a $2,000 jacket, gold Piaget watch, and close-cut hair, and he'd shaved like five minutes ago. He says, "You must be the Stone brothers. And you must be Tony." It was the cop, who'd *also* gotten there fifteen minutes early to have a couple of drinks and a couple of smokes.

WEB STONE, WRITING AND PUBLISHING PARTNER: To get revved up, for the meeting.

ROB STONE: These guys, in some ways were— it's unfair to say "birds of a feather," but they both were remarkable raconteurs, with a bit of a kindred spirit. Maybe the cop more as specimen, and Tony more as scientific observer.

After a couple of drinks, in the span of fifteen to twenty minutes, we go up to De Niro's office, and he's super relaxed, super quiet. Jane Rosenthal—a bit uptight, a bit busybodyish—welcomes everybody in. Tony, once he walked into that room, barely said a word. I think he was pleased that an ashtray was put out on the table and he could smoke and listen, but in the company of De Niro and this character, this cop—when he walked into the room, honestly, the cop didn't enter the office, he occupied it. He was this marauding force who walked into the room and sucked all the oxygen away from De Niro being in the room. As Tony said later, he worked his way into your brain like an insidious fungus.

You gotta imagine, this guy is maybe six feet tall, two twenty, and he's all muscle and gut, big, barrel-chested guy wearing this $2,000 sport jacket and Cole Haan loafers and the gold watch. And he made sure when he sits on the couch that you can see he's packing the Glock nine. And as Tony would say later, "You tend to listen a little more intently to people carrying guns."

The cop just started telling these appalling stories of remorseless criminality. His entire career, starting from the academy, in which he proudly did nothing but get his instructors some blow jobs— the guy's whole life is described in terms of greed, brutality, deception, and the constant pursuit of women. And all he did was basically rob, steal, lie, and ejaculate his way through life as a cop. And—

WEB STONE: And Tony, in a way, disdained him.

ROB STONE: After multiple meetings with De Niro, in which we would sit there and listen, dumbfounded, we'd then go with the cop and Tony to debrief for a couple of hours, in which we were drinking and smoking, but eventually the cop had to drive himself home, and then we got a couple more hours of debriefing with Tony. This meant that we started spending such a ridiculous amount of time with Tony that at some point he was like, "Listen, guys, you have to meet Nancy, because she's starting to think that you're a product of my adulterous imagination."

The reason the book ultimately died is that the cop had told too much of his story, and realized that, after the insanely corrupt deal that De Niro's company had done with him, he would make practically no money, and gain possibly a little bit of fame, and he became more worried about the security of his pension than the future assets that would be derived from his book and movie deals.

WEB STONE: At the same time, we were developing a sitcom. Tony liked crime stuff, and he liked chef stuff. The story was, "From 1984 to 1996, members of the Genovese crime family and the US government partnered to run a restaurant in New York's Little Italy. The food was not good. This is that story."

He worked hard on it. At the time, he was in deep debt. He had IRS liens against him, so we wanted to pay him for some of the work he was doing, even though we were all sort of creating it, and it was our baby.

ROB STONE: We had a deal with him, but it had to be not on paper, cash only. "You pay me, I write, that's it. And you pay me in a brown paper bag."

WEB STONE: Tony loved to do things like that, like we're all characters in *The Friends of Eddie Coyle*. So, we had to go to the deli across the street, to get those little brown sandwich bags, and we put real money in there, a couple thousand bucks, or whatever it was.

ROB STONE: And we trusted him.

WEB STONE: He wasn't morally self-righteous at all, but he was totally a moral, stand-up-for-the-underdog— I mean, you could trust him as far as the day is long.

ROB STONE: [He was] maybe the second-most-honest person I know. We went out with him several times, and also with our mother, and drank copious amounts of alcohol with her. She had a line, one night, that was, "I respect and appreciate every human flaw, except dishonesty." And Tony said, "I love that. You got me. I *have* every human flaw, but dishonesty."

WEB STONE: If we paid him, he did work, and it was good. Did it always work out? No, but, I mean, it was fun, and funny.

DAVID ROSENTHAL: Gordon called and said he had another book, and he showed me: Tony had just written the first few chapters of *Gone Bamboo*. It was a good sequel, and the idea of moving him to the Caribbean, to a drecky place there, was kind of nice. I thought, if one was gonna do this cinematically—which is what we were thinking at the time—it's a much better setting, gets you out of the *Goodfellas* realm.

WEB STONE: And this wasn't just his second novel; this was, in some ways, his tribute to his love for Nancy, because it was a thinly veiled memoir—not that he'd ever operated on the level of an assassin, but it was about Tony's love of CIA covert ops, military covert operations, circa the fifties, sixties, early seventies, and this novel was, as he said many times, "Tony and Nancy meet Nick and Nora Charles, with firepower, on an island of corrupt cops and insane mafiosi."

ROB STONE: Henry Denard *was* Tony Bourdain, and Frances Denard *was* Nancy.

WEB STONE: It was the ideal, what he wanted, in a way, for both of them. The highest embodiment of how Tony could see himself. There was a little bit of superhero to it.

DAVID ROSENTHAL: We published [*Gone Bamboo*] through Villard. Because I was running the imprint, we gave it more attention, and I had a whole separate publicity staff, and everybody liked him. He came into the office quite a bit; he liked hanging out there.

It was on the second book, that's when the *New York Times* did a profile on him [Enid Nemy, "Potboiler Dreams: Chef Hopes to Write His Way Out of the Kitchen," September 10, 1997]. I forget whether his mother [then a copy editor at the *Times*] was behind it, but it's a great piece.

But it's so strange—other than that, we couldn't get the media to bite. Here we have a working New York chef, and in his spare time he's written a novel; you name me one other chef who has done this. It's a big fucking deal. We had trouble getting him the attention, which was unfair, because the book was good, and he was a great personality.

"YOU'VE GOT A LONG CON GOING HERE"

THE GENESIS OF *KITCHEN CONFIDENTIAL*

KAREN RINALDI, BOOK EDITOR AND PUBLISHER: I met Tony around 1995 or '96 as a good friend of [my husband] Joel [Rose], when he was a working chef. I don't know where he was then, maybe Sullivan's.

We had a couple of dinners there that were extraordinary, really fun and festive, and Tony was just sort of fabulous. He was working hard as a chef, and really frustrated as a writer. He wanted to be a fiction writer. He had written and published, at that point, *Bone in the Throat* and then *Gone Bamboo*. *Bone in the Throat* did pretty well, or at least got some notice, and *Gone Bamboo* was very quiet. I think he was wondering, "Why are they not doing better?"

So when I met Tony in the restaurant environment, he had that kind of persona, and then "offstage," I found him sweet and shy and a little awkward, and I loved that about him. I thought, this is the kind of guy who can bring it when he has to, but there's a lot more going on, so that juxtaposition—I was charmed by it, for sure.

PHILIPPE LAJAUNIE, OWNER OF LES HALLES RESTAURANTS: My business partner Jose [de Meirelles] told me, "I hired this new guy; his name is Anthony Bourdain." I said, "Oh that sounds French!" I projected a short, kind of big-stomach French guy who had probably been here from France a long time and had changed his name from Antoine to Anthony. When I saw Tony in the kitchen, of course, it was the exact opposite.

I remember the first couple of weeks, being a bit unnerved, because Tony had just come out of working in an Italian restaurant. He was OK with the menu, and we had a strong kitchen behind him, but all his specials were pastas, Italian dishes, so that was rattling my cage a little bit. He turned out to be a very good cook, and he was managing the kitchen OK, and the kitchen was very quiet.

STEVEN TEMPEL: Tony and I worked together, from place to place, for years. Then I went into corporate, and for the first few months, working corporate, I missed working with Tony so much that on Saturday nights, I'd go to Les Halles and run the grill for him.

KAREN RINALDI: Joel had always encouraged him to write nonfiction from his point of view as a chef, because he had that window onto it. He had stories to tell. I think he had more stories to tell than time to tell them.

ROB STONE: Before *Gone Bamboo* was published, he wrote a short story, totally irreverent, sort of the chef-world version of *Trainspotting*.

It was at least six or seven thousand words, unpublishable in the United States, not a novella, neither here nor there, but about two-thirds of the way through it, there were a thousand to fifteen hundred words that were offset, that told what I would call his origin story, of how he decided to become a chef in Provincetown, Massachusetts, working in some tourist trap lobster joint, taking a job as a dishwasher but becoming completely enamored of chef culture, and looking at chefs as if they were samurais—marinated in alcohol, drug addled, sex obsessed—but when he describes these characters, he gives them chivalry. And he wrote with this clear-eyed, simple style. He wasn't trying hard; it wasn't self-conscious. This thousand or fifteen hundred words was clear-eyed, beautiful memoir writing.

I set a time to meet Tony for drinks at the infamous Siberia, a bar in a location that was built on generations of urine stains. It was a hole in the ground you poured alcohol and smoke into.

Tony spent a fair amount of time there, and I was going there to pitch him. I think he had only ever imagined himself as a fiction writer. I knew I had to get there as soon as he was off work, and be as punctual as possible, so that everybody was sober, to tell him, "You need to go nonfiction. You've got a long con going here, not just a short con."

WEB STONE: You want him maybe after one drink, and before seven, where he's gonna be receptive, a little less stressed, because the tension is cut, and you can pitch him and get him to understand that those thousand words of that story are where you hang your hat. Our whole thing was, "You're missing where the gold is. The gold is this stuff that you think is throwaway, that you're indenting and you're putting in fricking italics. That is where *you* are."

ROB STONE: And, and, of course, the night ends at six in the morning, and we walk out, and there's a fresh pool of piss right outside the door.

WEB STONE: He was scared to death of doing this, because it was like, "I'll never eat lunch in this town again."

11

"IT WAS PICKING UP A ROCK OFF THE RESTAURANT SCENE AND SHOWING EVERYTHING THAT WAS UNDERNEATH IT"

Tony wrote an approximately two-thousand-word essay about the restaurant business that he sent, unsolicited, to the Downtown Express, *a Tribeca-based community newspaper, whose editors rejected it. He then sent it to the* New York Press, *an alt-weekly paper that was in competition with the* Village Voice. *Sam Sifton, now an editor at the* New York Times, *was then the* Press *editor who received and greenlit Tony's essay, which ultimately didn't run.*

SAM SIFTON, EDITOR: One of the things that I was unable to explain to Tony at the time, and am unable to explain to you right now, is why [*New York Press* editor and publisher] Russ Smith declined to publish the piece. Tony was unknown to me. Les Halles, where he was working at the time, was four or five blocks north of where my world ended, as a *New York Press* reporter and editor. We were downtown kids being downtown kids, and Les Halles might as well have been Le Bernardin. It was not for us.

Nevertheless, the essay landed, and I read it, and it was great. It was perfect. It was everything. It was picking up a rock off the restaurant scene and showing everything that was underneath it. And it was telling the truth. And it seemed to me to be a really important, exciting, funny, brash, profane, and, above all, incredibly readable tale. Tony was a clean writer. We were soliciting first-person essays from the citizenry of New York, so I saw a lot of terrible copy. His was not that. It was like a slam dunk.

So I thought we should publish it. Russ Smith, I believe, was on vacation, or away. It must have been '98, and I'm thinking it must have been the summer. In any event, the *Press* was sent to the printer on Tuesday night, and Russ returned to the office on Monday, and the story was laid out.

It was the cover story, and Russ killed it. It's difficult to explain. The *New York Press* was a rowdy place, but it was run by a king. And what Russ said went. And there would be times when Russ was very clear about why he was killing something or championing something, and then there were times when he was not. And though I was very close to Russ at the time, and deeply respectful of him as an editor, I just didn't get it. And I still don't.*

But, I will tell you, I've dined out on the story a million times. I liked that story when it was a *New York Press* story, I liked that story when it was a *New Yorker* story, I liked that story when it became the book.

---

* *Russ Smith declined to be interviewed for this book.*

GLADYS BOURDAIN: David Remnick's wife was a colleague of mine at the *New York Times*—we were sort of chums—and I asked if I might use her name and send the article to him, mentioning that we were colleagues. I didn't want anything more than that. I do think that helped, to have David Remnick read the thing.*

---

* The New Yorker *published the piece, titled "Don't Eat before Reading This," in 1999.*

12

"HE WAS NOT JUST A COOK ANYMORE; HE WAS A REAL 3D PERSON"

DAVID ROSENTHAL: Gordon Howard called to tell me that he was no longer working with Tony, and he was very upset.

ROB STONE: Tony came to us and said, "I think it's time for me to move on from Gordon. Where do I go?" And we said, "Our agent is Kim Witherspoon, and she is true, and honest, and a straight shooter. She may not be the agent who will get you the biggest advance, but she will get you the honest advance."

WEB STONE: She did not exactly jump on the prospect of representing Anthony Bourdain.

ROB STONE: She definitely did not. It was a hard sell.

KIMBERLY WITHERSPOON, LITERARY AGENT: It was 1997 when I was introduced to Tony. That's a fair bit before he wrote *Kitchen Confidential*. When Web and Rob [Stone] introduced me to Tony, I don't think he had a book project ready to submit to publishers. He didn't come with a proposal for me to read. I think they knew they were coming to me with a bit of a mess, basically.

He needed help with a problem with Random House, which is that they had published two novels and had not—in spite of the fact that they were each *New York Times* Notable Books—they had not published them in paperback, and were not planning to. And there were no e-books at the time, there were no digital copies of the book available, so if you didn't have the book out in paperback, it was essentially not available, outside of libraries, after the first year of publication.

I talked to Tony on the telephone, and I was struck immediately by the fact that he was very bright, very funny, and I thought that his expectations were realistic. I also felt that he would be a good partner in letting me take the lead and trying to work this out, in spite of the fact that I wasn't the agent who had sold those first two books to Random House. It was a gamble, absolutely.

The first time I actually met Tony was in the lobby of Random House on our way up to a meeting that I'd set up.

He was early.

We got up there, and there was a new publisher. It wasn't David Rosenthal, who had originally acquired the novels, it was Brian DeFiore, who succeeded him. And Tony basically leaned back in his seat, stretched his legs out, and just glowered at Brian, while I explained that they either had to put the books into paperback or give us the rights back. That's not an agent's dream job.

I didn't have another book to offer them, so I had no leverage.

They didn't really have to do anything, but they gave us back the rights. The next book ended up being *Kitchen Confidential*. And that timing was brilliant, because we got the rights back, that piece got published [in *The New Yorker*], and then Karen [Rinaldi] signed him and put the novels back in print, in paperback.

PHILIPPE LAJAUNIE: When we opened Les Halles in Tokyo, I had a young French chef over there. I wanted him to have the exact same presentation as we were doing in New York, so I decided to take Tony with me for a week, to Tokyo.

I left a day or two before him, and just as I was leaving, he gave me two books: *Bone in the Throat* and *Gone Bamboo*. It was like he pulled the curtain back—the sort of work it takes, the focus, style, intelligence, a big mental museum of experiences and drive to write a book—I was very impressed. He was not just a cook anymore, he was a real 3D person. I read the books, and they were pretty good, and then I was really, really impressed.

In Tokyo, instead of leaving him in the kitchen on his own, I thought, *Maybe that's the guy to hang out with*. I decided to go around and show him my favorite places. Of course, he turned out to be ahead of me: one night he could not be in the restaurant because he had a presentation with his book publisher in Tokyo, which sounded very glamorous to me.

JOEL ROSE: Tony was working at Les Halles, and he sent me an email from Tokyo. First time he had been there, and he had just been to the fish market. He was standing in his hotel room, looking down on the street, and he wrote me an email. It was hilarious, it was great. Karen was in our living room breastfeeding [our son] Rocco, I'll never forget this, and I went in, I said, "You have to read this!"

KAREN RINALDI: It was about five or six in the morning and I was sitting on the ground nursing our then-eight-month-old son, and Joel was telling me, "Tony is sending me these amazing stories from Japan."

JOEL ROSE: And she said, "Joel, get the fuck out of here!" This was before the *New Yorker* article came out. We knew it was coming. Karen knew Tony, but not like I knew him, and she said, "Well, does he have other stories?" and I said, "He has so many great stories."

KAREN RINALDI: He handed me a printed-out email, and as I was sitting on the floor, nursing, I read the email, and it was just so fucking funny. I said, "God, he's good on the page in nonfiction."

Joel said, "I know, I've been trying to encourage him to do this." At that point, I had just started at Bloomsbury.

JOEL ROSE: She called Kim while Tony was still in Japan, and she made an offer on a book. The contingency was he had to agree to it before he came back to the United States, because she knew *The New Yorker* was coming.

PHILIPPE LAJAUNIE: The piece that was published in *The New Yorker*, it was really loaded with everything he had in him. The consequences were pretty amazing. It was not just the intellectuals commenting on it; the TV was there, radio was there, journalists came to interview him at the restaurant.

I could tell this was something way beyond writing a piece for intellectual enjoyment; there was something that was touching people differently. And because the kitchen was running perfectly fine without him, I was willing to give him the space he needed to grow into that new dimension. I did not see any downside for the restaurant.

DAVID ROSENTHAL: I left [Random House] to take over at Simon & Schuster, to run the whole adult trade division there, and one of the first calls I got was from Kim [Witherspoon], who said, "Tony wants to do a nonfiction thing about working in the kitchens," and I said no.

My immediate reaction was, had he been a chef at a really big, famous place, it would've been one thing, but he was sort of in a box. I felt that my credibility with the sales force would be somewhat damaged, because I had pushed very hard on his two novels, and they didn't work.

Kim had sent me over pages, and I thought there was very funny stuff in there. She called again to say that they had a big offer from somebody. I remember saying, "You know what, go with god." It's one of the phone calls I most regret in my life.

KAREN RINALDI: It was kind of a playful negotiation. Kim brought it to him and Nancy faxed him the offer, and he thought it was a joke. And I said, "No, this is no joke." So he accepted.

When he got back, Tony and I met at a bar, and I said, "So, OK, you've got this book deal, what do you want to write? Joel tells me you have these amazing stories that you've been telling all these years. Just write those stories down."

JOEL ROSE: He couldn't believe it. He was so happy. He came back from Japan, and he and Karen went out for a drink. It changed his life right there. I felt a little bit left out, because Tony and I had been so close, but also it was Karen, so I trusted her implicitly.

KAREN RINALDI: He was like a kid. He was so happy and excited. He said, "I already have the title for it: *Kitchen Confidential*."

It was teed up; it was one of those magical moments when things just all happened at the same time. You can't make that stuff happen; it was fortuitous on all ends. So that's it—we started working together.

13

"I'M NOT GONNA CENSOR THE GUY"

EDITING AND PUBLISHING *KITCHEN CONFIDENTIAL*

PANIO GIANOPOULOS, BOOK EDITOR: The stories were so good, and they were so polished. They were the kinds of stories that he had clearly told a thousand times to friends; they were tested the way a comedian tests a set, you know, over and over. The beats were there, and the moments were all there. The editing was fun. There were no structural, fundamental changes that had to be made.

Tony was the easiest author to work with, because he was so busy, he had no time to talk on the phone. He was still working at Les Halles. All these other authors who had nothing to do, they would just keep you on the phone for hours, but Tony was always like, "I gotta get back to work." So he'd call me really quickly and answer a question, and then, boom, he'd go back to work. So that was sort of a pleasure.

It came in—I think maybe half the book had come in at that point—and I went into Karen's office to give her an update. It's the only time in my life it's ever happened: I said, "It's incredible. It's so funny, it's so entertaining. If we can't make this a bestseller, we don't deserve to have our jobs."

One of the things I had to decide was, *How dirty are we gonna let this be? How filthy, how many drugs, how much sex, how much cursing and profanity?* I cut maybe 5 percent of the language, cleaned it up a little bit, cut a few things here and there, but really, we just let Tony be Tony, because that was his charm.

But I remember when we had it copyedited. That's part of the process where a person goes through and makes sure— Obviously, there's things like grammar, and typos, and little things, proofreading, but there's also bigger issues around fact-checking, and then there's also things around tone, right, and that's where the copy editor can have a big influence. And she went through, and she changed all the curses, she cut them out, and so then I had to go through manually, and just, like, *stet, stet, stet,* like, put back the *fucker*s, put back all the *cocksucker*s, put back all the *fuck you*s, and the this and the that. It was the PG version of it, you know, but we kept the R version.

KAREN RINALDI: People were objecting to the all-caps profanity in the book—COCKSUCKER, MOTHERFUCKER, all that stuff—and I just said, "I'm not gonna censor the guy. He uses these words. No one's gonna mind, because the book is so good."

PANIO GIANOPOULOS: I worked with Rose Marie Morse, his publicist. I remember her calling and asking me about the line about "making that fuzzy little Emeril my bitch." She asked if we could cut that, and I said no. She was a little worried, I think, about how it might go over.

KAREN RINALDI: What wound up happening, of course, is that his profanity and honesty were part of what drew people to him. That's the beauty of publishing, that you don't know what's going to happen.

PANIO GIANOPOULOS: He was the master of being provocative, yet it comes from a place of absolute sincerity, and it's such an interesting balance of provocation and macho bravado, but it's done in a playful way, too. Other people try it. You see it on Twitter all the time, and it's just not charming. Tony had a way of being absolutely charming. And I think part of that is just because he loved the real deal, and he was the first to praise somebody if they were great at something; he didn't care where they came from, and who they were; if somebody was great, they were great.

PATTI JACKSON: He was excited about the book coming out, because as much as he loved to cook, he also kind of felt like he had something inside him—I mean, obviously, he had a story, he had all those stories. I was like, "Nobody's ever gonna buy that book, Ton. You are out of your mind. You can't keep telling people not to order fish on Mondays, and what really goes on at brunch." And he was like, "Patti, it's a good story. People need to understand." It seemed like such a pipe dream. If he had said to me, "I will become this famous novelist, raconteur, travel guru, political commentator, you know, hero to everybody," I think we would have both laughed and taken a big drag on a cigarette. You know what I mean? Like, who would have seen that coming?

KAREN RINALDI: Tony wanted to please everybody. He wanted people to be happy—deeply, he wanted that—but I think on the surface it was like, "I'm gonna do it my way," and everybody let him, and he wound up being absolutely brilliant.

There are very funny stories about me pitching it at sales conference, and everybody saying, "His track [record] is not good," because of the modest sales on the fiction books. "Nobody knows him as a chef."

We didn't actually shoot him for the book cover. That picture was taken for something else at Les Halles, so we grabbed it and put it on the cover. I said, "Look at that guy: Don't you just want to know what he has to say?"

The book came out in August 2000. I remember printing eleven thousand copies, and it came out and hit the bestseller list at number seven, with very few copies in the world, which is all about velocity of sales. He didn't have a platform, he wasn't selling anything. That was just him writing a book, and people wanting it.

SCOTT BRYAN: When I opened Veritas in '99, he came in and said, "I'm doing a little synopsis on restaurants. Can I come into your kitchen and observe?" He hung around in the kitchen for five days; he saw how I ran my kitchen. I didn't know he was writing a book until *Kitchen Confidential* came out. He was like, "Oh you're in my book. Read it." I was shocked.

BILL BUFORD, WRITER: It was radical and fresh. It was the first frank look at this world that we all rely on. It was the first frank look at what goes on beyond the doors of the kitchen, possibly since George Orwell. And it made a lot of other books possible, including mine [*Heat*]. It was a whole new anthropology. He had a sense of voice, and a sense of word choice, and a feel for narrative, and it was very exciting to read.

ALEX GETMANOV: His description of me in *Kitchen Confidential* hurt, because it was spot-on. He called me "a bit of a mama's boy," which I was, at that point.

DAVE MCMILLAN, CHEF-RESTAURATEUR: Lots of kids dropped out of university after reading *Kitchen Confidential*, just to become line cooks. We saw it for a decade. Intelligent, sober men and women dropping out and making a lifestyle change to work in kitchens.

FRED MORIN, CHEF-RESTAURATEUR: Ninety percent of applicants in the restaurant business, in the last ten years, have Anthony Bourdain to thank for going into that job.

JOSÉ ANDRÉS, CHEF-RESTAURATEUR: Kitchens were dark places that, as cooks, we were not allowed to come out [of], so it was fascinating to see how he came from deep in the caves, to very high up in the world. Tony seemed to be a guy who liberated himself by being a great writer.

DANIEL HALPERN, EDITOR AND PUBLISHER: When I first met Tony, he was so excited about the reception of *Kitchen Confidential*; he couldn't believe his good fortune. I saw it in manuscript. [Editor] Karen [Rinaldi] had just gotten to Bloomsbury, and they needed money. I shouldn't say that, but every publisher needs money.

She said, "It's really good, and if you want to give us some money to buy the reprint rights . . ."

I had just gotten to HarperCollins, and I told the president of the company that I wanted to buy this book. She gave it to [cook-book publisher] Susan Friedland. Susan read it and said, "This is a piece of shit. Why would you even think about publishing it?"

I bought it anyway. It would take a moron not to know that was a great book. It was the voice. You can't edit that into a book, and if you don't have it, you're never gonna have it. From the very first page, the turns of phrase, the way his mind shifts from thing to thing, the speaking voice, and it's exactly his voice: whenever he gave a speech, whenever he was a master of ceremonies, whatever he did, it was always that Tony voice. That was in that manuscript. You couldn't put it down. Certainly one of the best books I ever bought.

PANIO GIANOPOULOS: We wouldn't have sold the paperback rights, frankly, if we knew how enduring and amazing it was gonna be. We were a new company, and we were trying to be profitable pretty early on, and so we sold it. I know Karen didn't really want to, but eventually she gave in; I think she got pressured into it. I mean, who knew? Cooks weren't a big thing yet. He was so ahead of the curve.

Immediately afterward, there were so many people trying to sell food books to us. Suddenly, I was getting memoir after memoir from people, these imitation books coming in to us, and I'm sure other publishers got them, too. I didn't feel like anyone really replicated the Tony recipe.

14

"THE BRASS RING COMES AROUND ONLY ONCE"

DAVID ROSENTHAL: He was ahead of his time. He was not a guy, back then, who one thought would have a TV career. He was not as outgoing as the Tony who showed up on TV. This guy was looking for himself, I think. And who knows? If the book hadn't worked, he probably would've tried [more] screenwriting or something. I think he did want to become famous.

HELEN LANG: After *Kitchen Confidential* was published, he invited my partner Carol and me to dine with him at Les Halles. He was really hyped up, because at that point the book was a big success, and he was getting offers from all over the place, and he said, "The brass ring comes around only once, and I'm gonna grab it with both hands." He knew this was his big opportunity, and he might not get another one.

NANCY BOURDAIN: Tony would always say that we were expecting everything to blow up, you know? He didn't want to slow down. He thought everything was going to be taken away from him real quick, that he had fifteen minutes.

JEFF FORMOSA: I was around his whole life, until he got famous. Right after *Kitchen Confidential* was published, it kind of went to his head. I remember he asked me to help him with a TV, help him buy it and hook it up. I went with him to buy it. We get out of the store, and he expects me to carry it for him, like he's too much of a star to help me carry this TV for him!

ALEX GETMANOV: Around the time that he started to get published, we got together a few times, and then just completely— You know, there didn't seem to be anything to pull us together. I lost touch with him. He was into this whole other world, the thing with the media and whatnot, and he didn't seem interested in cooking or the restaurant world or hardly any of his old friends, people from that era.

ROBERT VUOLO: When *Kitchen Confidential* came out, I hadn't really been in contact with him; we'd left messages on each other's machines leading up to that point. But once that book came out, he was untouchable, and never returned any of my calls.

JEFF FORMOSA: Once he got famous, nobody who knew him, like Sam [Goldman] and Nancy—he just didn't seem to see any of us. He did it on his own terms.

NIGELLA LAWSON, WRITER AND TV HOST: I met Tony at dinner, a long time ago, the late nineties, probably with the food critic A. A. [Adrian] Gill, in London. He didn't *frighten* me at first, but I found him daunting, because he was quite manic. He had his silver thumb ring, and [was] wearing black leather.

CHRISTIANE AMANPOUR, JOURNALIST, CNN: I first met Tony in London, in the early 2000s, when I was living there, through my very close friend Adrian Gill and his partner Nicola Formby. It was at a Chinese restaurant called Zen, which no longer exists; it was in Mayfair. My first impressions were that this was an extraordinarily charismatic and unusual fellow.

I remember Adrian and Tony being very key to what we all ate, and just having a whole different kind of experience at a meal with two obviously brilliant critics and storytellers.

NIGELLA LAWSON: I didn't feel we got to know each other very much, but he was very much being Tony, many stories. From that dinner, he told everyone that I'd eaten aborted lamb, which is an embellished story. I was saying there were practices in France where they take the lamb out before it's born and eat it. So he embellished that into a story about how that's what *I* had done. I can't tell you what trouble that got me into.

ERIC RIPERT, CHEF-RESTAURATEUR: I was fascinated by *Kitchen Confidential*, and I was also relieved that he didn't trash Le Bernardin, because a lot of people were trashed in that book. I read it very quickly, because I was totally absorbed by the book, and I called him, and I wanted to talk to him, and I wanted to know who he was. I invited him to Le Bernardin to have lunch, and he said yes, and I was very happy.

I was surprised, because he showed up with a film crew. He warned me a few minutes before, "I'm coming with a crew, is it OK?" They were supposedly doing a documentary on him already, and they were supposed to stay a few minutes, and then leave us alone. It's what happened.

So, I see this elegant man with good manners, smart, very articulate. We had a fantastic lunch together, and we really understand that we are very different, and come from very different backgrounds. I mean, the culinary backgrounds that we have are—opposite worlds. He comes from a ship with pirates, and I come from the kitchen of Robuchon, which is like the army. And we talk a lot on that lunch, and then we decided to see each other again, for drinks, and he took me to Siberia. And that was the beginning of the friendship.

MICHAEL RUHLMAN, FRIEND AND OCCASIONAL COLLABORATOR: Tony reviewed my book *Soul of a Chef* for the *New York Times*. It was a brilliant review, and it was a book-selling review. And then in February 2001, I was coming to New York, I emailed him and he said, "Come by the restaurant," so I did. I didn't see him, and I was sort of intimidated, and I didn't say anything. I had my steak frites, and then I saw that he was about to leave, so I went up behind him and said, "Mr. Bourdain."

We sat down and just started talking. We talked about veal stock. He sent one of his cooks out for a pack of Lark cigarettes. And then we went and met Eric [Ripert] at Siberia bar. He idolized Eric to an extent that I found almost a little weird, a little embarrassing.

ERIC RIPERT: It's interesting, because, with Tony, he would say a lot of nice things about other people, and he would be almost obsessed about certain people whom he will meet in his life, and he would create a portrait of them that would be very complimentary, and so on. With me, he would never speak about Le Bernardin, and never say anything nice, or bad, but he would totally ignore the subject of

Le Bernardin, and ignore the subject of my career or accomplishments. So, we will have actually a relationship that will be very interesting because we will not speak about those things. I think, in a sense, it was good, because it gave space to speak about other topics.

NANCY BOURDAIN: There was one time—he was starting to get famous— he had to go to a luncheon, and there was a lot of the food press. His reputation was as a bad boy, cursing, and totally different from the way the establishment did things. He's at a table with all these people, he gets up to go either have a cigarette or take a leak; when he comes back, everybody's gone from the table. I'd never seen him so hurt by people he didn't really know.

If something negative happens to you, and you get a little down from it, I just think, well, that's normal; not bouncing back is abnormal. It took me a while, but I got him out of it. I was saying, "What do you expect? Them to welcome you with open arms? You're changing their whole lives, and you're totally different, and now they have to pay attention, [after] phoning it in for a while. Just calm down. It means a good thing for you."

I remember early, early, early on. *Kitchen Confidential* had just come out. He went to a Queens library, a limo came and got him, and another author drove out there with him. Tony came back, and said, "He gave me really good advice: 'Stay public. You gotta promote, promote, promote, or it all dies. You just gotta be out there all the time.'" Tony embraced that, and he was really good at promoting his brand. I don't know if he was doing it consciously, but he had an innate way of protecting his brand, protecting his name.

MICHAEL RUHLMAN: We were doing an event together, at the CIA. He was, by then, a cultural figure, but not what he would become. We were both smoking cigarettes, with students hovering around, and he squinted his eyes and said, "Ruhlman, it's all about fame maintenance." It was half-joke, but half-true; I think he liked and wanted to keep being famous. He was ambitious.

PHILIPPE LAJAUNIE: After *Kitchen Confidential* was published, in a very acute way, he tried matching the persona for himself, maybe for the people working in the kitchen. Now we could hear him screaming in the kitchen, which had never happened. He would throw things in the kitchen, which had never happened. But funny enough, I could tell that it was just a game; in other words, it was not natural. He was trying to scream, but shyly. He was throwing something, but being very careful not to hurt anyone. He was exactly how he described cooks and chefs in the book, but not at all what he was. Even the vocabulary kind of changed, and he was using stronger words.

I was impressed by his writing, and the scope of his intellect. He knew he could count on me, and vice versa. I was myself interviewed about him, and I was always careful to have my stories fit the person he was becoming.

JOEL ROSE: It's not the first time that one of my best friends has gotten super famous, and it definitely puts some strain [on the friendship], just trying to figure it out. I thought Tony remained remarkably the same, at the same time that I saw this strain on him. How harried he could be, how frustrated and nervous he could be sometimes. It was a different iteration of what I had seen in him before.

15

"HE NEVER CAME OFF BOOK TOUR"

BETH ARETSKY: After *Kitchen Confidential* came out, he asked if I would be his assistant. I don't think Nancy enjoyed doing any of that for him. I was pretty thrilled to get out of the kitchen for a bit and see what happened.

It started off pretty small, doing the scheduling, making sure he would get to his appointments on time. Tony was always very early. Anytime he'd say to meet at 8:00, you'd show up at 7:45, and he'd been sitting there since 7:30.

DANIEL HALPERN: He'd always be early, which was amazing. I think it spoke to his respect for people. He didn't want to make people wait on him.

PHILIPPE LAJAUNIE: We all know about this obsessiveness with being on time. He had certain mental reflexes. He used to be a heroin user; heroin users have certain common traits and reflexes, which may or may not include obsessiveness. I had seen it very early on. In the seventies and eighties, I had too many people on my staff who were users. You know, you have a car accident, you keep walking funny the rest of your life; you have some mental reflexes that are noticeable.

BETH ARETSKY: I went on book tour with him. He was gaining some momentum, and he had a lot of fanboys who wanted to get him wasted, so we had this trick. They'd say, "Hey, Tony. Let's do shots," and Tony would say, "OK."

I'd go to the bar and get shots of Jäger with floaters of Bacardi 151 on top, and Tony and I would just have a straight-up shot of Jäger, or tequila, so we wouldn't end up too fucked up.

KAREN RINALDI: His line was, he published *Kitchen Confidential*, and he never came off book tour.

DAVE MCMILLAN: The first time we met Tony, he was hawking a book. This was kind of, like, pretelevision.

FRED MORIN: He was still the "no fish on Monday" guy.

DAVE MCMILLAN: He was coming to town [Montréal] with a suitcase full of books. He was still lugging them by hand. It was *Kitchen Confidential*, but at kind of the end of the tour. It was already a hit.

I think we'd figured out quickly, at L'Express, over dinner, that— Fred and I have obscure knowledge of old French cooking. We've been down that rabbit hole for so many years, and for so long, that we can converse with very few people about the deep, very historic French cooking. We clicked immediately with Tony, because, all of a sudden, Tony knew who Alain Chapel was. Tony knew who Michel Guérard was.

FRED MORIN: The *repertoire de la cuisine*, and everything.

DAVE MCMILLAN: Yeah, the mise en scène of dining. None of our peers have that in-depth, historic knowledge of French cooking. We've always been alone in that. We'd drive around and buy oyster forks, and geek out on plates, like two nerds, Fred and I, who had this affinity for the ashtrays, and fucking absinthe spoons, and just so much useless information about old, historical dining in our minds. Tony was the third nerd who could join our loser club of guys who collected oyster forks. Tony would jump right into the rabbit hole of Limoges porcelain and fish knives, you know? It was like, *Yay, we have another nerd to play with.*

So I think that we kind of hit it off, because, all of a sudden, we're talking about the seafood restaurant Le Divellec and Alain Chapel. You know how many duck press conversations we had with Tony? And from his upbringing, and where he worked, he shouldn't know shit about that stuff. But he knew it as much as me and Fred, who are scholars on it.

There's a code, kind of. It's hard to describe to outsiders. And I don't have that with young cooks, right? Tony understood that we were long-career line cooks, and we understood, as well, that he was.

DANIEL HALPERN: He wasn't pretending to be a great chef. He was very open about that from the beginning; he was a line cook. He was incredibly modest.

It was as if he felt all of this was happening, and he could see it happening, but he didn't deserve it. And that seemed to be right at the heart of so much of his affect. He couldn't believe he was Anthony Bourdain.

He always told me, when I'd invite him to dinners and things, "I don't really like being around writers." I think they made him feel insecure. He was certainly a much better writer than a chef; he would've been the first to agree. But he didn't really like talking about his writing. I think it made him nervous. We talked about it in the context of editing the essays, that kind of thing, and he was fine with that. He'd say, "Yeah, I gotta keep that," or "That sounds bad," or "This essay should be last." But the process, not so much.

Often he would say, "Let's just have a phone call, we don't need to meet." He was always kind of easygoing, but really, when you were with him, at least in my experience, he was uncomfortable enough with himself that *you* felt uncomfortable. It would be taxing, actually, to spend two or three hours with him, because you felt there was a part of him that didn't want to be there; that he'd rather just be alone.

ANDERSON COOPER, CNN ANCHOR: I remember, he used to do his thing with his hands, like a fidgeting thing, and I felt like he was always on the way somewhere, or felt like— I don't know if he felt uncomfortable, or bored, or what it was. But I felt like he was a very complex person. And we got to see a little bit of it, and what we saw was remarkable, and funny, and thrilling, and smart, and cool. I was always left with this feeling of, *I really wish I knew him more, and I really hope I can be like him one day.*

PANIO GIANOPOULOS: With Tony, I felt a little bit like a freshman, hanging out with a cool senior. Maybe he's friends with your older brother or something, and he kind of tolerates you, and he's decent enough, but you just don't really matter.

And it's already—when you're editing a book, you're in this weird position where it's collaborative, right? You're having these conversations that are pretty involved, and it would seem like you're peers, and yet, when I saw him in person, it was always weird. I felt like, *Did we not just do this? Like, have a whole thing?*

I think the most I noticed it was at social events. I ran into him at a party at Les Halles, and when I went to talk to him, he did this thing where he would sort of speak to me, but he was turned away, almost perpendicular. And you don't know if he's addressing you, or somebody near you. Maybe he's talking to his friends, and I'm just around? And he was such a natural storyteller, and then, as he became more famous, more and more people would come around, so he'd address five people at once, and tell a funny anecdote. You felt like you were always part of an audience. Even if you were talking to him one-on-one, he had a way of talking to you where you still felt like you were part of an audience, but you were waiting for the other people to show up.

That said, he was never rude. I want to be totally clear about that. He was never unkind, he was always really generous, and he'd answer any questions, when I got the courage to ask him a question.

DANIEL HALPERN: When he wanted to talk, there was nobody more charming, and he could make small talk better than anybody. Always had his metaphors, his analogies that were surprising and accurate, always penetrating.

It wouldn't matter if it was President Obama sitting across from him or some person in the street who wanted a selfie. It was the same kind of attention and energy he put into every one of those conversations.

A couple of times, my daughter's school had an auction, we

auctioned Tony off; he and I cooked dinner for twenty people. He was so generous, he came down there. Tony was very relaxed then. We made bone marrow and parsley salad. He and I were working together at the cutting board; he looked over and said, "Why don't you just sit down? Your knife skills are shit."

16

"I'D LOVE TO TRAVEL THE WORLD"

A COOK'S TOUR BEGINS

KAREN RINALDI: Not one bit of it was planned, from the moment he signed up for *Kitchen Confidential*, to signing up for [his next book] *A Cook's Tour*, and all the books that came after that. It wasn't strategized, it wasn't building a platform, or a brand, none of that stuff. We just kind of said, "We'll see what happens, wing it."

We were following Tony's instincts, which I thought were really good, with [Tony's agent] Kim [Witherspoon]. The three of us would have these conversations.

KIMBERLY WITHERSPOON: I think that he was truly surprised at the response to *Kitchen Confidential*, and that people were so positive about his voice when writing nonfiction. Prior to that, he pretty much thought of himself as a fiction writer. It took him a moment to adjust to the idea that there was going to be a consistent demand for his voice on the page, whether it was for magazines, or from his publisher, for another book. Karen was pretty quick about wanting another one. So before he had too much time to worry about it, Tony was thrown into a position where he had to produce another book, and that probably was one of the best things to happen to him. He didn't have time to get writer's block, or to start worrying about it.

KAREN RINALDI: Tony said, "I'd love to travel the world, and explore food all over the world; that's my dream, to do it and write about it. What if I pick ten or fifteen cities and do this?" And I said, "Sounds like a good idea." So that was *A Cook's Tour.*

NANCY BOURDAIN: The fights we had over my [*Typhoid Mary*] research! Tony wanted so badly to see her recipes, the things she prided herself on, personal things. But there's not much of that. She had no one but the state, so that's who tells her story. At one point, Tony threatened to hire someone to do the job he thought I wasn't doing—but I really was; I felt confident that I'd come up with all there actually was, though it was so pitifully thin and one-sided. So I said, "Go ahead." And he did. That finally satisfied him that that's all there was.

> In 2001, Bloomsbury published Tony's nonfiction book Typhoid Mary, *about the notorious Irish cook Mary Mallon, who is believed to have infected thirty-three people with typhoid in the early twentieth century, in New York. Tony enlisted Nancy Bourdain to conduct research.*

PANIO GIANOPOULOS: I did a line edit on [*Typhoid Mary*], too, but it was pretty clean. And it was such a short book, and it was a new series of urban historicals; we were just sort of figuring out what it was. I wish that book had done better. It was really sort of a charming and weird story, about this superfamous historical figure, done in an incredibly engaging way. It probably would have made a great little TV show.

I don't think we did a great job publishing that book. I'm not insulting Karen, she's a brilliant publisher, but I think we wanted to build a series, with these great authors writing about New York historical things, or any city's historical things. But Tony was such a superstar that I feel like we should have just done it as a Tony book; we really should have pushed the angle. I think it could have been a bigger book if we'd found a way to do it right.

KAREN RINALDI: Next was a Les Halles cookbook, and he had a very definite idea of what it would feel like. We broke the rules; he said, "I want it on uncoated stock." Nobody did cookbooks on uncoated stock, because they get messed up, which was the whole point. He said, "I want it to absorb everything."

And that butcher-block paper [cover] with the stamp on it, that was all Tony. So [*Anthony Bourdain's*] *Les Halles Cookbook* was really fun to put together. I remember the photographer, Robert Di-Scalfani, was so upset when the book came out at first, because at that point, nobody had done photography with uncoated stock. People loved that texture; that was Tony, that was his vision. And it's a small thing, but that's how he got, you know? "Let's get the cookbook all fucked up and dirty and the pages will stick together." That's what he wanted.

NANCY BOURDAIN: [Tony's mother] Gladys Bourdain called his publisher once. I think it was about the [Les Halles] cookbook. She [was] fluent in French. Loved living in France and working at the newspaper. She knew everything. So I said, "If you're using French, make your mother feel good—she can really help you out with any errors. She'll just see them right away." He wouldn't do it. Writing the first few novels, it didn't matter so much, but for people who care, it's a problem.

Anyway, she called the publisher, behind his back, to make corrections [to the cookbook]. Now, how's that gonna make anybody feel, right? Although, she was a really good editor. For a long time, Tony had his life run by women. I think that's a big reason he's done so well. I really mean that.

GLADYS BOURDAIN: I never gave him any guidance in editing or writing. He was never quite one to ask his mom for anything like that, anyway. [*Laughing*] He never wanted his mother to be involved in any of that, although I wished I had been, because of some of the language that he used. He was never one to ask his mother for advice, or take it if I gave any. I would have changed a lot of the bad language, which I really didn't like, but I just thought he was a terrific writer, always.

PATRICK RADDEN KEEFE: The luxury that I have writing for *The New Yorker* is that I can spend a year working on a piece and keep coming back. My promise to Tony was, "I'm gonna do the work. I'll talk to everybody."

And he, amazingly, for a guy who's so busy, was very obliging. The one thing he didn't want me to do was talk to his mom.

CHRISTOPHER BOURDAIN: Our mom was very intelligent and talented. She loved French film, and she loved opera, and she got to write occasionally about those things. She'd written articles in *Opera News* and *High Fidelity* magazine, interviews with opera singers, and little clips about French film festivals and things that she loved.

She had the perfect job for Gladys Bourdain: she was an old-fashioned grammarian, and she was a copy editor at the *New York Times* for twenty-five years. She was paid to be fussy and correct other people. It was such a great job for her. And she worked well until after normal retirement age. I think she needed the money. She was seventy-five, and was sharp as a wit until then. But she was never not interfering. She figured, *I have the better answer, and people should understand that I am giving them the right thing, and they should appreciate that I'm being helpful.*

I think she legitimately thought she was trying to help Tony by calling his publisher and trying to correct mistakes in one of his books. I mean, lady, just stay the hell out of it. You know, your son is already a global success story. He's already sold two books, or whatever, and his own TV show, and here Mommy is, calling the publisher to say, "There are some grammatical and spelling mistakes here that should be taken care of." That drove him bat-shit crazy.

17

"TONY WAS SO RELUCTANT TO DO TELEVISION"

KAREN RINALDI: Tony was so reluctant to do television. He would say, "If I ever do TV, that would be a big sellout." He was mostly just really funny about it.

LYDIA TENAGLIA, COFOUNDER AND EXECUTIVE PRODUCER, ZERO POINT ZERO PRODUCTION: We met Tony in 2000. Chris [Collins] and I were working as producers on a lot of medical shows.

Kitchen Confidential was the big smash it became, and we had heard he was going to write a second book. It may have been named, too, at that point—*A Cook's Tour*—and we were eager to get out of doing medical shows, so I called him and said, "I'm a producer, I work together with my partner; would you meet with us? We would love to talk to you about making *A Cook's Tour* into something."

Tony had no designs, I think, on making television; it was never even in his mind. He was kind of, "Yeah, sure, whatever," about it. I met with him at Les Halles. It was between the lunch and dinner shifts, and he was sitting at the bar. He had the chef jacket on, it was unbuttoned. He had a very tall drink in front of him.

I asked him, "Would you even consider making [*A Cook's Tour*] into a TV show? No guarantees, but the next steps, as producers, we'd come in here, shoot some B-roll with you, do an interview." In typical Tony fashion, he was kind of unfazed by the whole thing.

We made an appointment to shoot with him; it was a pretty busy night at Les Halles. Chris and I went with these small-format cameras and we ended up shooting with him in the kitchen. There was a lot of banter. It was clear he had full command of the kitchen, there was tremendous camaraderie, but he definitely kept things moving.

We shot from a fly-on-the-wall perspective; we weren't directing him. It was a wonderful juxtaposition of somebody who was in control but also having fun with the crew. After the dinner shift, we sat him against a brick wall and started asking him questions: "Have you ever traveled before?" He hadn't, really; he'd traveled to France as a kid, and once to Japan.

We said, "What do you hope to accomplish with *A Cook's Tour*?" and he said, "Well, I owe the publisher another book; I want to travel around and experience other cultures and the way that they eat."

What was clear was that Tony was very well read, he had a deep love of film; those were his points of reference. It was like, "I want to go check out the places that loom large in my mind, from the things I've read and the films I've seen."

PANIO GIANOPOULOS: With *A Cook's Tour*, it's funny, because even though it was the book after *Kitchen Confidential*, so you'd think "sophomore slump," and expect it not to do as well, it actually had a totally different feel to it, because there was [eventually] a TV show attached to it. And he was really kind of wrestling with that.

LYDIA TENAGLIA: We sold *A Cook's Tour* to Food Network, and we were on our way.

EILEEN OPATUT, FORMER EVP OF PROGRAMMING, FOOD NETWORK: Tony was the person who exemplified exactly what I wanted to do on Food Network. He clearly had created a persona for himself. I wasn't really clear whether that really was him, or whether that was a character, but I found him, like a lot of people who have a bravura personality, very soft-spoken, very intelligent, very well read, very serious about what he was doing, yet at the same time, still squeezing everything that he could out of his life and his experiences. He was very gentlemanly. In talking about the creation of the show, his intent was philosophical, and I loved that.

Some people are born with charm; people want to do for you. He was born with that, and you just knew it. The camera loved him. He always knew where the light would hit him.

It really was my reading of *Kitchen Confidential* that got me so enthused [to make television with him]. When I was asked, in an interview for the *New York Times*, if he was really that impudent and arrogant and a terror to work with, I said, "You know what? He's totally different from that. In fact, I kind of think of him as a mama's boy."

Well, the phone rang very quickly after that printed, and it was Tony. He was not really sputtering, but he might as well have been. He said, "Why did you call me that?!" And I said, "Because it's kind of true! You're a really nice, smart, warm, intelligent person."

LYDIA TENAGLIA: Chris and I got married, and we left a week later—it was December 2000—just me, Chris, and Tony [to begin shooting *A Cook's Tour*]. We didn't know each other very well. I look back on it now and the whole thing was so ill conceived. We had no real game plan. There was no real format to the show. We had no fucking clue what we were doing together, and it became quickly clear to us—

CHRIS COLLINS, COFOUNDER AND EXECUTIVE PRODUCER, ZERO POINT ZERO PRODUCTION: Neither did Tony.

LYDIA TENAGLIA: In the back of his mind, he's thinking, *Somebody's flying me over, fantastic. I'll eat a few things, go back to my hotel, write my shit*, with no sense of, *We're making a television series; I have to be really present for this.*

Our first location was Japan. We were set up with a fixer who had a tremendous amount of well-studied protocol and etiquette, and was hypertyrannical about it. I think Tony felt awkward and weird and uncomfortable; he was avoiding me and Chris, not talking to us, not looking at us. He kept us at an arm's length.

CHRIS COLLINS: We'd shot with him only once before, when we shot the demo, and he was in control of that environment. He understood where everything was, how everything moved, how he could interact with people, where he could physically move. If you look at it today, he was actually playing with the camera, and us. He was giving us a heightened version of who he was; maybe that was the version he became over time, but what we were confronted with, in that first shoot in Tokyo, was a guy coming to terms with the fact that he didn't know what he was doing, or what he was supposed to do.

And we might not have been as helpful as we could have been, at least those first couple of days. We kind of threw him into the boiling water and watched him squirm. Today I can laugh about it, but at the time, it was painful for all three of us.

I can still see the three of us, sitting, waiting to board a plane at JFK. Frankly, Tony looked and dressed like a kid who went away freshman year and came back sophomore year and had grown six inches over the summer but was still wearing the same jacket. His clothing—everything looked too small on him.

On the plane, we were about five rows from the toilet in the back, and Tony was three rows back from us. I don't think he realized there was another way to travel. He was always open for that rough-and-tumble, in the early years. In fact, he did everything to have us stay in some of the dumpiest hotels, so he could experience it as close to the ground as possible, and write about it later.

LYDIA TENAGLIA: He seemed very jittery. He was constantly fidgeting with his thumb ring, and— I don't know if *shy* is the right word, but when we put him in these Edo sushi scenes or at the yakitori place, it didn't necessarily come naturally, for him to engage.

CHRIS COLLINS: He was uncomfortable.

PANIO GIANOPOULOS: It's really easy to think that it's the best gig in the world—you get to fly around the world, and meet cool people, and eat amazing food. And Tony was the first to admit that it *is* the best job in the world, right? But at the same time, there's the showbiz side of it, which is so much more intense for TV and movies than it is for books.

So that was a big theme when he was working on the book, and I remember thinking, *How do we integrate that, how do we get that tone in there and still make it fun, and not apologetic or disingenuous?*

LYDIA TENAGLIA: You could see this wide-eyed enthusiasm for what he was being exposed to, but in combination with nervous energy and insecurity. It was a constant through line, from the day we met him to the very end; those basic traits were always there, this combination of extraordinary intelligence surrounded by a vulnerability at the core of things.

CHRIS COLLINS: We shot in Japan for two weeks, and then he flew back to New York, to cook Christmas dinner for Nancy and her family. And it was like, "Why is he leaving now?" What was that sense of responsibility, or guilt, to do what was an incredibly generous act, physically grueling, to go back and forth?

LYDIA TENAGLIA: We overheard a few conversations; there was tension there with Nancy. I don't think she was particularly happy that he was gone on this long trip.

There was a funny incident in Japan. He said, "I gotta get a gift for Nancy," so we go into this jewelry store. He sees a pair of jade earrings. I don't remember what the price was in yen, but he thought that they were, like, $300. He said to the clerk, "I want the earrings in the window," and all of a sudden there was a big movement of people, and champagne came out, they put a velvet cloth out, it was like a tremendous ceremony—

CHRIS COLLINS: He gave his credit card over and we're drinking—

LYDIA TENAGLIA: And he's like, "Oh, she's going to love those," and of course he made a mistake with the currency. They were extremely expensive earrings. They tried to run his card, and he didn't have that amount available. It was all very embarrassing; the fixer was very embarrassed. I think he laughed it off, then took a plane and went all the way home.

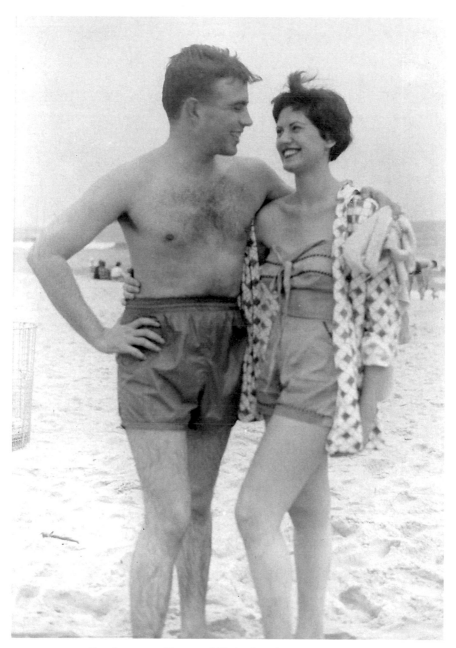

Tony's parents, Pierre and Gladys Bourdain, summer 1954.

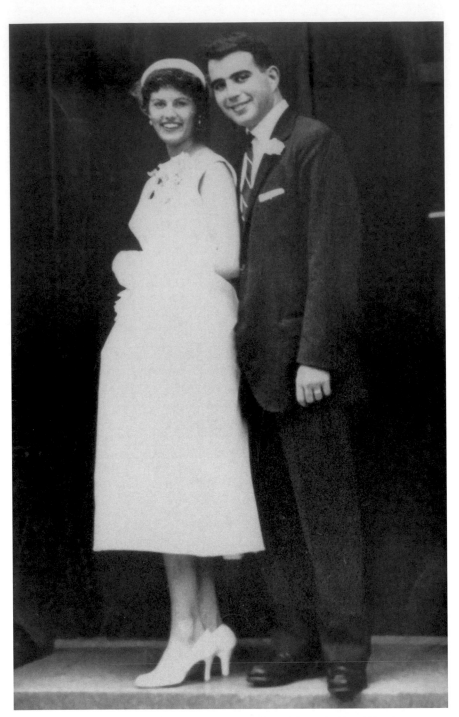

Gladys Bourdain (née Sacksman) and Pierre Bourdain on their wedding day,
August 20, 1954, in New York City.

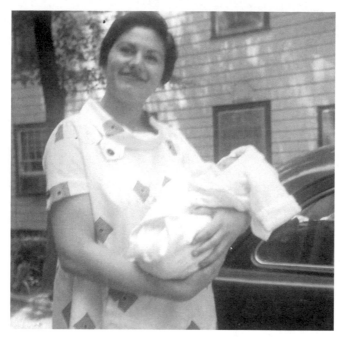

Gladys Bourdain at home in Leonia, New Jersey, with newborn son, Anthony Michael Bourdain, June 1956. Gladys was very close with her parents, both of whom died during her pregnancy. Later she would speculate that Tony's dark outlook was a result of her profound grief during pregnancy.

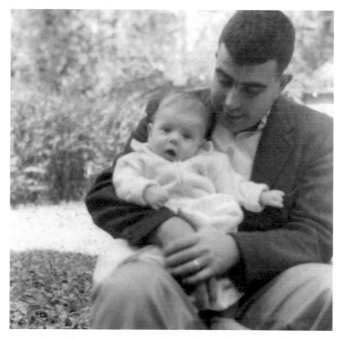

Pierre Bourdain at home with infant Tony, summer 1956.

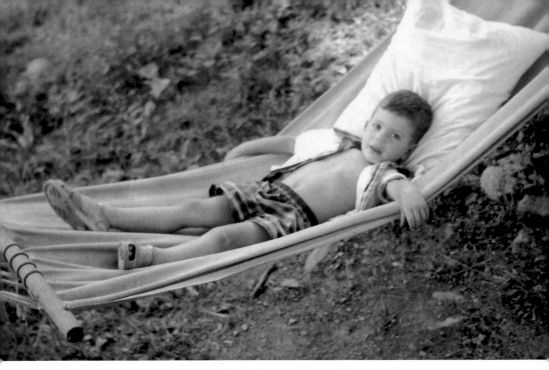

Tony at home, summer 1961.

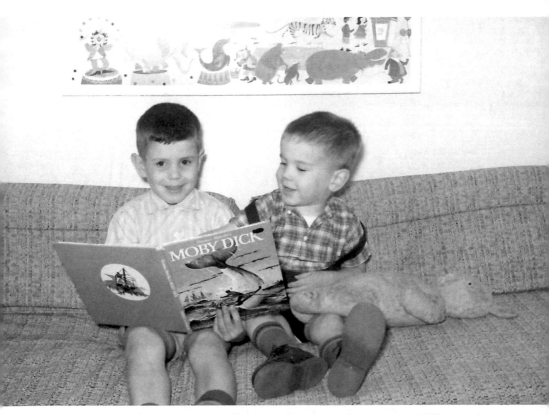

Tony and his brother, Christopher Bourdain, at home, summer 1962.

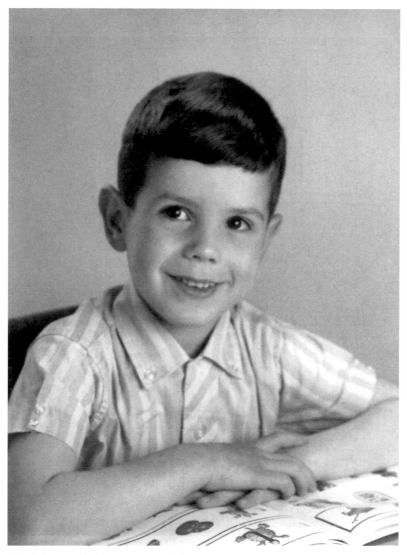

Tony's first-grade picture, spring 1963, from the Anna C. Scott Elementary School in Leonia, New Jersey. According to Gladys, Tony was academically far ahead of his classmates and, according to Christopher, he was mercilessly bullied, to the point that administrators suggested that his parents enroll him in private school.

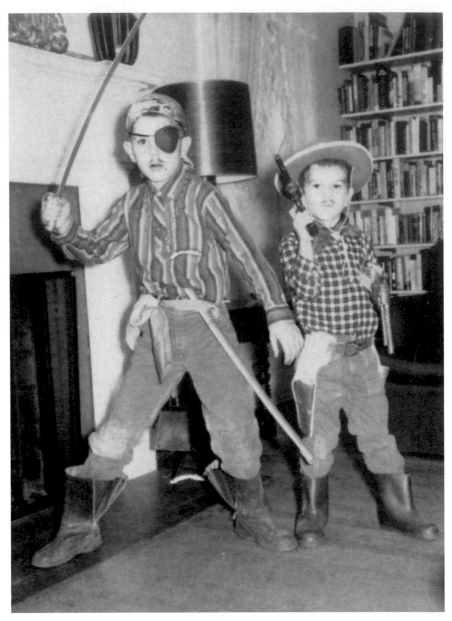

Tony and Chris, Halloween at home, 1963.

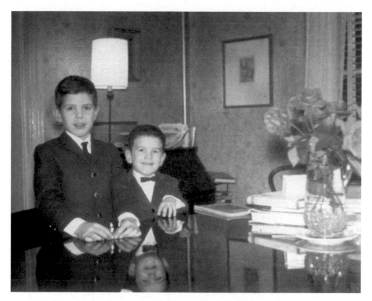

Tony and Chris Bourdain, smartly dressed as usual,
at the home of family friends, 1964.

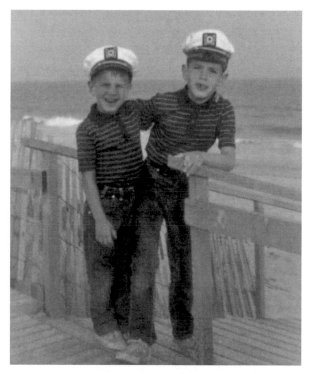

Chris and Tony in Amagansett, New York, summer 1965.

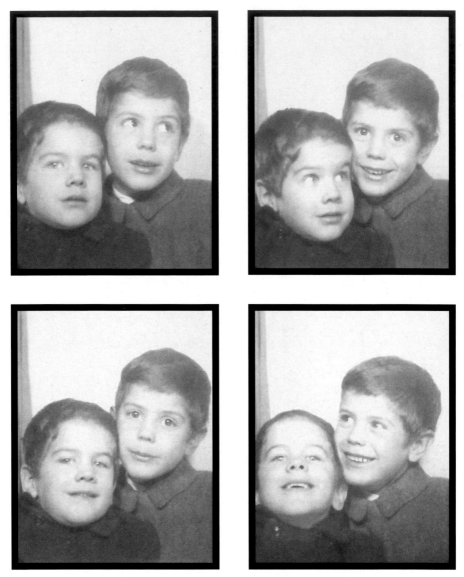

Tony and Chris, 1964.

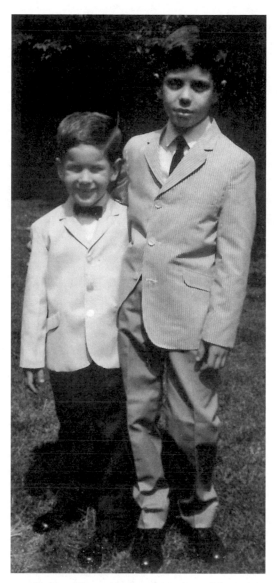

Chris and Tony at home, dressed to celebrate
Chris's birthday, 1964.

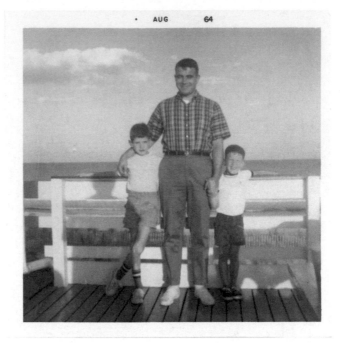

Tony, Pierre, and Chris Bourdain in Barnegat Light, New Jersey, summer 1964. The family would regularly vacation at the New Jersey shore, renting a modest house for a few weeks, with Pierre taking the bus down from New York on the weekends.

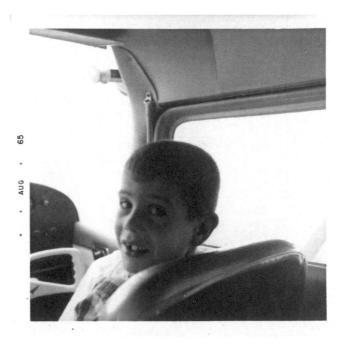

Tony on a family trip, exploring the Wisconsin Dells by plane, summer 1965.

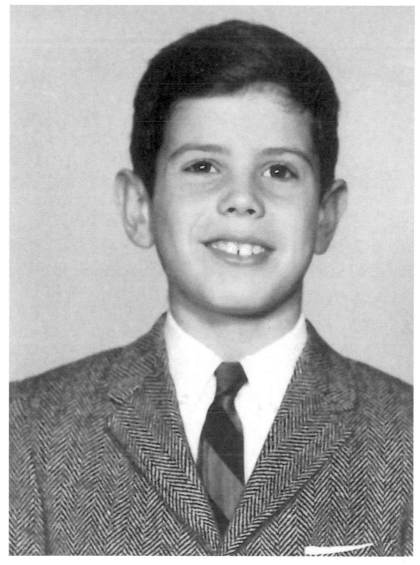

Tony's passport photo, taken in 1966, in preparation for the family's first transatlantic trip, which would have a transformative effect on his relationship to France, food, and travel.

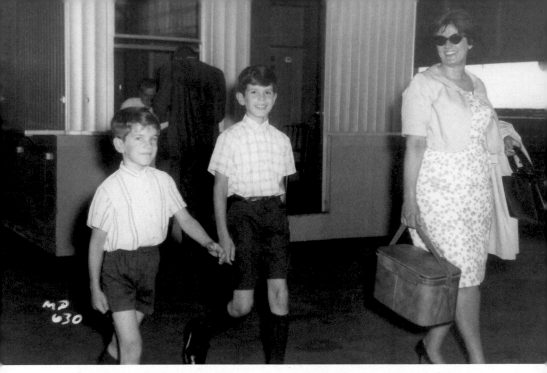

Chris, Tony, and Gladys en route to France aboard the *Queen Mary*, summer 1966.

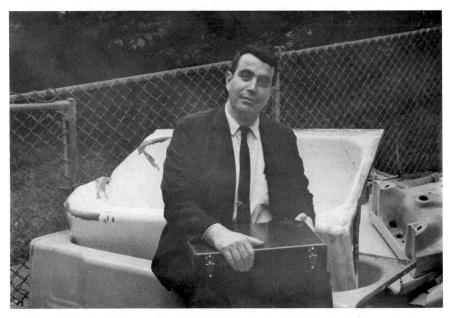

Pierre Bourdain, 1966, outside the family home in Leonia, at the start of an extensive renovation, which was left incomplete when they ran out of money.

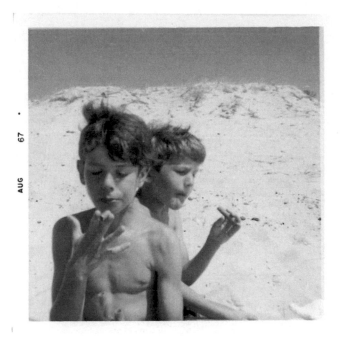

Tony and Chris on the beach in Cap Ferret, France, August 1967, enjoying cookies called Cigarettes Russes.

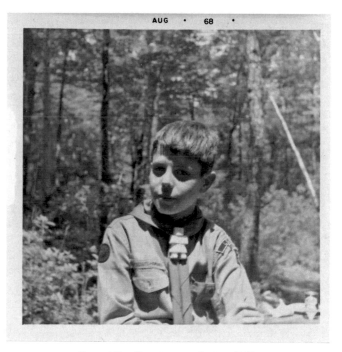

Tony at Boy Scout camp, August 1968.

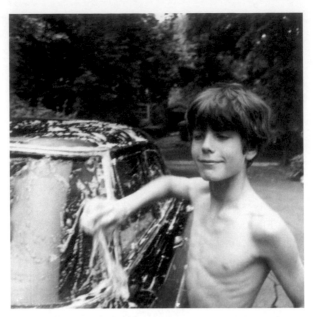

Tony washing the family car at home, June 1969.

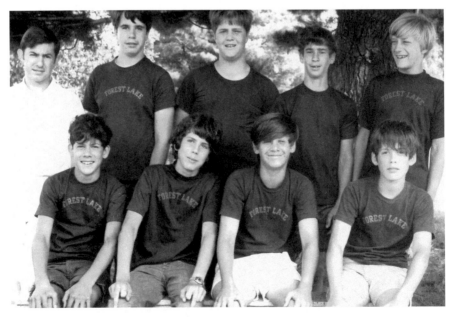

Tony (*bottom row, second from left*), showing off his signature subversive style
at Forest Lake Camp in the Adirondacks, summer 1969.

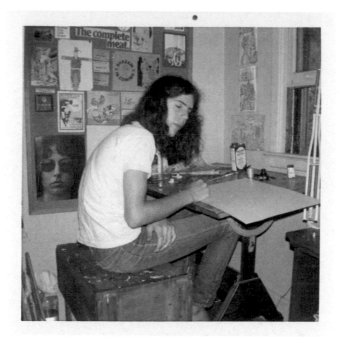

Tony at his home drawing desk, September 1972. He long harbored the dream of becoming a professional cartoonist, but he became discouraged in early adulthood.

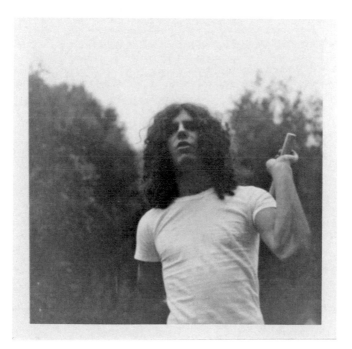

Tony at home, 1972.

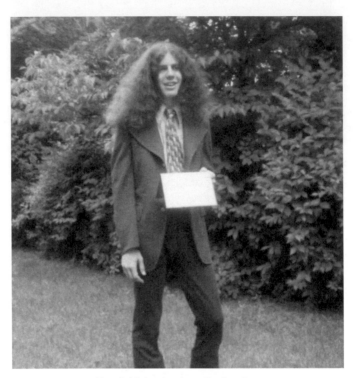

Tony's high school graduation day,
from the Dwight-Englewood School, 1973.

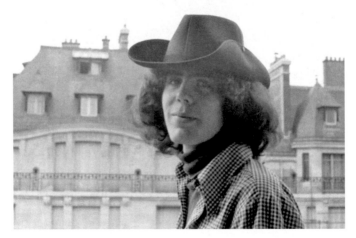

Paris, summer 1973.

CHRIS COLLINS: He flew back and met us in Ho Chi Minh City. We always say that's where the show really started to happen, because he had read so extensively about Vietnam, knew so much about its history, that when he flew into that airport, which remained largely unchanged since the Vietnam War, there were all these interesting points of reference that started to percolate—films and books and what have you. We were grabbing on to that energy. If you look at that footage, he's coming alive in the field for the first time. His ability to communicate began to open up a little bit.

I think he began to understand, "I can actually have fun with this. I can do something that has some meaning."

PHILIPPE LAJAUNIE: There was an implicit trust; there was no ambiguity in our relationship. Tony was trustful enough to take me, a few times, with him filming episodes—very early, on Food Network for *A Cook's Tour*, in Vietnam and Cambodia.

What was remarkable is that, as big as he was—he was a tall guy with a huge head—he was doing his best to disappear behind the people whose stories he was showcasing. At the beginning, he's a big kid having plenty of good fun, and it's about him going around on behalf of the viewers.

When we arrived in Angkor Wat, he was, in a way, not in paradise, but he was in the world that he wanted to be in. I had never seen anyone happy like this, except a four-year-old to whom you give his first bicycle. It was unbelievable, and the whole trip was absolutely magical, because of the state he was in. It was extraordinary, although I should mention, in the middle of that trip, I saw him fall into the abyss. It lasted just a few hours, but in those two weeks of complete elation and happiness, I saw him fall, like falling from a plane, down deep dark, and then he climbed back out.

We talked very little about it, but the little we spoke, he opened the window, the door, to what was inside, and it was dark. He partially knew where it was coming from, or he might have made up a certain logic for why it was this way.

CHRIS COLLINS: Tony's sort of swinging in emotions—it reared its head, even in those early years, where you thought you were sure of your footing [with him], but don't be too sure, because you don't know what door is gonna open up.

> *In 2000, Dmitri Kasterine, a filmmaker, began to shoot footage of Tony, with the intention of making a film about his life. A short version of the film, called "Out of the Pan, into the Fire," debuted as a special episode of* No Reservations *in 2010.*

NANCY BOURDAIN: We both really liked [Dmitri], maybe me more than Tony, since Tony was the focus. It was new, and I think he felt a little like the bug under the microscope, for the first time.

CHRIS COLLINS: The film about Tony, which Dmitri was shooting, part of that was shot after we came back from those first six weeks. I didn't see that footage until a decade later. I got to see Tony reflecting on what he'd just experienced with us, out on the road. There was a certain sadness, and this dawning realization that *my life may be changing*.

We would see that over the course of our decades with him; it would draw back in him, and there would be a sadness. I'm not suggesting it was depression. It was reflection about, *How am I going to change? What does it mean to the people around me? What does it mean to my current career?*

LYDIA TENAGLIA: He would often say, "The kitchen is a meritocracy. You're as good as what you accomplish in a shift, and it's palpably measurable."

I think at times he struggled with the transition. Part of him was like, "Can you believe my friggin' good luck, that I'm getting the opportunity to leave the kitchen?" versus, "Who am I, and what value am I creating in this scenario?"

PATTI JACKSON: The last serious conversation that I ever had with him, kind of mano a mano, before he really took off, he said to me, "You'll never know the consequences of getting what you want until you get what you want." He was super enthusiastic about all the changes that were happening, and who wouldn't be, right? He was also, obviously—he knew that it was a breaking point, that he was separating himself from his old life in that way.

PANIO GIANOPOULOS: We had this whole kind of running gag in *A Cook's Tour*, the book, which was, "reasons why you don't want to be on television." It was a series that went through the book, and it was about selling out, and about the bullshit, and the artifice, of making a TV show.

And this was before reality TV was just an everyday thing. So I think he was dealing with the kind of compromises inherent in it, and he was writing about it in a typically brutal Tony way, being completely up front and revealing about it, which I thought was really charming, and I imagine readers did, too.

NANCY BOURDAIN: I remember he said to me, "I have to go talk to my agent, because she wants me to decide whether I'm an author or I'm a TV personality." Things had started to develop, and I think he was very uncomfortable.

CHRISTOPHER BOURDAIN: When Tony hit it big [with *Kitchen Confidential*], and suddenly had money, he and Nancy rented a fantastic private house with a pool, in a really, really nice neighborhood in Saint Maarten, up the street from one of his favorite beaches, where there was just a guy with a chicken shack and Heinekens. We visited them then, and my kids totally loved it. They loved their uncle Tony intensely. He and Nancy were just the best aunt and uncle. They spoiled our kids. We liked that. They let them do everything we wouldn't let them do. That's what aunts and uncles are for, as long as it's not dangerous, or going to get them killed, fine.

I'll never forget, my son was afraid, at age six or seven, of getting his head underwater in a pool, and it impeded him learning how to swim well, but somehow Tony got my son to be unafraid of getting his face underwater, in the pool at that house. He was just so good with him, and so much fun with him.

CHRIS COLLINS: In 2002, we flew to Saint Maarten, which had deep meaning for him. He invited Lydia and me to spend some time with him and Nancy, just socially, prior to shooting what would be the first episode of the second season of *A Cook's Tour* [in Saint Maarten].

It was a really fun time, having dinners together and going to the beach. They seemed to be getting along well. They were finally in a position to rent this villa that they had always admired but were never able to afford.

LYDIA TENAGLIA: We were there for a couple of days, then we shot the episode, which had all these characters whom he had known from his years of going to Saint Maarten, and we left. Then he called us.

CHRIS COLLINS: Something happened after we left. They'd had a fight. I think she split, and he said, "Can you come back down? I don't want to be alone."

LYDIA TENAGLIA: He had gotten, I think, really drunk, and walked into a glass door and split his nose. He got a tremendous amount of stitches in his face, and he was starting to reel in the aftermath of it.

CHRISTOPHER BOURDAIN: Tony and Nancy invited us to be in Saint Maarten with them as a family one more time, but they were sort of in the middle of separating at that point, and the plan had changed up at the very last minute, and we found out that we were going to be there alone with Tony, which was still very nice, but it was awkward. I don't think we wanted to tell our kids about it, because I didn't know at that point: Was this permanent? Could they fix this? Somehow, we lied about it; we didn't want them at that point to know that Tony and Nancy were splitsky, because they loved them so much, and identified them with everything that is fun; people who weren't telling them what to do.

It was kind of obvious that the whole fame and TV thing was not for Nancy. She didn't like the attention, she didn't like the intrusiveness, she didn't like, "Oh, we have to be places at a specific time."

I was very uncomfortable that week in Saint Maarten, because (a), we were kind of hiding stuff from our kids; and (b), we had nailed down a certain kind of routine that we expected, being with Tony and Nancy, and it was just a little more awkward being only with Tony. And then the other thing that made it very awkward—you know, it was emotionally trying for him. I don't think he was happy that he had just split from the woman he had known since the age of fourteen. But, anyway, we'd come home from dinner, or have dinner at the house, and then we'd play poker or hang out or something, and Tony would basically go out and get banged by prostitutes. He'd ride out somewhere at ten p.m., and he'd be back by the time we woke up.

He was very up front about it. I don't think he was saying it out of pride or shame; it was just matter-of-fact. I think he felt he needed it for some reason. I mean, you know, that was not my scene. I was uncomfortable with that.

NANCY BOURDAIN: We were both very compartmentalized. I think that's why we got along. Life, when it worked, it worked. Once the [chance to make] TV came along, he embraced it. I think it took a little while, but Tony was very smart, and I think he realized, *This is the way things are going.* It does weird things to a marriage.

There were times when Tony would just want to go to movies. It didn't matter what movie, any movie. Looking back, I realize this was an escape. He just couldn't handle whatever he wanted to tell me, or not tell me, or whatever was going on. He would go to a movie and really get taken away. That was a red flag for me.

As I watched his career develop, he seemed more at ease with giving all of himself, which, I hate to say it, gave me pause. You've gotta save something. You just have to have something that's your own—and Tony didn't. Sometimes I would die of mortification when my parents were still alive. I didn't want them to know some of the things. You know, they were happy living in disbelief. I wanted that to continue.

We were together a long time. The plan was for Tony to write books, and us to travel all around, go to all these places, and have a great time. Traveling in Russia with Tony was a good experience. Spain was terrible.*

CHRIS COLLINS: We went as a group to Barcelona, to shoot Ferran Adrià. In the midst of that, there was another fight, and [Nancy] showed up at a meal; her eyes were swollen from crying. They had obviously been arguing, and there was a lot of discomfort.

NANCY BOURDAIN: Everybody went to El Bulli, and I wasn't allowed to go. And I said, "Tony, can't you just pretend I'm somebody else, and I'll take notes?" It was like, I couldn't be the girl just taking notes at the restaurant; I couldn't even go.

I said to Tony, "I want to be included." Tony would do terrible things like make me sit on the damn floor, because he didn't want a camera guy to not have a seat. I mean, I just felt like I was the lowest of the low, and after that happens for a while, you don't want to go.

When we were teenagers, we made fun of TV. Ted Baxter was on *Mary Tyler Moore*, and everything was goofy. It wasn't something you aspired to, the little screen. But that changed over the years. Once it was offered to Tony, he grabbed it, and he was pretty selfish with it.

I think he was confused a lot. Looking back now, he handled it as well, I guess, as he could. No, that's not quite true, because, he [could] be very iron door, you know? Once Tony's closed that iron door, it's never coming up again.

---

* *Tony, Nancy, Chris, and Lydia went to Spain in 2003, to shoot what they hoped would be the first episode of season 3 of* A Cook's Tour. *When the network and the production company (New York Times Television) balked at underwriting the cost of the endeavor, they decided to self-finance the project, eventually releasing it as a stand-alone film, called* Decoding Ferran Adrià. *It would later appear as a special episode of* No Reservations.

LYDIA TENAGLIA: Who knows? They were together for a long time, but I certainly think that him shifting gears in his career had something to do with their coming apart at the seams. It's inevitable. He's this person, and now he's becoming someone else.

PHILIPPE LAJAUNIE: I have known very well [Tony's] first wife, Nancy, and he was very much in love with her. They were extremely sweet and loving; there was a fundamental bond between the two. Then they were going through rough times. His universe was changing so dramatically.

18

"HE WAS AHEAD OF HIS TIME"

THE END OF *A COOK'S TOUR*

EILEEN OPATUT: Tony and Chris and Lydia tried to push the boundaries. One of the episodes starts with him on the floor of the toilet. Well, my god, the people down in Knoxville [Tennessee, the home of Food Network's parent company, Scripps], where they still had prayer meetings even though they weren't legally allowed to, almost murdered me for that one. They would say, "He can't smoke on TV!" and "He's cursing!"

He knew how to write mysteries, and maybe I am romanticizing it, but he created mysteries that led you through a half hour, so that you were always waiting for some surprise. The intellectual rigor, that literate approach, the ability to reference other cultural elements—art, music, writing, sculpture—for me, that was heaven; for Scripps, it was hard to justify.

[*A Cook's Tour*] was not something that Food Network really stood behind, as opposed to, say, Paula Deen. And because I was in charge of scheduling, I gave it a very prominent position in the lineup, so that the most eyeballs could see it, but it didn't really explode. It had a moderately good number of viewers, but it didn't have a breakout number of viewers, and it was an expensive show for us, so as the years went on, I was really pressed by management to cancel the show.

I hate the phrase "He was ahead of his time." He was on the wrong channel! He was on the channel *I* wanted to make, but it wasn't the channel for the audience that Scripps wanted to sell advertising to.

CHRIS COLLINS: Once we said our goodbyes to Food Network, in classic Tony form, he said, "When you figure something out, let me know, because I'll be there."

We started to pitch what became *No Reservations*. It took a long time to sell it. Tony went back to Les Halles; it was a solid twelve months. The first place we pitched was Travel Channel, and we thought, *This is going to be a slam dunk*. They were intrigued, but they said, "We don't do food."

Somewhere in that twelve months, we went to A&E and got an offer to do a pilot. This was at the beginning of their ascent into the docu-follow reality world. And they said they would give us a few hundred thousand dollars, but "there's one thing we would like to change. We're wondering if you can make it New York based." Tony was still with Nancy at that juncture. "You're hanging out and arguing with your wife, seeing your chef friends"—

LYDIA TENAGLIA: They wanted a reality show. "All the worlds you explored in *Kitchen Confidential*, the mafia underground, out carousing with different people, I'm sure that puts a lot of tension on your relationship at home . . ."

At that point, a year had gone by and none of us had been out in the field. Tony was thrust back into the rhythm of his old life. He had just gone two years around the world and then was just thrown right back where he started, so he entertained the idea.

He said, "What do you think? Should we do this thing?" and we said, "This is not what the show is, and if we do it and we fail, that's it, we're done, and frankly, what they want, it's really kind of egregious." So we said no.

Very shortly after that, Travel Channel came back around, and we were out in the field again.

CHRIS COLLINS: It was very quick. They called in September, and by the end of October, we'd signed the contract to do three pilots. And we went out in the field in late November.

LYDIA TENAGLIA: Tony and Chris did the first [*No Reservations*] pilot in Paris. They ended up having this huge fight in the field. It was an existential crisis. Tony was like, "This is all bullshit. I don't know what this is. What am I, a TV personality now?"

CHRIS COLLINS: It was the first day.

LYDIA TENAGLIA: Chris talked him off a ledge.

CHRIS COLLINS: I wasn't doing talent management as much as saying, "Fucking pull it together. Somebody just paid for us to be here. You better get your head around this thing." We were in the shadow of where the original Les Halles market was, and we went for a walk. There was the simultaneous smoking of two cigarettes.

It was probably a forty-five-minute postponement. And then we went back in—it was that restaurant with the catacombs underneath it, and the skulls. We thought Paris was the great reentry for us back into the field, that it would be so much fun, but it was anything but fun in the beginning of that shoot. [*Laughs*]

And it happened again on the next shoot, when we got to Iceland. It was just Tony and me eating dinner; we might have been shooting in the restaurant and then the scene was over, everyone was gone, and it was just the two of us sitting at a table where he, again, kind of fell apart, with tears, questioning what we were doing, and what it meant.

It was obviously upsetting for him, and for me as well, because, between Tony and me, there wasn't a lot of emotional maturity. We were not those guys who could talk it out in a productive way. But at the time, I just saw it as, "We're all scared of our new venture; we're trying to figure it out." I think the underpinnings of his relationship falling apart were really coming to the surface at that point.

JOEL ROSE: I was close with him and Nancy. Nancy had a really hard time when Tony began to get famous. She was not into that. When they split, it hurt me. And then I saw him with a bunch of different women. As handsome and as great as he was, he was not a ladies' man. He just was not. He was so shy and awkward and loving and needy.

SAM GOLDMAN: Tony had somehow developed this magnetic sex appeal.

HELEN LANG: I was completely surprised; I had no idea. It just seemed like he and Nancy were soul mates, and I never expected that to happen.

BETH ARETSKY: When he and Nancy split up, I was really surprised. They'd been together for so long. It was a little awkward and uncomfortable, to say the least, but I did not see him in any dark place. He moved into [producing partners] Chris and Lydia's old apartment, and I helped him outfit the whole place, from soup to nuts. He gave me his credit card and said, "Get me everything I need."

I got him 1,000-thread-count sheets. He had no clue about these things. I turned him into the princess he became later on in his life.

Tony was always completely respectful. He never hit on me. And he was never rude or crude toward me. We just had a mutual respect. One week we were working in Saint Maarten; we'd go to the nude beach, sitting there naked next to each other picking out recipes [from *Anthony Bourdain's Les Halles Cookbook*] that would be best for TV spots.

STEVEN TEMPEL: I knew him before he was famous, before he had money. The first couple of years after he got famous were fun. In the beginning of *A Cook's Tour*, he was grounded, but then when *No Reservations* came out, he turned into a real cock. He did reach out to me once in a while, but I think he just got caught up in what he was doing.

I got married. I bought a restaurant. I called him and said, "I had a child!" and he said, "Yeah, that's nice, I'm four-wheeling in the desert with Ozzy Osbourne," and I was like, *Fuck you*. To see pictures of Tony Bourdain in a tux at the Emmys or whatever—to me, that's not Bourdain.

MICHAEL RUHLMAN: We were together in Baltimore, speaking at an International Association of Culinary Professionals event in 2004. My book *The Making of a Chef* had been optioned, and Tony was working with Darren Star on developing *Kitchen Confidential* for TV. He says, "So what's going on with that show of yours?" and I said, "It's not going anywhere," and he said "YESSS!" So, I mean, he was competitive like that.

ERIC RIPERT: He was very competitive, yes. When we were together as friends, no competition. But when I realized for the first time he was competitive, obsessed with winning the challenge, it's when we were in Peru. We were in the mountains, we were about to do a scene cooking for the farmers, doing a kind of a coq au vin, or something similar to that. We were supposed to slice garlic, and I took my knife, and I started, and I realized that he was going like a machine, extremely precise, and very fast, to beat me at my own game. And each time he would have an opportunity to beat me at my own game, in cooking, with the speed, he would do that.

And in pétanque, he would be extremely competitive. We would play together, it would be fine, and he will be kind to others, but when he was playing against me, it was no pity. We were in the Cayman Islands, in the finals against my son and myself and someone else. And he looked at me, and he said, "Look at me in the eyes." I look at him in the eyes, and we exchange some words, and then I look down for some reason, and he says, "You're gonna lose." And I say, "Why?" He said, "You look down. You jinx it. You'll see, I'm gonna beat you." And he did.

19

"HE WAS PREPARED TO PISS OFF EVERYBODY"

TRAVEL CHANNEL

PAT YOUNGE, FORMER PRESIDENT AND GENERAL MANAGER, TRAVEL CHANNEL: I took over the Travel Channel in 2005. The network had been without a boss for nearly a year, and when I joined, the cupboard was pretty bare. Bill Margol was the head of production and development, and he had been the one who stalked Zero Point Zero [ZPZ] and Tony from their Food Network show, and persuaded them to do a pilot for the Travel Channel. It was clearly the only bullet in my gun; there were literally no other new shows— well, there was one other new show, which I didn't like—coming through.

I'd heard of Tony, and I read him, but I'd never met him. When I first met Tony, it was at the day of the upfronts, and we had brunch in a restaurant, but I didn't really get a measure of him. The next time I properly talked to him was when I saw the pilot. The pilot was done, in the bag; it was France. It starts off in black and white, and Tony is walking down the road, smoking. I understood it to be an homage to the French New Wave. And Tony said his aim was to show Americans that the French didn't suck. We were betting the shop on this.

And, I thought, *How does this work?* And I engaged with the team, and they said, "He's got a vision. It comes together. It works. Trust us."

Then it sort of drifted out of my sight for a few weeks, until it came to the final edit, and my marketing guy came to see me, in a bit of a lather, and he said, "What should I do about this?" Tony had written, in an email, "The new title sequence, which you promised me would be modern, hip, and edgy, is, in fact, dated, trite, and wouldn't have been edgy in 1962. I do not know the ninth circle of hell that the creators of this abomination inhabit, but I feel my enthusiasm for this project draining by the pint. Best, Tony."

And I'm like, pardon the language, but, "Fuck me." This guy, he's *talent*, you know? My marketing team are obviously upset, and I'm the new guy, and they're looking at me, saying, "What are you gonna do?"

I left it overnight, and I came in the next morning, and decided that this thing was a judgment call; there was no right or wrong. So I wrote to him: "Your judgments on all the other issues with the show seem to have been OK, so I'm going to go with you on this, but you need to understand that if this proves to be slightly slower and less impactful than we want, then I reserve the right to change it. Best, Pat."

He emailed me back: "Sir, you have a deal. If, however, your opinion is going to be based on the output of some focus clusterfuck group, then we should all bend over now, hold on to our ankles, and pass the lube. Best, Tony."

These emails, they're burned into my brain. He was giving me a sense of the level at which he wanted to operate, and no detail was too small. When he believed in something, he really went with it and put his all into it.

He did some great marketing for the show. We came up with his tagline for it: "Be a traveler, not a tourist," and he did some great little vignettes for us. He even did one that he was pushing sort of various tchotchkes that people bring back from their holidays, like a stuffed donkey, and a snow globe, he was pushing them into a sort of wood-chopping machine.

MUSTAFA BHAGAT, EDITOR: I'd been working on *No Reservations* for like two weeks, Tony wanted to have a meeting with everyone who worked in postproduction, so we gathered together in this little conference room, and he proceeded to tell everyone to ignore the network. He said, "Completely ignore everything they're saying about music, about story, about shots. Let me deal with it all. I'm gonna make the show I want to make, across all fronts."

I had already been editing for at least ten years, and this was the first time I'd heard anything like this. Everyone is always just trying to make the network happy. That's how production companies stay in business, by making the network happy. For me, it was the beginning of understanding how Tony empowered his team, using a kind of military-style, "band of brothers" approach. He demanded ultimate loyalty, and he gave it back in return.

PAT YOUNGE: He was prepared to piss off everybody; he was going to make sure that we knew what he had to say, and let him say it. We agreed with him that there would be no product integration, and that he would sign off on any sort of correlated marketing propositions. His personal integrity was important to him, and we weren't to do anything that was going to compromise that.

I think you can get quite cynical in television; you can sort of get to a place where, "That's good enough." And for Tony, good enough wasn't good enough. He really did raise the game, and that's why that show stood out. It became definitional for our channel, a channel that had been a poker channel became a travel channel, and that show was like our north star, and it allowed us to build other shows around it.

I do remember, he did an episode on the Tex-Mex border, and a car brand wanted to integrate their brand-new car into the show. I can't remember what the deal was, but it was a good deal. And he said he'd do it, only on the basis that he had every right to talk about the car as he felt fit. And the way Tony felt fit was that in the show, as he walked up to get into the car, he said, "The advertising guys and bigwigs at the network want me to drive this car. So they've done a deal for me to drive this car." But the car brand was really happy with it, because they liked the authenticity of it. *Authenticity*, I mean, it's the word du jour now, but he was there a long time before lots of other people were.

JEFF FORMOSA: He didn't ever do the Imodium A-D commercial. He wrote his own ticket, he wrote his own ending. He wanted to maximize his chance and he did, whatever it cost him.

DANIEL HALPERN: He could've done any number of things. He could've done commercials, backed products. He did it only a few times, for things that he really liked and believed in. But he was not motivated by money.

RENNIK SOHOLT, PRODUCER-DIRECTOR: He would always make fun of people who did cheesy commercials. I asked him about product placement, if he'd consider doing it, and I remember him saying, "I'm going to wait for the big payout."

20

"HE WAS VERY UNTETHERED"

THE EARLY *NO RESERVATIONS* YEARS

CHRISTOPHER BOURDAIN: After he and Nancy separated, I remember Tony fell fabulously in love with somebody in another part of the world, and had this notion of, "We'll go and live in Vietnam together, and we'll have a kid, and the kid will be running around barefoot on the beach in Vietnam." I mean, he had a whole scenario built for himself. He had gotten a publisher to give him an advance to go live in Vietnam for a year and write about living there. And it was a book that he never did end up writing.

ASHA GILL, TV COLLEAGUE: I had just started working for Discovery Channel. I get the call from the editor for one of the newspapers I used to write for, and she's like, "OK, this chef's in town. He's on his book tour." This was in Malaysia, for *Kitchen Confidential*. "He's also a TV host. Do you want to interview him?" For years, I was an anchor for Asia's version of MTV, Channel V. So I wasn't worried so much about meeting someone who's this big celebrity, but I was a little bit daunted by the fact that I'd have only ten minutes.

He's sitting in his chair, and I walk in, and he sort of unfolds himself, because he's such a lanky spider, and I'm like, "Fucking hell, you're tall."

At twenty minutes or whatever, the press people were going, "Come on, come on. There's more important press here. There's Reuters coming in. Get out." But it was just the most hysterical conversation. I'd read the book before I went to see him, and I knew how he felt about vegetarians. I'm like, "I'm not fucking leaving this room unless you give me one fucking vegetable that you like." And he was hysterical, he was patient, he was gracious, and he was kind of shy, in the way the nerdy kid at school got famous, and he was awkward, with his tall gangliness.

He was supposed to be having drinks at this other place, and he invited me. I walk in, there's all these network executives at the bar, everyone's drinking. And then I see him there in the corner. We just sat and talked bollocks, and really got on.

We kept in contact. And if we were ever on travels or whatever, we'd connect. I think he delayed his flight one day in London, or something like that, because of something else he had to do, and that was fantastic, because I managed to see him for dinner in London. I'd just flown in to do a show, and he was on his way out. We just kind of cross-connected wherever we could.

We used to call it, when we used to do stuff for Discovery, the dog and pony show, right? So we did a couple of dog and pony shows together. I remember the one in Taipei.

We had to do a lot of sort of functions and stuff. This one night, afterward, we were like, "Dude, let's go hit karaoke."

And, you know, off duty, Tony's kind of chill, funny, but not in the centerpiece so much, right? This particular night, I was dying with laughter. I was like, "Come on, baby, sing me a song." And he gets up and goes, "This one's for you." So we're sitting there, and he, oh my god, he sings "White Wedding," Billy Idol. He was fucking insane. And the minute he stopped, he folded himself back in the chair, going, "OK, who's going next? Get me a drink."

MIKE RUFFINO, COMPOSER FOR *NO RESERVATIONS* AND *PARTS UNKNOWN*: When I met Tony, he was very untethered. It was at the Chateau Marmont, in 2003 or 2004. I don't remember the actual point of collision, but, as I recall, I fell into his table, we wound up talking, and then, within minutes, I do remember this, we had a plan to make a film. I had no clue who he was. It was like, "This guy's funny. I should hang out with this guy."

And we just spent, I don't know how many days—you know, back in the day when he used to go pretty hard—there were a lot of very late night, early morning, you know, weird times. Very rarely leaving the Chateau, unless absolutely necessary, and it just wasn't all that necessary.

He was in LA talking to some producers, and he wound up kind of dragging me into the meeting with these film guys, thinking that I was a film producer of some kind. Of course, I was nothing. And I just thought he was a writer; I didn't really put together the whole chef thing at all.

And then he read my book [*Gentlemanly Repose*], on the way home, on the plane. I was supposed to be on a book tour, but I just never—the first interview was at the Chateau, and I never did the rest of it.

Tony wrote me this email, a lengthy, very funny—really one of the better emails I've ever received. In that email, he said, "If I'm ever in a position to republish this book, I promise I'm gonna do it." And then, almost unbelievably, [in 2011] he actually did get a publishing imprint, and, true to his word, republished my book [an updated version, retitled *Adios, Motherfucker*].

At some point, it came up, on maybe the second or third visit—each of which was many days long, of getting completely screwed up together—he suggested that I do some music for his show. He was shooting the Los Angeles episode [of *No Reservations*]. I told him I had no idea what I was doing. He said, "It's all right, neither do I." And so, that was encouragement enough.

Our musical tastes were identical, pretty much, and all the reference points were the same, and all our formative music was pretty much the same. He just wanted everything to sound like one band, like a live band doing it, but he didn't know how it worked, and neither did I.

It was all so casual. I think he just felt lucky to even be doing one more episode; he just had a feeling that it was gonna end soon, and he was gonna be back in the kitchen, and that was that. He wasn't concerned or nervous; it was just something he'd already accepted, and, you know, "There's no way this could keep going."

He was living it up while he could, and he used to try to convince me all the time, "Don't get used to it, it's gonna go away." And I never really thought that was the case.

ASHA GILL: I think when you get friends who do TV for a living together, it can be like a couple of teenagers being idiots. So it was a great laugh. He wanted to get a new tattoo. His Ouroboros on his shoulder actually is a copy, more or less, of a pendant that I had.

Tony and I were extraordinarily close. I loved him. He's an extraordinary man, chivalrous, just such a gentleman. We connected.

I think that things conspired to make it just extraordinarily difficult, with me doing all my travel hosting stuff, and there was crazy talk of him relocating to this side of the world. Because I'm like, "I'm not fucking moving. I don't know where to move. I can't work in America." So it was hard, you know.

He loved, like, old-school love. And through loving, he filled up that hole inside himself, and connected back to himself. He was able to do that. And he was a hopeless romantic.

Having said that, the kind of presents I got [from Tony] were coming from a loving disdain. Like a pan for omelets, because he couldn't believe I didn't know how to make an omelet. He shut down the kitchen in a very posh hotel in Singapore one time. He spoke to the chef, and I didn't even know any of this. We were having some beers by the pool. He was like, "I'm going to teach you how to cook a fucking omelet." I'm like, "Really? This is cutting into my beer time." So he had me there, cracking eggs, and then I wasn't doing it right. I finally did it. I think I must have, I don't know, gone through a couple dozen eggs, but I finally made an omelet that he was OK with. And then I get a present through the post once he'd gone back. He sent me an omelet pan.

BETH ARETSKY: Tony would go out a lot to Siberia [bar]. I would get phone calls from him at two in the morning, three in the morning: "Beth, I locked myself out of the apartment. Can you come down with keys?" There were a lot of those. There was one night he was actually locked down in the private room at Siberia, and he's calling me to call them to let him out. He was a little out of control at the time. That was prekid, premarriage. He was a single guy looking for love.

I think it was in *Medium Raw* where he wrote about the crazy cocaine model. I was still working with him then. He was calling me from Saint Barts, telling me, "You've got to get her out of here on the first plane. The Russian mob is going to kill me. Get me back to Saint Maarten, and get her back to England."

I managed to get it done. Whatever he needed, I always managed to get it done.

PAULA FROELICH, JOURNALIST: We met at Siberia, the old bar with the toilet hanging from the ceiling, Tracy Westmoreland's place. And he was friendly with my [*New York Post*] coworker Chris Wilson.

There was some big after-party there, and I just show up, and Chris is like, "Hey, man, you gotta meet my friend Tony."

Tracy said, "Hey, guys, come downstairs. I got something to show you." Tracy, by the way, is this huge—he looks like this ginormous biker. He looks like kind of an overgrown Campbell's soup kid, you know. He's got that solid body, and he had this big ZZ Top beard. And he was wearing a Bamm-Bamm outfit. By that I mean, literally, a tiny little loincloth with maybe a sash. It wasn't Halloween.

We hover into this disgusting toilet, because everything Tracy did, he liked to do everything to level eleven, like, "All my bars have to be gross. It's authentic." It was like a hepatitis swimming pool. So, we go into this bathroom; we're all super squished in, elbow to elbow.

Tracy lifts up his loincloth, showing us that he had no underwear on. And from between his ball sack and his thigh, he whips out a bag of coke. And I said, "Dude, I don't do drugs." And he goes, "Tony?" Who says, "Ah, man, I don't do drugs anymore." And Tracy goes, "Merry Christmas. I do."

Tony and I go upstairs, have a few drinks; I ended up making out with him. I didn't know who he was or what he did at the time, because I didn't have time to watch TV. We ended up going home [together].

He was the one-night stand who never left. I woke up in the morning, was like, "You can go now." He said, "You don't want breakfast?"

I was like, "I guess. All right."

Then we dated for three months. We broke up, and then we dated for another eight or nine months, before I broke up with him again.

But then, the second time I broke up with him, I realized I had fallen in love with him, so I got back together with him to fall out of love with him, and then broke it off for good.

I took Tony to India for the first time. I had a wedding I was invited to, at the Devigarh hotel in Udaipur. We'd been dating three months. This is a guy who couldn't pick up a phone in a hotel room, and hated answering doors. He was like, "I don't really talk to people."

He had never been to India. I went to Delhi for a few days by myself, and he met me, we went to Jaipur. There was this rinky-dink restaurant, dating back from 1897, on the second floor of the port. You had to know people who know people. It was really good food. He asked, "Are we gonna get sick?" I told him, "Nah, dude. You get sick at five-star hotels."

Later he was feeling pretty good, wheeling and dealing for scarves and bargaining. They strike a bargain, and the guy holds out his left hand. And I go, "Absolutely fricking not," and I slapped his hand away. "This guy just insulted you. After all that bargaining, he gave you his left hand." Which is considered unclean; it's very rude to offer it. He was like, "But I like that scarf!"

He cooked for me only three times. Twice he gave my dog the runs, and once he gave me the runs. But, to his credit, he always said he was never a great chef. He made it very clear.

LYDIA TENAGLIA: Our relationship [with Tony] was—there was a lot of love and fun, and we fought like siblings. He was like that friend who went to a party, got too high, and needed you to come get him, because he found himself in a place he shouldn't be. We got a call one night; he was somewhere on a superyacht, somewhere in the Mediterranean with a bunch of, I think, Saudi royalty. He called from the boat and said, "Can you help me get home? I might be in over my head here, can somebody please come help me out?" It was like three o'clock in the morning. I don't know how much of that was fueled by having fun and drinking and so on.

CHRIS COLLINS: That was the beauty of Tony—"You're *where*?" He found his way into some weird places. We kind of laughed about it, got ahold of him the next day, and he said, "I'm OK, I'm on my way home, it's all good."

LYDIA TENAGLIA: He was prone to hyperbole, though. He had that amazing gift of taking a story and turning it into an epic adventure.

WEB STONE: It had to be 2004, 2005, I threw a big fortieth birthday for my brother, in Charlie Chaplin's old house above the Chateau Marmont. And, you know, god bless, Tony was there. I was there for the week, with Jay McInerney, who was staying at the Chateau. And that's what Tony was built for, a night like that.

PAULA FROELICH: Listen, I loved him. He was great. We were very similar, in different ways. I don't think he ever said a bad word about me. We're both outgoing but very private. We had similar egos. And we did end up traveling well together.

I have very fond memories, and I know I changed his life for the better, and he changed my life for the better. But at the time, I said, "What are we gonna do? Get married and have kids?"

He said, "I'll get married, but I never want to have kids."

And I said, "Then you can leave right now, because I want the option. I mean, your children are your legacy."

He said, "My books are my legacy."

And I said, "Oh, shit, Tony, please. That's baloney. Do you know how many people write best-selling books?"

He said, "Let's do it. Let's have a kid." And then I said no.

By the end, he was very much into having a child. I'm glad he met Ottavia and that they had a kid. It's really important.

21

"BASICALLY, HE KIDNAPPED MY CAT"

TONY MEETS OTTAVIA

OTTAVIA BUSIA-BOURDAIN, WIFE (2007–2018): I used to be the manager at this restaurant, Geisha, and Eric Ripert was the consulting chef. I had known Eric for a few years, because one of my first jobs in New York, when I first arrived, was being a hostess at Le Bernardin for a few months, so that's when we met. We weren't friends or anything.

Then, when Eric became the consulting chef at Geisha, we started seeing each other at work, quite often, and his wife, Sandra, used to come in most nights and hang out in the lounge. And coincidentally, [Tony's assistant] Beth [Aretsky] was coming in at Geisha, because she lived two blocks away, and her neighbor Dwight would come in, more often than Beth, and he would always tell us all these crazy stories about Tony, all this drama.

I didn't really know who Tony was. At Geisha, most people work-ing in the kitchen would talk about the book *Kitchen Confidential*, which was like a bible for the people in the restaurant industry.

So there were all these little connections—Beth, and Eric, and everybody talking about *Kitchen Confidential*. So I read it, and I thought it was great, it was hilarious, and brutal, and I had this idea of Tony in my head that didn't quite correspond to reality. I thought he was just like a no-fucks heathen, you know, bad boy, leather jacket . . . but I knew he had a girlfriend at the time, because Beth's neighbor was, like, [the] official gossip. So I knew everything. But then, one day, he came in: "There's this big drama. Tony broke up with his girlfriend."

I was completely unattached, because I was working a million hours a day. I thought, *That would be interesting to meet him; maybe we'll get along.* Sandra [Ripert] actually made the connection. She talked to Tony about me. On Thanksgiving Day 2005, he sent me an email, asking if I wanted to go out with him.

A couple of nights after, he picked me up at work, and we went to Merchants, we drank a lot, and then we went to his apartment, and we had a lot of fun.

On our first date, he actually told me that, after his marriage ended, he was in Saint Maarten, and he was suicidal. He rented a car, and he was driving, in the middle of the night, on these really, really tiny roads, going up the hill, and he was like, you know, "If I die, I don't care."

I think he really liked the fact that I worked in the restaurant business, because he missed it, all these stories, and the drama, and he enjoyed listening to me talking about things that he also lived. So we really hit it off, having that in common.

The day after, I woke up with a horrible hangover, and he asked me if I wanted to go out that night to have sushi. I was just so hung-over, the thought of sushi—and I was just, like, "You know, we had this perfect night; I think it's enough for a while."

So we didn't talk to each other for maybe a couple of weeks. And then, I don't remember if he texted me, or I texted him, and we went out again. And it would happen every few weeks, and then more and more often.

He started asking me to spend more time at his apartment. It was nothing fancy—it was a one-bedroom railroad apartment in Hell's Kitchen, a walk-up, but it was filled with things from his travels.

I worked, and I had to go home at night, because I had a cat, so he asked me to bring the cat. I brought the cat, and then he didn't want me to take the cat back home. Basically, he kidnapped my cat. He was like, "If you want to see your cat, you have to come see me now."

So me and the cat spent a lot of time at his place.

MIKE RUFFINO: When he met Ottavia, there was a shift. I don't know that his overall behavior changed that significantly, but certainly his general attitude toward life changed. His cynicism was a bit tempered, and the conversations wouldn't necessarily twist toward the dark as quickly. He seemed very happy.

ASHA GILL: I knew that he'd met somebody. He used to call her his Sophia Loren, and just was like, "She's amazing." I was so happy that he found that connection.

MICHAEL RUHLMAN: I met Ottavia at Tony's fiftieth birthday party— that would have been 2006. I loved her outspokenness, and I loved that she was quoting Noam Chomsky. I called her "the fascist."

ERIC RIPERT: I was extremely surprised by how fast it went, and how strong their relationship was, and how much love was in that relationship from the beginning. And I have an anecdote about that. It was my birthday, they're dating for a few months, and everybody was about to make a toast for my birthday. Then Ottavia stopped the toast, and she said, "No, I want to do something else." She said, "I want to toast to the love that I have with Tony," and went on, and Tony start to cry. I was very surprised. It was very emotional, extremely emotional, and I was like, "Whoa, she really created something powerful."

22

"LET'S SPIN THE WHEEL AGAIN"

BEIRUT, A BABY

OTTAVIA BUSIA-BOURDAIN: It was July 2006, and Tony went to Beirut. We were more seriously dating. I never thought about getting married, or anything like that.

We talked about having children in a really hypothetical way; we had, like, no plans whatsoever. He said, "I always liked the idea, but I never thought I was going to be a good father." He also told me he was afraid that he was gonna die young, like his father. So he didn't think it was fair, you know; it would have been selfish for him to have a kid.

BETH ARETSKY: In the beginning, I think doing TV and traveling was very exciting for him. And then in 2006, when he was in Beirut while there was a whole war going on, we were having difficulty being in touch with each other. Things went really out of hand.

PAT YOUNGE: It was just a normal day in the office, and I'd seen the events around Beirut, on the border. But then, when James Ashurst, the head of communications, came in and said, "The Israelis have just shut down Lebanon, and Tony's trapped in Beirut," I just remember that was a whole—What do you do?

Luckily for us, we had access to all sorts of high-powered, international extraction bodies, safety experts, and they said, "You've got to get him to this hotel. Get him to keep his head down, because he's probably the highest-profile American in the country at the moment, outside of the embassy."

DIANE SCHUTZ, PRODUCER: I was on the Beirut shoot with Tony in 2006. It was surreal. We were stranded in the city; there was a naval blockade at first, so we couldn't leave by ship. You couldn't just drive over the border to Israel, because that's "shoot first and ask questions later." And we'd heard stories about Americans getting turned back at the border of Syria. At the same time, the network was still asking us to pull some kind of show together, so there was a sense of, "Well, let's do our best, though we're not war reporters, and we don't want to be."

PAT YOUNGE: So we got them all into this hotel, and then Tony asked, "Why can't we drive to Syria?" Now, Syria, at that time, wasn't Syria like it is now, but I said, "A high-profile American, and four other Americans, of which, I think, three are Jewish, driving through Lebanon to Syria probably isn't a good idea."

And he said, "OK, fair enough. But this place is killing me, it's driving me nuts. I can't get any decent cigarettes." So next thing I know, I'm in charge of getting him cigarettes. Then, the *next* thing I know, he's on CNN. And I said, "I thought I told you to keep your head down!"

He said, "This is so boring. You have to be here to understand how boring it is."

STEVEN TEMPEL: When he was over in Beirut and the bombs were hitting a mile away, I remember talking to him after that; he said that he wanted to slow down and have a family. The bombs going off that close made him realize that he wasn't immortal.

PAT YOUNGE: We got our international [fixer]—I don't know where this guy came from, but he appeared at the hotel, and he's the sort of guy who drives Tony mad. He's telling him all these stories about when he was in Baghdad, when he was in Syria, and when he was in Russia. And Tony's telling me, "This guy, one, he's fucking nuts, and, two, he's driving me bonkers. He won't shut up and leave me alone."

Then the Americans got an agreement to take this ship, to take people out, and the guy says to Tony, "All right, we're getting you at three in the morning." And then Tony told me it was just incredible: this guy was turning right from the wrong lane, and doubling back on himself to make sure he's not being followed, and all this sort of stuff. And Tony says, "It was the ride of my life; this guy might be a boring old bastard, but he really knew what he was doing."

And then they get to their rendezvous point, and there's chaos, and the guy disappears underneath some truck, and then, finally, he comes back, and says, "OK, I've got it sorted." And he takes Tony and the crew through some bizarre pathway, and then they're through, they're processed. The guy waves goodbye to them, and then they're on the ship, and on their way home. And when they got to Cyprus, we had the company jet there, and we flew them all back to Teterboro. And I met Tony at Teterboro, with two packets of Lark cigarettes, which he was interested in, but not as interested as meeting this very gorgeous young woman whom he then went on to marry.

BETH ARETSKY: When he got back, he was pretty shaken up. At that time, he was dating Ottavia. And he said to me that shoot changed his life. He decided that he wanted to have a child. He said, "I definitely have to leave a legacy after this. Life is too short and you don't know when—" That trip really scared him.

OTTAVIA BUSIA-BOURDAIN: He got stuck in Beirut, and I remember I would see everyone leaving—every other country was leaving, and the Americans were still there, and there was less and less contact. I was really panicking, and he was telling me, "Maybe we are not going to be able to be in touch anymore. Maybe this is the last time we talk to each other."

So it was really, really dramatic. And when he came back, I went with Chris [Collins] and Lydia [Tenaglia] to Teterboro [airport], and they landed, and I was so happy. It was one of those moments when you realize, things can happen any moment, you know—life is fleeting, let's really try to make the best of every day.

And so, we went home, we had sex, and we didn't even think about protection or anything. We just went for it. And that night, I was thinking, my calculations in my head, I said, "I think that I should take Plan B, because, you know, it's those days."

And he told me, "No, let's spin the wheel again." So we did it again. And I said, "OK, maybe you're right, because, after all, your sperm is old, so it's never gonna make it." I used to really make fun of him, torture him a little bit, in a loving way. We had that kind of a relationship.

But then, two weeks after, I was like, "OK, I feel really weird. My breasts are really hurting me."

I did a blood test, and then we went to LA—I think he was

shooting *Top Chef*. And on our way to Chateau Marmont from the airport, my gynecologist called and said, "From your levels, it looks like you're pregnant."

We went to the pharmacy and bought two boxes filled with pregnancy sticks. I still have the pictures of Tony with the million pregnancy sticks, with a big grin on his face, saying that I was actually pregnant. And I couldn't believe it, because, I mean, what are the chances?

But, you know, I was happy. And I thought we could make it work. And he was really happy. He was like, "Yeah, it's gonna work. We're both adults, good jobs . . ."

If Beirut hadn't happened, I don't know if we— I would have probably taken the Plan B that night. And I don't know if we would have even had children, honestly, because it was not really in our mind. We really liked to drink, and smoke, and party.

So I had to quit smoking and drinking. It was a big change. We had been together only seven months. Through those seven months, we were just having lots of fun. Things changed quite drastically. We got an apartment together on the Upper East Side.

It was a surprise when he proposed. In December [2006], we were supposed to go to Miami—the Raleigh, because we loved going to the Raleigh. I was watching *Dancing with the Stars*. He went to the closet, and he came out, and he opened this ring, and he asked me if I wanted to marry him, and I was like, "What the heck?"

He said, "I wanted to ask you in Miami, but I couldn't wait." I said yes. It made sense. I was pregnant, and it was like, why not?

We thought maybe after Ariane was born, we could have a barefoot ceremony in the back of the Raleigh, with our close friends coming. Then we actually got married before I thought we were going to, right after we had Ariane, because Tony was going to shoot the [*No Reservations*] Tuscany show, and he wanted me and

Ariane to come, but I was in the middle of getting another visa, and it looked like it was not gonna happen for me, the Tuscany show. So it was like, "Fuck it. Let's just get married now, and so you can come with us, and not worry about any of this."

Ten days after Ariane was born, we just went to City Hall and got married.

BETH ARETSKY: I think I was their only witness, and then we all had hot dogs after. And they weren't even, like, Papaya King dogs, they were just the dirty cart dogs, right outside the courthouse.

LYDIA TENAGLIA: While Tony had this lifestyle that required him to travel around the world, the fact that he had that anchor point of family was actually really meaningful for him.

We saw this shift in him, experiencing a real love, probably for the first time in his whole life, an unequivocal love that's not based on how it comes back to you. For the first time, when Tony had Ariane, he actually asked us, "How are you guys? How are your kids?"

When he had Ariane, it was the first time I saw him engaging in a way that felt deeply authentic. The way he talked about her, the way he spent time with her, their interactions felt deeply real.

TODD LIEBLER, CINEMATOGRAPHER: He would talk about Ottavia and Ariane in the most idealized, most precious light. His eyes would sparkle. And it was lovely to hear and to see him engaged with someone. Of course, it left no room for anyone else's engagement. He'd ask, "How was your summer?" and I'd say, "Oh, great, we went to—" and then he would start talking. It was really an excuse for him to tell me all about his summer, you know? His expression of interest in others was short lived, let's just say it that way.

23

"IT WAS NOT THE EASIEST THING"

LIFE ON THE ROAD AS A FAMILY

OTTAVIA BUSIA-BOURDAIN: Ariane was a few weeks old when we went to Tuscany, and everyone was there—family, friends. Tony wanted me to be on the show, and I didn't want to.

Before I was pregnant, we went to Miami, because he shot an episode of *Miami Ink*, and he really wanted me to be in the episode. We went there early in the morning, and we had mimosas on the plane, so I was not completely sober when I agreed to do it. And then I didn't think much of it, but when the episode came out, people were merciless.

They were saying, "Who's that bimbo with her midriff showing?" and, "She's wearing a wig," and, "She's so young. What's he doing with her?" So I was like, "I don't want to appear on TV ever again." I am not about this life. I want to be private.

He wanted me to be on the Tuscany show, so I said, "OK. I'm gonna just be some random person at a dinner table. I don't want anyone to recognize me and make comments."

But they did anyway. And it was even worse, because—the first time, I was all skinny, with the belly button ring, and fit, and everybody was like, "She's probably just a whore—some young—" It was horrible.

But now this time, it was, "She's so ugly. She's so fat," because I just had Ariane. So it was not hard when we were there, but it was hard once the show came out, and I was just like, "I don't want to do this ever again." But then, I ended up doing the Sardinia show, and he asked me to be in a couple of scenes of the Rome show as well.

For Sardinia, I was a liaison between [production company] ZPZ and my crazy Italian family. It was really, really hard. Organizing it was hard. I think we were on the brink of World War III at a certain point. It was the first and last time I did something like this. But once we were shooting, it was actually really nice. We had no issues when we were there. We had a good time shooting it. It didn't really feel like work.

For the first year after Ariane was born, I would barely leave the house. I just wanted to be with Ariane, and I had no family in New York, and Tony's family was not really helping, so it was me and Ariane, and occasionally a nanny.

It felt really isolating to raise a child in New York with no family. I grew up in Italy, surrounded by family, my aunts and my grandmother living next door; there was not a moment where I was left with a babysitter.

We went with Tony to Hawaii, and we went to Jamaica. We

went to France. It was the only way for us to spend time together, because he was away so long. Especially after he added his speaking engagements.

But there were a lot of occasions when we just stayed in hotel rooms, and after a while it was like, *OK, maybe we are not gonna do this anymore*, because it was really hard.

I was basically stuck in a hotel room most of the day. In Brittany, in this little town in the middle of nowhere, we were in a hotel where there was no one. We were the only guests. And everything was closed in town, and it was really creepy. There was no one at the reception. You had a key to go in and out. And it was just hours and hours of waiting for Tony to come back.

ALEX LOWRY, DIRECTOR: I remember one night in the house in Provence— we had a big crew house—and I came into the kitchen one night, and Ottavia was sitting having a glass of rosé and she asked if I wanted to join her.

I asked, "How are you, how's it going?" and she said, "It's really difficult. You all go off and do your own thing, and I'm with Ariane all day, and I feel the crew, they all resent me a bit, because I'm taking Tony away from what he's supposed to be doing, as his job."

I said no, but she was right, because if he was giving me half his attention because he's worried about what she's doing, that's a difficult situation. On a shoot, it's a trench mentality—you're all on the road together, and you're buddies, and maybe you act a bit differently on a shoot than you do with your family.

OTTAVIA BUSIA-BOURDAIN: At a certain point, when Ariane had really started school, it was also an issue for her to leave all the time, so we kind of stopped going. There was one year where we barely saw each other.

KAREN RINALDI: When Ariane was young, we used to spend time together; he would come to the house during holidays, and come down to the beach a couple of times, and then he was never around. He was never just off the grid for ten days with family. I mean, maybe he did that once in a while. I think he tried to do it. I think that got less and less.

OTTAVIA BUSIA-BOURDAIN: I wanted to go back to school, but then it was like, I'm going to have to spend five, six hours a day there, and then I have to study. Going back to work was out of the question, because working fourteen, sixteen hours a day in the restaurant business was insane. And with him always gone, it would not have been fair for Ariane, for both parents to be out of the house. We were lucky enough that I could stay home with Ariane, so that's what we decided, but it was not the easiest thing.

It was always horrible when he left. But then, when he would come back, of course, everything was wonderful, but he would leave again, and it was really sad. And the constant up and down eventually really took a toll on our marriage. And then it was like, "You really need to get yourself a life, because you can't just be home waiting for me."

So I started Brazilian jiu-jitsu, and I really got into it. But then every time he would come home, I had to stop, because I felt like I had to be home. And if I was not home, then I would feel guilty. And when he was home, he was home all day, basically, besides doing some voice-overs.

SAM GOLDMAN: Jeff [Formosa] and I were having lunch with Tony at some outdoor café on the east side, and we were just like marveling, because people would walk by, catch Tony's gaze, and we would see them clutch their pearls, like, *Oh my god, it's Tony Bourdain!* And a couple of minutes into this, Ottavia comes down with the kid, right? And the nanny.

Tony says, "Would you like to hold my child?"

Jeff sticks his arms out, and, like the world's best football corner-back, Ottavia shifts through, intercepts the kid, and keeps walking. I understood that we were the bad old days personified. I think that was the only time I ever met her. It was clear she didn't want, you know—and I get it. I get it.

I had no resentment about the fact that he got famous and became less and less in touch with us. I had seen it before, and it was expected. Shockingly, Tony wanted to come to a reunion of the bad kids from high school, at the Plaza Diner, in Fort Lee [New Jersey]. It must have been 2012 or so. When it was just the two of us, I gave him a little shit about being out of touch with Jeff [Formosa], and I remember this really well: he looked at me and he said, "You guys don't get me. Mario gets me. Eric gets me."

And I looked at him and I said, "Not only do we *get* you, we fucking *made* you." But I was so proud of him, and the discipline he developed. I don't know where the fuck that came from.

24

"DON'T BOTHER TONY"

NAVIGATING FRIENDSHIPS AND FAME

CHRISTOPHER BOURDAIN: Apart from filming a few episodes of TV with him, I took one other trip with Tony, on my own. We went out to Park City, Utah, for two or three days. That was actually a fun trip, because it was just me and Tony, and I think it was my idea. I said, "Hey, would you be willing to meet on a Thursday at LaGuardia, and we just go to Park City?"

I always had a lot of fun on trips with Tony. I think it was José Andrés, at Tony's memorial service, who said, "If you got to travel with Tony, you were then waiting, for the next three years, asking, 'Is he gonna call me again? Am I gonna get to go travel with him?'" It was very true. I mean, I felt that way even before he was famous.

This is a very personal thing with me, and it impeded my relationship with Tony in many ways for years, but I never wanted to ask him questions in a way where I sounded like our mom. I never wanted to ask the question that was riddled with bad feeling, or, "I'm feeling slighted," or, "I want more of your time." I just never wanted to be that type of voice with him, because our mom was always grumbling about something that was making her unhappy, and I just didn't want to be that way. Every conversation between them, there was always a loaded question of some kind.

I screwed myself, honestly, because probably if I had been a little more pushy, I would have seen Tony a lot more. And I wanted to, but I never wanted to be the resentful-toned person who was feeling slighted, or wanted something from him, because everybody wanted something from Tony, you know? Everybody wanted a piece of him. And I didn't want to be one of those people who wanted a piece of him.

HELEN CHO, PRODUCER-DIRECTOR: I started out as a production assistant. I was asked to help produce an episode of *No Reservations*, and it was a special. The specials were always an excuse to get weird. This one was called "Burning Questions." Tony had written a specific list of things that he wanted to include: a deranged child who's into exotic pets; a rodeo clown, wielding a bong, in a wheelchair; a crazy stalker with security guards. So I had a weird list of things to find and cast.

Then I wrote a crew blog about my experience acquiring all those things. I had thought it was a hazing thing, but I took it very seriously, and found the seediest basement, cast a clown, found a bong, an exotic pet store, everything.

Chris Collins came back from [shooting with Tony in] Istanbul, and said, "Man, Tony's been talking about you." And I was like, "Why, what did I do?" And he said, "No, he really liked your crew blog post. He said that's the standard to which all crew blog posts should be held."

I was so young, still in college, and one of two Korean Americans working there, and I think Tony really championed the underdog.

I had worked up to the point where I was associate-producing on *No Reservations*. Then Chris and Lydia said, "Tony wants you to head up the social media department, as well as his personal social media." It was pulling me off the production track, but I was young and new at the company, and I appreciated that Tony saw me as capable of being the head of something. I wasn't trained or that interested in marketing or in social media; I saw it as an opportunity, and I took it.

By the nature of the job, I had to get close to him. I had to learn his voice, because if you're gonna speak for somebody or post for somebody, you have to get to know him.

It kind of naturally moved from that to a real friendship. I related to him a lot on the loneliness level, feeling like a misfit in ordinary situations. Maybe that's why he opened that door. We'd sit and talk, and it didn't feel like a work thing. He'd say, "Hey, there's this weird music video I just saw, you would like it," or he'd ask to have dinner or go for a drink or watch a movie or something.

Meanwhile, I was still helping produce along the way; I wanted to keep that muscle alive.

I started to become dissatisfied doing social media. At the same time, I saw how many requests he'd get, and how much time was demanded of him, and how many people were just trying to take, take, take constantly. And I never wanted to be that person; I wanted him to feel like he could trust me, so I never asked him for anything or crossed that line. And I never said that I was unhappy, but he just picked up on it. He was that hybrid of having so much empathy and being hyper all-knowing, but at the same time, he could be pretty unaware or one-track-minded. It's a weird mix. I'd hear from other people that he would never ask how you were doing, or how your family was doing, or anything like that.

When I look back, he had an intuitive sense, and would ask, "What's wrong?" It meant a lot to me that he seemed to care, but I did not want to cross that line. I was trying to make the transition back into production, but I didn't quite know how.

Unbeknownst to me, he made sure that I went on the [*Parts Unknown*] Korea shoot. And he would say things like, "Well, if you wanna be in the field, I know exactly who to fire." But I didn't want to put other people out of work, because these were my friends, and I also didn't want to violate our friendship, and the working relationship.

Maybe that's why we had such a close friendship, because I treated him like a human being. I saw, also, how lonely it was to be him. He would make me go to events with him. When you first start going, you're like, "Oh, this is kind of cool." And then after the third one, you're like, "Got it. This is just people grabbing at him, and it's really alienating."

And to be fair, he was super tall, so he kind of stood out no matter where he went. But regardless, I understood, on a very granular level, how lonely and alienating that must have felt for him.

When we would go out to eat together, I would always offer to pay, and he would never let me, but I was serious. Like, *This is not you providing for me constantly, this is not what this is about, you know. We're friends, there has to be some sort of equality.* He let me pay for things that he thought that I could afford, like a smoothie or a beer or something.

SCOTT BRYAN: One good thing about Tony is he always picked up the phone. Guys would say, "Hey, do you think you can get Tony on the phone, hit him up with an idea to get me on his show?" And every now and then I would call him. I didn't want to bother him, though, with other people's little things like that.

DAVE CHANG, CHEF-RESTAURATEUR; FREQUENT TV AND PUBLISHING COLLABORATOR: I wanted to make sure I never bothered him. I knew in my life, all I wanted was for people to just not talk to me, and I know Tony was like that, too.

FRED MORIN: We all had the same level of friendship with Tony, and that was the Tony level of friendship. We knew that we had to exert a certain restraint in the display of friendship, you know? We have a lot of people who say, "You're friends of Tony," but we never used it.

DAVE MCMILLAN: I believe Tony was my friend. I was Tony's friend. But our friendship was a special friendship, because it was a friendship on his terms. We understood that. We were all sous chefs. No one could get him to do anything that he wouldn't want to do.

NATHAN THORNBURGH, EDITOR-WRITER; BUSINESS PARTNER IN *ROADS & KINGDOMS*: There were a lot of different rooms in that man's brain; you always knew it was a big mansion. Once in a while we'd have dinner and drinks. It was always a good time, and I loved being with him, but I tried to not get carried away.

ADAM EPSTEIN, LECTURE TOUR PRODUCER: I didn't know him well enough to know if he liked being alone, but I did try to leave him alone. I didn't want to be a star fucker.

DAVE MCMILLAN: I never asked him for anything, because he'd already done more than any person had ever done for me in my career, so—

FRED MORIN: —and we knew people who used the Bourdain acquaintance, you know? It's easy to fall for that; we had, like, an offer a week for some shit.

DAVE MCMILLAN: "Do you think Tony would come to my wedding for twenty thousand bucks? Can you give me his email address?"

FRED MORIN: It was unspoken, but there was, for us, a cardinal rule that, we're never gonna call him up, and say, "Hey, we have this idea for a show"—

DAVE MCMILLAN: We knew the golden rule was "Don't bother Tony." If he calls us, we're there, but we don't call. Don't ask.

JOSH HOMME, MUSICIAN: I met Tony in Berlin. We [Queens of the Stone Age] were playing a show, and he was in town doing *No Reservations*. He came to the show, and we just— [*snaps fingers*] It clicked, it was immediate. We stood outside in the relative cold, smoking cigarettes, drinking beers, and talking about what we liked. There was a hearty, good exchange of possibility between us that was immediate.

I think what we were bonding over is kind of wanting to live outside the system, you know? Even though what you do in the kitchen, what you do in a band—everything is a system of some sort. But there was a pirate-ship mentality to both of these things, where you go from town to town, giving as much as you can, taking as much as you can.

We showed each other our worlds, and there was a bunch in my world that he really loved. I introduced him to [musicians] Alison [Mosshart], and to Dean [Fertita], and Jack White, and to [Mark] Lanegan. We were the doormen of worlds the other one wasn't in.

DEAN FERTITA, MUSICIAN: We ended up doing a Christmas episode of Tony's show. Both Troy [Van Leeuwen, Queens of the Stone Age guitarist] and I were predominantly vegetarian at the time, but when

Tony cooked us a meal, we just totally went off the wagon. That experience alone opened me up to the idea of how important it is to let things take you where they take you. That came up a few times with Tony. Just being available to try new things with him, that still affects me daily now.

MIKE RUFFINO: Even among celebrities, he was a celebrity. He never complained about it, that I recall. Whenever we discussed it, it was always in a broader context of just how absurd the whole idea is, and on the more practical level, where he would express some regret that he wouldn't want to go to a place, because he would destroy it, you know? There was a night that I was at the Chateau, with Tony, and Eric Ripert, and Ludo [Lefevbre]. None of them had ever been to Irv's, this hamburger place in West Hollywood.

It was [run by] this great lady. She made the best burgers, and she would do your portrait on a paper plate, in pen. If you ordered one burger, sometimes she would charge you for two. "You're gonna want another one." And she was right every time. She was hilarious, and the burgers were better than In-N-Out, I thought. And we were gonna go there, but Tony realized that if he went there, it would be all done. Everyone would take his picture and put it on the internet, and Irv's would be jammed all the time, and that poor lady would be a little overwhelmed. So I went and picked up the burgers.

It's a weird life, and I'm sure it contributed to his overall exhaustion.

NATHAN THORNBURGH: We ran a heavy risk, one that I didn't fully appreciate, in getting involved with Tony [at *Roads & Kingdoms*]. Kim [Witherspoon], every once in a while, to her credit, would say, "Just so you know, this guy throws a real big shadow. Best-case scenario, people will start to look at you as Bourdain's publication. If you do this right and it works out well, you'll be Bourdain people."

Tony had a weird effect on the things that he loved—like a restaurant that he dug—the reason he was there was not so he would overshadow it, but things that he was interested in got changed by his interest in them, and that's not a predictable force.

PETER MEEHAN, JOURNALIST, FREQUENT PUBLISHING COLLABORATOR: Around 2010, we had dinner together [in New York] at Ko, back when it was in a little space on First Avenue. We walked after dinner down to PDT, my brother's bar, to have a drink, and he was stopped by eighteen people to take pictures, in the course of two and a half blocks. And he was fucking gracious to all of them.

Everybody has that line, that they're "thankful for their success and the people who put them there," but he genuinely seemed, every time I ever hung out with him, he felt like his success was a gift of people's attention, and if what he had to do was take a picture with someone to thank them for it? Then he had the time for it.

SAM SIFTON: I ran into Tony at a couple of industry rat-fuck events, to use a Bourdain term, over the years. And we had pleasant repartee.

One notable evening was the twenty-fifth anniversary of Alan Richman's employment at *GQ*. And there was a roast of Alan at Le Bernardin, at which I spoke, Tony spoke, and he was really funny. That was the night when I really realized the bubble of celebrity in which he was living. He was there with Ottavia, and they were sitting with the Riperts. There was sort of a force field of glam that was all of a sudden surrounding him. He had passed over from being a writer guy with a working-class background into something that made him 120 percent of the people around him. He was the same as the rest of us, cracking jokes, but in his relationship to the crowd— This is an industry crowd, right? It's all chefs and journalists. So he's sitting amid chefs and journalists, but even there, he was not interacting with chefs and journalists. He was in the bubble, and then the bubble drifted out of the room, and that was that.

And if you're socially awkward—and I think he was—you know, that's got to be kind of weird. I don't resent him that bubble. I'd use it, too.

JOSH HOMME: Tony had a guarded nature about him. In this thing we do, this travel, and that life, there's a bit, like, "Is it still safe to speak to you? Are you in the same spot?" And I think, sometimes the trouble with going back home, when you travel a lot, is that they've moved down the track, and you're still in the same spot. But bonding with someone like me and him, we're in the same spot, bouncing around, so you just click back together.

KAREN RINALDI: Watching Tony in public, if you were out with him and he got stopped on the street, every once in a while, he got aggravated. Certainly when Ottavia and Ariane were around, he really didn't like people interfering. But mostly, if you walked down the street with him, he handled it well.

DANIEL HALPERN: I guess being that famous at a certain point, the loss of anonymity takes over, and that can become devastating. You want to walk down the street without twenty people stopping you for a selfie. And he would never say no.

ARIANE BUSIA-BOURDAIN, DAUGHTER: When he was with me, I think he just liked to focus that he was with me, and not focus on the fact that he's on TV, because when he's at work, that's the time that he acknowledges that. When he's with me, then he just wants me to be the center of everything. So he didn't talk about work too much.

When we traveled together, I think we kind of liked staying in the hotel, but we'd usually go to the beach, if there was a beach, and to the pool. And when we would go outside, he'd get recognized. I think he got recognized more in New York than when I was traveling with him, but yeah, he got recognized sometimes, and I didn't really mind.

Sometimes he would just really want to hang out with me, but I kind of felt bad for his fans, because if I met a celebrity, I would want to do the same thing. Or if it was a kid, then I'd feel like, "Oh, Dad, go and take a picture with them."

It wasn't really bad; it was OK having fans come up to him. The only thing that was just kind of disrespectful was when people would film from afar, or when he'd tell them to stop, especially when they'd try taking pictures of me, and he'd already specified, "No, don't do that," and they'd still do it. That really annoyed me. Why would you? Why would you try and show this [child], who's chosen to stay private? Because there are a lot of just people out there who are weird, and they're gonna stalk you. I think of that all the time, and I don't even know the answer. There are benefits of being famous but, you know, I feel like I'd rather have a private life.

It's kind of unhealthy, for me, if I look at the things about him [online]. I used to always look him up, and I don't really do it that much anymore. There are a lot of false things for sure, and it's crazy how they can really make up things, and people, a lot of times, just trust the internet. People back up their statements with just a search from the internet. I've learned that a lot of things aren't true, because I've seen things about *me*, saying I was born on a plane, that I had blue eyes—I learned that you really just can't trust it. They make mistakes about my dad, they make mistakes about me, they could be making mistakes about a bunch of other people, too.

ERIC RIPERT: He was a good sport, very respectful of the people, and what the fans are asking. But he will lose patience, and he will lose his cool if people were becoming physical with him. So, for him, soon as some women, a bit drunk, will start to flirt too much with him, or touch him a little bit, or something like that, that will be the end, and it will be, like, drastic. He will be immediate, no more interaction. "I'm going to my car." He will stop it, immediately.

TOM VITALE, PRODUCER-DIRECTOR: "The kissing booth" was what Tony called it when one person wanted a picture, or a selfie, or an autograph, and then everybody would line up. That was pretty much the worst-case scenario. It would cause him to panic. So he would prefer to just disappear, which unfortunately could be misinterpreted as rude. Back in the day, when we finished a scene, Tony used to go and thank the kitchen staff on his way out. That ended a long time ago. In later years, like Elvis, we would have to extricate him from the building.

JOSH HOMME: It's hard to make friends when you don't know why someone wants to know you, because you have some notoriety. He was in the beginning stages of that, which really, at the end, was a major contributor to why we're talking *about* him, and not *to* him.

25

"WE GOT SHIT DONE"

MAKING *NO RESERVATIONS*

NARI KYE, PRODUCER-DIRECTOR, CODIRECTOR OF *WASTED!*: In the early 2000s, I took a production assistant job on a show called *28 Days in Rehab*, which, as you can imagine, was horrendous. The only silver lining was that I got to meet Chris [Collins] and Lydia [Tenaglia]. They hired me as their production manager for their brand-new company. They had just gotten green-lit by the Travel Channel to start making *No Reservations*.

On my second or third day, Chris Collins said, "Tony's coming in today. He has this one weird thing—you should never look him in the eyes when you talk to him."

Chris was totally scaring the shit out of me. I was twenty-two, just out of NYU film school. I didn't know anything. I was sitting there sweating, thinking, *I'm going to make a horrible impression and this guy's going to hate me.* Then, as Tony was walking through the door, Chris leaned over and said, "I was just kidding. He's great."

For me, whenever I was around Tony, I felt like I had to be "on." I had to be witty and have something relevant to say about politics and art and music. Going toe-to-toe with him required a lot of energy. I would have a running list of jokes in my mind.

He made us do our homework, and he always had this grand idea in mind. We did our best to try to make that a reality, but oftentimes we didn't have enough money, or time, or both. So it was a scrappy production, but I think that made it cooler, it made it more authentic.

RENNIK SOHOLT: Tony had already lived a substantial amount of life, and in some ways had nothing to lose, but he knew where he was going. That really served him well, even though he ruffled some feathers. He used to write emails to the network, and I guess they could be pretty articulate, in a . . . *sharp* way, if he disagreed. No one wants to make any enemies in this business; it feels like no one's actually saying anything, and he was willing to say things and stick up for what he wanted. Had he had a less sordid background, he might not have been as fearless.

JARED ANDRUKANIS, PRODUCER: Usually this industry is about following the numbers, checking off the boxes to get things done, and he allowed this sort of crazy, no-lines approach to creativity, like, *OK, you want to serve fresh eggnog to Queens of the Stone Age while they practice their new single in your basement? You want to call Josh Homme your son, and oh, you're also gonna stab your brother over the piece of skin that covers a chicken's ass at a holiday dinner? OK, sure! Let's try all that.* And it worked.

TODD LIEBLER: My first shoot [for *No Reservations*] was in New Zealand. We all sat down for lunch. I don't know if I had even shot anything yet. I was really excited, because my son had just hit a home run in baseball, and so I shared that with the table, and Tony just looked at me like, *Why would I care?*

I was pretty much petrified of him. He had a huge personality; it was intense, overwhelming. Those were my first impressions. Then, when we started shooting, things got better. We were shooting a bear-hunting scene. The bear was shot, and he and I went down the hill, and the bear was on the hood of the car. I was out of breath, and a little in awe, and nervous, and he said, "OK, Todd, just pan up from the bear," you know, just gave me a little direction that centered the whole thing. It started on the bear, I pan up to him, and he does his thing. I was really happy that he reined in my nervous energy, you know?

It's unusual to have talent directing camera, and he rarely did that, but he clearly knew that I was a little lost. This was maybe day two of shooting with him, and he just saw that I needed a little structure.

TOM VITALE: I started off as a tape logger on *A Cook's Tour*, and then came back for the first season of *No Reservations* as postproducer. Every Friday I'd go to Chris and Lydia's office, saying how much I wanted to travel instead of being stuck in the office. I must have worn them down, because they gave me the chance to go on the Moscow episode. I spent about a year as a segment producer before moving on to producer and ultimately director.

It could take years for Tony to make direct eye contact and say people's names. I think that came from his extreme social anxiety.

He was quite observant, much more so, I think, than we gave

him credit for. He had bat hearing, and he sometimes overheard things from across the room. I wasn't always sure if he was being willfully oblivious, or actually oblivious, or distracted, or how present he was. It could be very hard to tell.

I took my job very seriously. Eat, sleep, dream the job, and Tony appreciated that. It was how he approached the shows personally. The line between Tony and the show was very thin, if it existed at all.

We used to ride in the same van together, but that was before it took three hours to set up in order to hit Record, because of lighting, et cetera. His spot in the van was always the one behind the driver. He'd never actually ask for it, but you just sort of knew. All our production vans, they always had this sort of grease spot on the window from his hair gel, in that one spot, because he used the transportation as an opportunity to take little naps.

NARI KYE: It was three Pelicans—the cases you put all the equipment in—and five people total, including Tony. He would play music. He would always be DJ. Back then it was a little iPod and speakers, and he would put it on his lap. And we would always tell fart jokes and be gross and silly. We'd all fit in one van, and we went everywhere together.

MATT WALSH: The first episode [I worked on] was Beijing and Chengdu. The second episode, Shanghai to Shangri-La, was also multiple locations. I was trying to fit in as much as possible, because I had no imagination that the show was gonna go on and on like it did. In those days, Tony was much more accepting of doing road shows, whereas later, he would insist on posting up in a five-star hotel and coming out when needed. And that limited the possibilities.

But back in the early days, we could do a series of days in Beijing, then hop on a plane across the country to Chengdu, do a series of days in Sichuan. And that was terrific. A few days in Shanghai, and then to Yunnan Province. We packed up the van, and went from Kunming, the capital, to Dali, where we shot, then up to Lijiang, where we shot, and then up to Zhongdian, which is what the Chinese government, for commercial reasons, is now calling Shangri-La. These were all four-hour drives from each other. Everyone was quite happy in those days. I thought that the actual traveling from point A to B to C helped the spirit of those shows; he was all about it. He was very curious, very excited, and wide open.

TOM VITALE: We all worked as hard as we could to make him as comfortable as possible. He complained about a lot of things, but not the sorts of things you'd expect from a famous person. He could also be himself around us, which must have been a relief. He didn't have to perform.

He used to never sleep, early on. If I gave him a book at dinner, say, a novel about the place we were filming, he would have read it by breakfast. And I'm not talking about skimming; I mean, there were parts he could almost recite verbatim.

JARED ANDRUKANIS: Tony seemed very polite at first, and businesslike until we got to know each other, which was pretty quickly. My first shoot with him, in 2007, we were flying out to film Queens of the Stone Age in LA, and I think he was nervous about that, in the way Tony could be nervous, but I wouldn't know that then.

This was for the first holiday special. We went out there for a day and a half to film at the band's studio in LA, and then we cut it into the show as if it was Tony's basement.

I got the impression that he doesn't really focus on new people that much. He pretty much wanted to just talk to Chris when I was with Chris, and talk to Rennik when I was with him.

When you would see him call, you'd be like, *I don't know, should I pick it up?* Because he was never really calling you to say "Good job," or anything; it's usually when something's on fucking fire.

For the [*No Reservations*] New Orleans shoot, I called [assistant] Beth [Aretsky] to see if we could get an extra day with Tony, and she said he was free, and I changed his flight without checking with him. He called me as soon as he found out, and the first thing he said was, "I don't know who to blame for this, but whoever it is I'm gonna cut off their head and shit down their throat."

I've worked in restaurants, and on big sets, so that sort of thing didn't rattle me, though Tony can rattle someone pretty easily because he's tall, foreboding, says a lot of words, big, deep voice. That day, I answer the phone and he's fucking screaming.

ALEX LOWRY: Lydia Tenaglia told me, in the beginning, "I think you and Tony are going to get along. He likes stronger women, and he likes being told what to do by them, and it works well." I did kind of stick to that. He liked people who stood their ground or had an opinion; he respected that, I think.

SALLY FREEMAN, DIRECTOR: I took a jokey, kind of piss-taking approach with him in the field. I was never too worried about kind of placating him, which I think he was fine with.

JOSH FERRELL, PRODUCER: I was a very new production assistant, brought on in *No Reservations*. I didn't know who Tony was; the first time I met him was in Belém, Brazil. I didn't really talk to him, because he was such an imposing figure, but then we were in this market, and I was this big guy, new to the crew, right? In the middle of filming, this bird takes this giant shit on my shoulder, like a *giant* shit. Tony noticed; this was the first time he really made eye contact with me, and he said, "Hey, big guy!" and pointed to my shoulder. I said, "Oh, it's good luck!" and he gave me the head nod and said, "It's Josh, right?"

ALEX LOWRY: We were in Prague, and it was just terrible. It was freezing fucking cold, and he was not into the food there, and this side-kick we'd set him up with was such a wanker in the end, and they just did not get along. You could always tell with him if it was gonna go well, or when he wasn't gonna click with the person.

No Reservations used to have a "final meal" scene, so we go to this house, an hour outside of Prague, and Tony's sitting on the couch, fucking miserable; he just wants to get out of that house, and I'm like, "Dude, they're doing all the prep, we're here for hours. You just need to suck it up, buttercup; we're not going anywhere."

I'm getting pissed off, because he's just complaining and moaning, and our poor fixer had to keep smoothing it over with the hosts, because they could tell he wasn't happy. I was like, "This is embarrassing. They can tell you're miserable. It's not a good look," and to his credit, when I said that to him, he snapped out of it.

Then this massive dog bounds over, jumps on him, and just kind of lies there. And Tony just freezes, and puts his arms up. And the dog looks at him, and gets up off of him, and then there was a huge bloodstain on his pants. The dog was not spayed, and she had her period. I look at Tony, and he looks at me, and we just keep each other's gaze for like ten seconds wide-eyed and I start to go, laughing, and then he just bursts out laughing.

He didn't storm out; he didn't get mad. Of course, he ranted and raved about it in the van on the way back. He had his moments, yes, when he could be unhappy, or a naysayer, or rude, or whatever, but it never lasted that long, and it was always tinged with a dark humor.

SALLY FREEMAN: The rule was, no surprises were allowed. He always wanted to know what he was walking into. We'd been at Cook It Raw in Japan [in 2010], and he'd had a lovely time. It was such a bro fest, with all these best chefs in the world. For the crew, it wasn't the most interesting—it's a bit of a chef conference, and it's all very fancy.

Tony had been going on to Dave Chang the whole time, saying, "They've figured out the most amazing cocktail bar, when we're back in Tokyo, classy balls carved out of ice, blah, blah, blah."

He'd made it all up, because I had never said that. I said we would go to a bar, but he filled in the gaps, and I let him believe that's where we were going.

And then we found something called the Kagaya Frog Bar. It was this guy who was probably in his thirties, and his mom sat there and watched him—he'd come out dressed as a frog, with a smaller frog attached to his front, and then he'd sit you down, and give you these beer tankers with gyroscopes on the bottom, which when you picked them up, like, started spinning around. They walked in, and immediately Tony gave me a look; he knew that this was not as promised, and he was kind of furious, but he did actually go with it. The guy comes out, and he's doing all these weird sexual drawings, of himself, I think. He's doing this whole show, this weird cabaret, and his aged mother is watching from the kitchen, and it just got worse and worse. And he's getting in their faces with these frog dolls, and simulating things on them. Tony was laughing, which, you know, didn't happen that often. I think he also enjoyed how deeply uncomfortable Dave Chang was. The crew were shaking while they were trying to film it, because it was so funny. We knew it wouldn't be able to go on TV. It was the thing we'd always been warned not to do, and we did it. He came up to me at the end and said, "Well done. Good one. That is never going to see the light of day."

MICHAEL STEED, DIRECTOR: In 2009, I was working on this show called *The First 48*, which is a murder cop show, hanging out with homicide cops; then I was hired to do two special episodes of *No Reservations*. Me and one shooter would meet Tony in a city, shoot one scene with him. We did that for maybe eight locations, and then made an episode called "Heartland."

My very first impression of Tony? He didn't look me in the eye, and he had a limp handshake. I think he was just uninterested, or just kind of shy, and wondering, *Who is this person? Is he going to be part of the gang?*

I mean, what did he have to say to me? He probably had twenty things on his mind. Once you'd established with Tony that you could back your ideas up, then you were pretty good. I brought stuff to the table, and I think he picked up on that, because at a certain point [executive producer] Lydia [Tenaglia] said, "So I talked to Tony the other day, and he's like, 'The fucking new guy's all right.'"

I wasn't real chatty-chatty with him. I was always directing Tony. Always. I always saw Tony as a muse of sorts.

I think we agreed on a lot of aesthetics, and I liked fucking with him. I would defend John Hughes purposefully, or if they got too filmy at their dinner discussions, I would bring up *Meatballs Part II* or something stupid, and talk about it seriously. Or I'd bring up Steely Dan.

Tony never asked about me. Never. And I didn't judge him for that. I just took note of that. I loved the man, I respected him, and I loved working with him. He made a lot of fucking money. We worked our asses off for him. Local crews liked us; we got shit done.

MORGAN FALLON, CINEMATOGRAPHER-DIRECTOR: Someone had dropped out from a *No Reservations* episode in 2008. I got called to go, because I was on a list. It was a quick turnaround; I think it was a week, and then I arrived in Egypt and met Tony.

I remember the first night, and almost immediately getting cut down by him, on some piece of misinformation that I'd tried to add to his story regarding the narcotics trade in Southeast Asia, and I was like, *Well, that didn't go well.*

He didn't talk to me for the next few days, and then we had to drive out in the western desert, and I said, "Oh, I'll get on the roof, and we'll shoot car to car."

I get up on the car, and these cats proceed to go across the desert at like eighty miles per hour. I was clinging for my life to this four-poster bed that, for some reason, they had on the roof of their car. And when we stopped, I had this huge hematoma on my arm, where I had been hanging on to that bed. I think that act—well, first of all, it's stupid, and I would not recommend that any camera operator do something so dumb and cavalier—but I think that Tony respected those kind of things, the willingness to take physical risks, create risks, the desire to be out there on the edge and have experiences.

I got an email from Chris and Lydia that said, "He knows your name, and seems to like you, and we have another show coming up." And it was ten years, from that point forward, that I worked with Tony.

SANDY ZWEIG, SERIES PRODUCER, *NO RESERVATIONS* AND *PARTS UNKNOWN*: Lydia got in touch with me about *No Reservations*. It was in late 2010. At the time, Tony was in the field, so I didn't meet him before being hired. The first time I met him was at a voice-over session, and it was very funny, because Chris [Collins] said, "When you meet Tony, he may not look you in the eye, he may not look at you at all. Don't take it personally. He's a little socially awkward."

I said, "I'm socially awkward, too, so it's totally fine." I went into the session, sat in, and I met him, talked to him, and he looked me in the eye.

At the point I came in, I think Tony, he wasn't *quite* over Travel Channel, but was getting to that point. One of the shows that was in edit was the Haiti episode; Tom Vitale was editing it. The first set of notes that we got back from the network, there was a beautiful sequence, obviously a gorgeous sequence, and they were like, "Well, we're not really sure about this. This could be cut down."

TOM VITALE: For *No Reservations*, Haiti, we went there shortly after the 2010 earthquake, and Tony had really been dying to stretch his legs, tell different stories. Haiti was quite an intense environment. Being there after the earthquake, it had a postapocalyptic vibe, and of course, there was a hurricane heading toward us. But Tony was inspired by getting to flex some different storytelling muscles.

Having traveled as much as he did, Tony could be a bit jaded, even if he was seeing something amazing, so the times I remember him being really excited were usually the most intense locations. Haiti would be a good example of that. It was certainly one of the more dangerous and unstable places we'd been to at that point. Seeing that kind of suffering takes an emotional toll, so I'm not saying Tony was having a good time, but he was very engaged, which was contagious.

Travel Channel wasn't particularly happy with what we delivered. In addition to Haiti being a different kind of location, we didn't do it in a typical travel show format. Instead, it was all about atmosphere and texture. We got some pretty hilarious notes like, "Are there any parts of Haiti that *are* touristy?"

Worst of all, the network wanted a traditional sum-up at the end. Tony, very passionately and eloquently, argued that the entire point of the show was that there *was* no answer. No neat, tidy sum-up to the situation in Haiti. That was a bitter pill for the network to swallow.

SANDY ZWEIG: I emailed Haiti notes to Tony, and said, "Here are my thoughts on these notes. They want us to cut this thing. We're obviously not going to do that." And then he sent back just one line: "It's a pleasure working with you."

TOM VITALE: Ultimately, Tony prevailed and they didn't gut the episode.

SANDY ZWEIG: That really established our relationship, which was, I felt, like one of mutual respect. He would not always agree with me, and there were often colorful emails as well—like, "I need a sharp object to stick in my eyes, because this cut is making me hate myself so much," those sort of things—but I always felt, ultimately, we could have an honest exchange.

He was very decisive. He stood by what he believed in, you know? He was smart. He knew who he was. He knew what he wanted from the show. And he delivered. I wasn't always in 100 percent agreement with him creatively, but it was clear that he had a vision for it, and that vision reflected who he was.

And that is so not the case with most people on television.

As hard as he was, sometimes, to work with—and he could be difficult, demanding—it elevated all of us to do better. He was not a perfect person, he could be an asshole sometimes, but I've dealt with people who were far less talented, and far more high maintenance.

26

"YOU SEE A PERSON WHO'S COME FULL CIRCLE, AND HE'S SEEN THE WORLD"

MEDIUM RAW

DAVE CHANG: There was a whirlwind of Bourdain around these years in my early thirties. I think Tony took a shine to me because he saw a lot of me in him, and I idolized him. Some of the best moments of my life were with that guy. The best hang. Man, drinking, smoking—Tony was the fucking best. There was a five-year stretch where more often than not, Tony was going to be there and we were just hanging out a lot, and getting blind drunk together, and smoking so many cigarettes. Almost all our conversations were based on happiness, and the elusiveness of it.

The first time I did TV with Tony was at Ssäm Bar, for the [*No*

Reservations] "Food Porn" episode, and then we did Queens, and then we did the overnight at PDT [bar in Manhattan]. I saw him in Australia and a few other places. San Sebastián [Spain] . . .

It was Gastronomika [an annual culinary conference], and we were filming, so it was probably 2010. We had dinner at Elkano.

It was me, Daniel Boulud, every chef who was at the conference, Tony was there, and it was packed. And Tony and I were like, *We don't want to go to this fucking dinner.* They make you go to all these dinner junkets, and we're drinking these giant gin and tonics trying to get out of it, but we couldn't, and I was like, *Fuck, if Tony has to go, then I definitely have to go to this fucking thing.*

I do think it was the best dinner I've ever had in my life. Grilled turbot. Elkano has a special place in my heart to this day. Everything we ate—and I remember we were drunk—but we were just eating it with our hands, and the whole thing was magic. It was like amazing cheese, and lobsters, and everything you would want to eat at that moment in time. I remember looking around the room, at Tony, looking at Daniel—there was just utter fucking joy. Perfect lighting, and I remember saying, "Even the most jaded, cynical motherfucker can be knocked on their ass," and at the time I didn't think there was anyone more jaded and cynical than Tony. And he said, too, "This is the best meal."

DANIEL HALPERN: I loved *Medium Raw*, which was a follow-up to *Kitchen Confidential*; I think it was written in the same way. These chapters, he wrote them and sent them to me. They weren't in any order. I just edited the manuscripts and put them into an order, and we talked about that order.

He wanted to call the book *Medium Rare*; I suggested *Medium Raw*. It didn't do quite as well as *Kitchen Confidential*. Nothing would. That book is one of the iconic memoirs of the last fifty years, really. There's just nothing like it. *Medium Raw* is the closest thing to it. *Medium Raw* did well. But it's not *Kitchen Confidential*. There's just one.

DAVE CHANG: Probably the best thing he's ever written in his life is the chapter about Thomas Keller and his meal at Per Se, in *Medium Raw*. Because if you mirror that with his earlier writings about Thomas Keller, you see a person who's come full circle, and he's seen the world, and he's no longer impressed. I thought it was some of the most beautiful prose he's ever written. I was like, *Shit, where does a guy go from here?* Food's dead to him. There's only so many bowls of soup. Even going to Southeast Asia, I think, hurt him, because it was no longer the place he fell in love with, because it had become developed and urbanized.

When he first started to travel [on TV], he's basically just this fucking bro, and all that travel made him worldly and wise. I think he saw that things are relatively meaningless. I think the travel was him running away—every new culture, every new TV project, was to fill the heroin void, so everything had to become more difficult, more extreme, more challenging, and you could see that throughout his entire television career, and the more he traveled, the more he saw the pain and suffering of it all. It gave him deep, deep humanity, but I think it fucked him up even more.

27

"I KNEW I COULD WRITE THE STORY I NEEDED TO WRITE"

TONY AS PUBLISHER, GRAPHIC NOVELIST, AND SCREENWRITER

In 2011, Tony established Anthony Bourdain Books, a publishing imprint within Ecco, his longtime publisher, which is itself an imprint of HarperCollins.

DANIEL HALPERN: He said, "I've always wanted to be a publisher. I would love to be a publisher," so we made the deal.

We never had any conflicts over his writing. We had conflicts, when he was publishing books, over books that he would like, that I thought we wouldn't be able to sell. But they weren't fights. We never got to that place, ever. We did a lot of the books that he wanted. I wish he had been able to do more. He wanted to do a reprint of *Ashenden, or The British Agent*, a collection of W. Somerset Maugham stories that he loved, and we tried to get the rights, but it was still in copyright.

I think he just loved having access to a publishing house, and could say to people, "You have a book?" He would meet people and get excited about them, and sometimes there would be a book, sometimes not. He brought in [comedian] Bonnie MacFarlane, Roy Choi, José Andrés.

ROY CHOI, TV AND PUBLISHING COLLABORATOR: The first time I met Tony was for *The Layover*, the Los Angeles episode. It was at Ham Ji Park restaurant, in K-Town. Tony came in and sat down with the camera already rolling. We were already five minutes into the conversation before I asked when the shoot would start.[*]

I was just about to pitch my book, and I asked him if he had any advice for me. That's when I first saw the compassionate and tender side of Tony, and that's the Tony that I grew to know, who always showed up on time, returned your email within five minutes, always gave you a hundred suggestions, pointed you in the right direction, and that happened that first night, when I barely knew him.

I don't think he had the publishing company fully ready yet, but now that I look back, he was telling me that he had a publishing company without really telling me, because I don't think it was official yet, and the next time I hit him up, he said, "You need to come with me." He introduced me to Dan Halpern, and Dan said, "You want to make a pretty book? Make a fucking pretty book with another publisher. You want to make a real book? Come over here." And Tony echoed that.

---

[*] *Chef and entrepreneur Roy Choi wrote a hybrid cookbook-memoir, L.A. Son, with coauthors Natasha Phan and Tien Nguyen, that Tony published through his imprint in 2013.*

It all felt right. I knew I could write the story I needed to write with Tony. I didn't know how involved he would be, and then a lot of anxiety started popping up, like, *Oh, now Tony's my boss; what's that relationship gonna be like, and what if I don't agree with him? How am I gonna fight with Tony?*

Tony never really gave line edit notes or anything. He would just basically say, "Fuck, yeah, keep it fucking going!" But he would read every single chapter, and he'd say, "I want to learn more about this," or "Why are you dancing around that?"

NATASHA PHAN, ROY'S BUSINESS PARTNER AND COAUTHOR: We knew we could take risks with Tony. Everything we did was the antithesis of cookbooks. It was a memoir and a cookbook, and we wanted Bobby Fisher to photograph it, which at that time was a completely different style. He let us use our own organic way of knowing how to put a book together.

ROY CHOI: I remember when we announced the book, we were in South Beach, at the Raleigh. He loved that hotel. I met him there and we talked by the pool; it felt very *Godfather*-like. He was swimming with his family, and he got out of the pool and sat with me and talked, and then he got back in the pool.

BONNIE MCFARLANE, COMIC, WRITER: Someone asked if I would do a roast of Anthony Bourdain, for the New York Food and Wine Festival in 2012. I had to do a lot of research to make jokes about him, and he did seem like a really great guy, so I decided, *I'm not gonna do too many jokes about him; I'm gonna make fun of everyone else on the dais.*

I guess he liked what I did, because he and his agent asked me to meet them for lunch a couple of weeks later, and during that lunch he said, "I want you to write a book. I want you to write about your life."

It was really an incredibly easy process. He just read all the chapters, and would, every once in a while, send me a message to say, "I love the book. I love what you're doing," and that was it.

That was the way it was writing for his stage show, too. He would ask me for jokes, send me a list of topics that he needed, and I would write, you know, one hundred jokes for him, and he would send me a check and say, "Thank you." There was no negative feedback, ever, from him.

At that lunch, he did say to me that he had never heard a woman who could do that before, meaning, to roast him. He said, "I've never heard a woman with that voice before." I wanted to say, "Well, I'm not like that all the time," but I didn't want to lose his respect, so I was a little bit mean to him every time I saw him. He loved it. Once he was on board with me he was completely supportive, 100 percent.

He made a video when my book was published and said, "This is why I have a book imprint, to publish Bonnie McFarlane."* It was over the top, but that's the thing about him, is that he still comes across as genuine. I was nervous around him, because I didn't want that approval to go away. I have a little bit of an issue with saying things I really shouldn't say, and doing things I really shouldn't do, and I never got to know him really well, because I was scared of severing that mutual respect.

YEGANEH REZAIAN, JOURNALIST: Tony was really supportive of the idea of a book. I think Jason started writing it the very first night he got

---

* *Bonnie published her memoir,* You're Better Than Me, *through the Anthony Bourdain Books imprint in 2016.*

released from prison, and they took us from Iran to Switzerland and Germany.* So he was always writing. The first thing he asked for was a pen and paper.

JASON REZAIAN, JOURNALIST: [Literary agent] Kim [Witherspoon] and I spent a ton of time on the phone, developing this idea for a [book] proposal. That process is not easy in the best of times, but when you're just out of a year and a half in a foreign prison, it's even more complicated. We took it to twelve or thirteen different publishers, and Tony was really adamant about wanting to read the proposal. We got seven offers, including one from Tony's imprint.

I got an email from Tony—he was in Laos—and it was like, "I'm gonna be a vociferous supporter of you and [Jason's wife] Yegi no matter what you do, but give me some serious consideration."

Yegi and I were going to some event, sitting in the back of an Uber, when this email came in, and I read it to her, and she said, "Jason, were you even *considering* going with anybody else?"

So that started this journey with Tony, writing my story. He wasn't reading my pages or anything like that. I don't know how much of the manuscript that he actually read. All I know is that Dan and Zack Wagman, my editor at Ecco, they wrote to me the day before Tony died, and said, "We're accepting your manuscript." Everything was starting to really come together.

JOEL ROSE: We used to have Thanksgiving together every year, and he would just bug me, saying, "Let's do a graphic novel together. Let's write comic books together." And I was always like, "Dude, what the

---

* In January 2019, Tony's imprint published Jason Rezaian's Prisoner, his account of being arrested and jailed for eighteen months in Iran.

fuck? I'm not doing that." I consider myself a novelist; I didn't want to write a comic book.[*]

He was over for Thanksgiving one year, and Ariane was little, she was like four, and she was sick, and she was on the couch. He caught me by the elevator and pitched me *Get Jiro*. He gave me the background, and I wrote to Karen Berger at Vertigo and said, "Would you be interested, Tony Bourdain and I have this idea . . ." and she went, "Are you crazy? Of course!"

I don't think I've ever seen him more happy and jazzed than that day when we went in to talk to Karen Berger at DC. We put that together, and it was really fun. And with *Hungry Ghosts*, it was the same thing.

When I worked with him, he was so responsive. Writing is hard, and it's lonely. I felt totally comfortable when I reached a place of difficulty for myself, that I could say, usually by email, "Hey, I'm having problems right here. Can you write a scene in front of the dojo, or in front of the ramen shop," or whatever, and it would come back to me in, like, fifteen minutes.

And it wouldn't be polished, it would just be pure Tony. It would be a blast. And for me, it was like a smorgasbord, because I could just pick and choose what he had sent me. Some of it sucked, but most of it was brilliant, and I could take those brilliant things and plug them in.

DAVID SIMON, COCREATOR, *TREME:* As a writer, he was so good. Prose, dialogue; you know, he overwrote scenes. "Tony, I can't do four and a half pages in this kitchen scene. It's got to be one and a half pages. We got to get there faster." But it was always there. He knew exactly why the scene was there, and he knew how the characters should

---

[*] *Tony and Joel Rose coauthored a total of three graphic novels together over the span of seven years.*

talk. His sense of who these characters needed to be, and what they needed to say, was so acute. I admired him as a writer, and I loved the engagement there. It was just a matter of delivering the economy of scale for a sixty-page script.*

LOLIS ELIE, JOURNALIST, WRITER, *TREME*: Tony would tend to fly in [to the writer's room in New Orleans] for a day, and he would solve somewhere between 75 to 100 percent of the problem of what's going to happen to Jeanette [Desautel, the chef character on *Treme*]. His scenes always came in long. It was kind of like if I told you, "OK, you're going to be onstage for five minutes," and you're like, "I'm going to get out there and do everything I can."

ERIC OVERMYER, COCREATOR, *TREME*: Tony was wonderful company; he was a wonderful writer. When I got a Tony scene to polish, I had very little to do except to trim it. They were always too long, and too full, but all good stuff. He had a real sense of the shape of the scene; he had a sense of the dramatic flow, and how to take some unexpected turns in a scene. He had a sense of characters' voices. He was a natural. Most rewriting is not a pleasure, but it was always a pleasure to polish his scenes; they needed very little work.

LOLIS ELIE: What Tony managed to do was devise the kinds of tortures that would happen in the kitchen, that you don't really know unless you work in the kitchen or talk to a lot of chefs. I don't think we ever used it, but we talked about the grease trap as an issue. I would never have thought of that. I think he liked the idea of

* In 2010, David Simon asked Tony to join the writing staff of the HBO series Treme, *beginning with the second season. The series, which ran for four seasons, depicted life in New Orleans after Hurricane Katrina, and it featured a chef and restaurant storyline.*

simultaneously talking about the glories and the hell of chefs' lives, and how, as much as they hate it, they also love it.

ERIC OVERMYER: Tony would bring detail [about restaurants], both in front and back. In the last season, Anthony Anderson played a very smart, savvy waiter who could predict how big his tip would be by what kind of shoes the customer was wearing. That was Tony; he was just full of stuff like that. He was a joy to have in the room, and his stuff was just gold.

LOLIS ELIE: He and I had one run-in, which was kind of funny. Part of what we were doing—*Treme* was simultaneously a totally fictional show, and in a sense a documentary about what actually did happen in those months and years after Katrina. Alice Waters is important, in terms of, she opened the Edible Schoolyard [in New Orleans], and I got to know her and be friendly with her. So I suggested in an email, "Hey, we're talking about all these chefs coming to town; maybe we should have Alice?"

Tony's response was, I'll say, "scathing light." In essence, he said, "Her stuff is old, no one would ever do that again, this is a terrible idea," et cetera. But he didn't shoot it down entirely, and so I had a response. Part of this also was Tony saying Desautel was a woman chef who could run with the boys, so I might have said it would be good to have a woman chef.

Eric Overmyer was like, "You should just leave this alone," but I sent my response, and then I think we went from Tony at a level two, to Tony at a level seven. Again, Eric Overmyer said, "You should've left this alone," and I was like, "I lost the battle. I'm not worried about that, but I ain't gonna let this motherfucker tell me I don't know the show well enough to pitch a good idea."

So it got to be that kind of thing; I'm trying to save a little face.

And then it was sort of funny, because we were in the room, and he's saying, "You know what I think would be good is that there's some dish that she starts off loving, that's so important, but it takes over, and she wishes she could take it off the menu, and then she's trying to figure out how not to make it not be such a pain in the ass."

And I say, "Maybe a pasta dish, and she goes from making fresh pasta to making it with using dried," and Tony says, "Yeah, that's a good idea." And I really felt that was Tony throwing me a bone. I think he believed he was right about Alice, but that he was harsher than he could have been, or should have been.

DAVID SIMON: He constructed all those storylines in *Treme*. He argued for what he argued for. He took possession of those things in a very heartfelt way. Wrote his way through all of them. There were times when, because of the rush, or because he was out of the country, and we had to reverse some scenes or maybe a storyline, I would have to pitch him stuff cold and send it to him. It would always come back better. But when I could land one in the pocket, where he was like, "This is good. This is funny," I was like, "Geez, I ducked a bullet."

I had absolute confidence in his ability to write anything. He'd have been great on *The Deuce*. He'd have been great on anything. He was funny. He was ridiculously self-effacing about his writing and his narrative abilities.

ERIC OVERMYER: I remember we were at some Spanish restaurant in the warehouse district [of New Orleans]. Lolis handed Tony the wine list, and Tony handed it right back, and said, "I don't know shit about wine." That was a very endearing moment, just genuinely modest. And he was fond of saying that being invited to write for us on *Treme* was like playing shortstop for the 1927 Yankees, which was such great hyperbole. He was a master of highly entertaining hyperbole.

28

"I FELT LIKE I KNEW HIM ALL MY LIFE"

DAVID SIMON RECALLS TONY

DAVID SIMON: The moment I fell in love with Tony as a person, I just wanted to go sit beside him. The TV shows, to me, were journalism. And incredibly political, without being didactic or ideological. But there was a general ideology, one that was very humanistic and very antihierarchical.

I remember this image: he's in some urban center in South America. I want to say Montevideo, but maybe it was Buenos Aires. He's sitting against the wall of an alley. Gangly and tall. He's got his arms wrapped around his knees. And they're all drinking the *siete y tres*, seven and three, and the kids are kicking some sort of ersatz soccer ball.

And he's sitting there, and the footage of kids, and the men drinking, and him, and there's this look of incredible sadness and love. It was a moment of *duende* for me. It's like, *This guy loves people.* He's trying desperately to connect in ways that great journalists and great writers connect. And also, the writing is so good, the narration was so well written, that I just wanted to be his friend.

I'd already met him once, in Manchester; he'd written a crime novel and I met him then. [My wife] Laura [Lippman]'s the mystery writer; I was there hanging with her and just looking for people to drink with. *Kitchen Confidential*, I think that book was just out, but I hadn't read it. So all I had was this tall guy, who was very charming and playful. Nice guy, he used to be a chef. I didn't remember him.

Then I'm watching the show and not connecting it to having met him. I watched, like, twenty hours with our son. We just couldn't get out of our fucking underwear. We sat on the couch.

Laura came in and she saw us and asked, "You guys pissed away the whole day?"

"Absolutely not! We watched this guy Tony Bourdain. He's the coolest guy on the planet, and he needs to be my friend."

It took a couple of days, and she said, "I know how you can meet him."

Laura probably went through a publisher, and got something. When I first got him on the phone, I was talking so fast. I felt like such an interloper.

The thing is, I know foods that are sort of hot and taste good. I hear about the new shit, because I chase it down, because I like putting new food in my mouth. I don't know how kitchens work. I love eating, but I often felt like I disappointed him; there were moments I felt like I just revealed myself to be an incredibly disappointing rube.

He interviewed me one time for a show. He was out doing this boucherie in Opelousas, western Louisiana. I had hooked him up with these guys, Joel Savoy and that group. They'd helped us make *Treme*.

Anyway, my son and I got there early in the morning, to watch it. Got to the campground, watched Tony shoot the pig, watched them film it. At some point, just before the band played, starting the celebration, he said, "We're filming some extra video for the website. Can I interview you?"

I sat down, he asked me a bunch of questions, and some of the answers I gave clearly amused him. But then he said, "OK, you're going to die tomorrow. What's your last meal?"

I said, "The first time that I had a couple of dollars to scratch together to buy any meal I wanted, somebody took me to Nobu to have a meal. And I'd had sushi, but suddenly there were these *sauces*. I put this food in my mouth and I was like, 'This is new. I wasn't expecting this.'"

I realized, as I was answering, he was just so disappointed in me. I could see it in his face. It was so uncool an answer by the standards of a guy who finds himself in some back alley, hunting for the perfect noodle dish in Hong Kong. It was such an un-Tony answer. He wasn't mean about it, but I could just see, *You're letting me hang. You have really distinct opinions about people, politics, and food, and you're picking the perennial number-one listing in New York in the* Zagat *guide.*

I felt like I knew him all my life, and I've known nobody like him. Does everybody else feel that way? He was so accessible in his intellect and his humor that when I watched him on the screen without knowing him, I felt like I knew him, and I needed to hang out. And I am not seduced by television—I am engaged in this industry. I understand how attenuated reality is from what we put on the screen.

His journalism was so good. His voice was the voice of people

I've loved in my life before I met him—my cousins from New York, the retort, the hyperbolic and outrageous statement that nevertheless makes you perceive just how wrong or right something is. Which he could do about food or drink or politics. I felt like I knew him so well, even before I made that first phone call, and then everything fell into place. Sometimes you think that's going to be the case, especially with actors, because actors are so good at pretending. I don't think Tony was particularly good at pretending. That's not what his skill set was.

It's a rather rare thing for people to feel, *There's no way you can flip on me as a person. This thing you're giving me is not a persona, it's really you.* And for it to have so many edges, because he wasn't trying to be likable at all points; he was just trying to be truthful. And he was trying to be generous with the people, for the most part, who were leading him around, showing him the world, talking to him, feeding him.

29

"HE COULD HAVE SAT IN A SANTA'S THRONE IN A SHOPPING MALL"

THE ONSTAGE EXPERIENCE

SAM GOLDMAN: Tony was masterful at speaking to a group. I remember the days when he would hold court at restaurants, at one place in particular, Nikki & Kelly, up on Columbus. There was staff meal, and then there was staff meeting, where we'd tell the waiters what was going on, and, I mean, you were a captive audience, they didn't have any choice, but Tony was brilliant.

DANIEL HALPERN: He was an unknown when *Kitchen Confidential* was published, but he turned out to be such an appealing man, an amazing speaker—an amazing speaker, given how shy he was. I think he was really shy.

BILL BUFORD: He was fantastic impromptu. Really probably at his best. His spoken narrative was virtually as good as his written narrative, but it had the virtue of being spoken, and it gave his shows their poignancy and their poetry and their moodiness, their sense of reflection. He's got a feel for language, which can come only from having a command of language, and knowing what you can do with language. He understands word choice, and he understands kind of the beauty of combining unlikely words.

LAURIE BARNETT, LECTURE AGENT: Tony was introduced to Royce Carlton, the lecture agency where I was working, by Kim Witherspoon. That was at the onset of *No Reservations*. To be honest, no one else on the team wanted him as a client. When Kim walked him in the door, the response was, "Who's gonna pay money to listen to a cook?"

I had to beg for the first $5,000. "We don't pay cooks," you know. On our watch, we set a bar that Tony's heroes in the food world had not raised. They were out there doing quite a bit for free, in that style of, "OK, they're my patrons, so I have to give them everything."

So there was an arc from $5,000, to the end, fifteen years later, a whole lot more. The very first event was in the Boston Convention and Exhibition Center. Six hundred people. When we pulled up in the cab, the cooks were lined up on the sidewalk.

They'd put him in a rangy exhibit hall, with lots of ambient noise. It was standing room only. The voice on the page from *Kitchen Confidential* leapt out as the voice on the stage. It was all there, the heart and the scathing humor. He was magic onstage, and it became pretty clear, pretty soon, that this was going to become a big, exponential deal.

I [met] with a rep from Guilford College, which is a Quaker college. And I said, "If you want a capital campaign, this is the guy." These were the Bush years; everyone wanted high-profile news correspondents from the *New York Times*. But they put him in his first theater, two thousand seats. And that shifted the game. Promoters who fill those kinds of seats, and performing arts centers, started to come to us as customers.

ADAM EPSTEIN: It was in Denver, in 2009, it was the first time we did a show with Tony. We did a few more dates—Ann Arbor, Michigan, and New Orleans—as part of a speaker series. We really started to understand how his audience was incredibly passionate for him, for his narrative and his delivery. They were excited by the energy he brought to the stage. He didn't need any sort of presentation; he just commanded attention the second he walked out there. He just paced back and forth, and it seemed like stream of consciousness to me, except it had a beginning, a middle, and an end, but it didn't feel rehearsed, and I don't know if it ever was. It seemed to flow from him authentically.

I would have thought twice before giving him any criticism, but at the same time, I didn't need to. He delivered. His presentation was so good, from start to finish.

From a ticket sales perspective, when we first did Denver, we didn't know how much the audience was comfortable paying, so we priced tickets very, very inexpensively. We had a $99 postevent meet and greet where he just shook people's hands and posed for pictures, but most of the tickets were $40.

At each venue, we sold about sixteen hundred tickets or so, but the thing was, we lost piles of money. On the second round of dates, we knew there was something there, people were buying tickets, so we raised the prices, and we sold exactly the same number of tickets.

They didn't hesitate at all. And these weren't golfers, they weren't high-net-worth people; these were working people, pulling significant resources from their budgets to dedicate to a night spent with Tony.

Our tickets started showing up on secondary ticketing sites like StubHub for hundreds of dollars more than what we were selling them for. And we're talking large numbers, and they were moving. It became a serious way to generate revenue for him.

LAURIE BARNETT: Tony came into my office, and said, "There's someone I want you to meet. His name is Eric Ripert. It would make me very happy if you worked with him, too." I said, "Absolutely."

For that first gig with Eric, Tony said to me, like a week before, "So, who's the local yokel who's going to interview Eric and me onstage?" And I said, "Uh . . . we, we don't have one." He said, "OK, no problem. Go to the hallway of the theater and find me the creepiest, most beat-up old metal chair. Put it downstage center. Put a klieg light on it. And then put two comfy chairs behind it."

He wrote this thing for Eric, a little script, an interrogation. He asked Ripert—a Buddhist and a strong proponent of sustainable seafood—what he would do if he were offered the last piece of endangered bluefin tuna in the world, an endangered species. "Would you eat it? After all, you not eating it won't bring it back alive."

It was taunting, teasing. Eric was a newbie at the stage thing; eventually he got more comfortable with all of it, and he started turning the tables, and asking Tony crazy things, and writing his script himself.

ERIC RIPERT: When we did the show "Good versus Evil," he made sure that I was in very uncomfortable situations, and was taking advantage of it, for the well-being of the show.

When we were together privately, just Tony and me, he will be extremely respectful, and never try to make me do something I don't want to, or even suggest it. When we were in public, sometimes he will be playful, and go to a situation where it was like a tease, basically. We went to Paris together [for *No Reservations*]. In that one, he put me in a tough situation, because he put me with that guy from Le Fooding, who was trashing fine dining, and Tony knew it, and basically set me up, but I didn't play the game.

On "Good versus Evil," I was not comfortable, because I didn't like the fact that Tony was saying bad things about people, and I didn't want to deliver to him the opportunity to do that. It was bad karma for him, and I don't like gossip, and I don't like people who are saying bad things about others. It bothered me a lot, and we had many, many discussions, Tony and me, about that, during the duration of the show.

It was nonscripted, but we knew the gig by heart, of course, and we will surprise ourselves onstage a little bit, and sometimes add a little component to it. But the show was basically in our heads. Tony never changed. For instance, he liked to pick on Guy Fieri, and he will make fun of his sunglasses, and his hair, and say that he has to "de-douche," and I really didn't like that, and I will actually defend Guy Fieri onstage. People will think it's part of the comedy, but it was not. So Tony had those victims lined up for himself, and despite what I will say, we will go on with it.

We did, I don't know, maybe thirty shows. We were sold out in every theater that we were doing, including Las Vegas and so on. And we were making good money, and it was a struggle for me, because I didn't want to do it. And, at the end, actually, it was me who said, "Tony, we have to stop. I don't want to do that anymore."

MICHAEL RUHLMAN: He came up with the Golden Clog Awards, at the South Beach Wine and Food Festival, to make fun of the Food

Network. Tony convinced Rocco DiSpirito to accept the Golden Clog award for worst career move, but the execs were furious, and I was kind of blackballed from the network for a while. And Tony felt really bad about it.

SAM GOLDMAN: It blew my mind to see him onstage. I get to the Pantages [Theatre, in LA] and it's sold out; there's all these people milling around outside, and it smells like weed. They flash the lights two times; Tony had gotten us VIP seats, so some usher grabs us. "Gimme Shelter" is blasting, and this was like every concert we went to at the Capitol in Passaic, or the Fillmore in New York. This was like exactly what we did as kids, and the next thing I know there's Tony Bourdain onstage. That blew my fucking mind. That's when I was like, *He's there, he's a fucking rock star; god bless.* By the time I saw him live, he'd been doing it for a while, and he was great.

People ask me if I'm envious now, and I say no, he had the vision, he did the work, and it was a long time coming.

BONNIE MCFARLANE: He asked me, "What makes a great comic?" and I said, "Well, you can't just do it once in a while, for your own fans. You have to do it every night, do it in front of people who don't know you." And he said, "Get me a set at the Comedy Cellar," and so I did. I couldn't make it that night, I couldn't get a babysitter, but he went to the Comedy Cellar, and went onstage one night, like a real comic, and I guess he did pretty well. I don't know if he used the jokes I wrote for him; I never asked him. He didn't do it to get attention; he just wanted to be a real comic for a night and see what it was like.

ADAM EPSTEIN: Did he enjoy it? I never could figure it out. I mean, if he didn't enjoy it, I think he wouldn't have done it, but my instinct says that maybe he wanted to be at home. It was one of the reasons we got him a private jet, because we knew that this guy travels for a living, so the last thing he wants to do is get on another fucking airplane. It was an extraordinary measure for somebody playing theaters, very uncommon, but we knew that the only way he'd even consider doing it was if I took away the pains in the ass of traveling. And the money was definitely great on those last few tours.

FRED MORIN: When we did the live show at Place des Arts [in Montréal], that was a bit of another thing, you know. That was, uh— Tripes and Glory?*

DAVE MCMILLAN: We sold out. It was super expensive. We sold out the Place des Arts theater. It was fucking $300 a head, or something like that.

FRED MORIN: It was packed. Packed.

DAVE MCMILLAN: And he won't say a word to us. Like, "You wanna tell us the questions first?" He goes, "No, no. It's cool. I do it with Ripert all the time."

FRED MORIN: He's like, "Don't worry, guys. I got it."

DAVE MCMILLAN: We're standing at shitty wood podiums, we know nothing of what he's gonna say. And it was a very traumatic hour, sweating onstage; the jokes weren't working. He underestimated that the crowd is French Canadian. So what he was getting laughs for in the United States, an American crowd, was just *thud, thud.*

And me and Fred, we said, "We have to live here once you leave.

---

* *The name of the tour was, in fact, Guts and Glory.*

We're gonna have to hear 'I paid three hundred bucks. This was a lackluster performance.'" But he shook everyone's hand, and took a picture with everyone—

FRED MORIN: Which, ultimately, is what people paid for. Like, he could have sat in a Santa's throne in a shopping mall, and people would have paid a hundred bucks just to tell them about their grandma's brownie, you know, and it would have been the same thing.

30

"HE WAS A CURATOR OF PEOPLE"

NIGELLA LAWSON: There are so many people whose lives he did try and make better. That's what I mean about kindness. The worst sort of charity is giving and wanting to be applauded for it. He was very much at the upper echelon of the Maimonides table, because he didn't make a noise about it. There were so many people he helped, silently.

JOSÉ ANDRÉS: You could see that he had other interests beyond the kitchen, beyond a TV show. Tony was here to be more than just a face on TV. He was the voice of those people who are voiceless, people whose story needed to be told. Tony was here to do many more things.

He supported a lot of things, for a long time, in very generous ways, in ways that people don't even realize. He really fell in love with DC Central Kitchen. When we created Food Fight [a fund-raising event] and I asked him, "Why you don't join me?" he didn't even hesitate. He didn't even look at his schedule.

He was super important in the making of that event, raised millions of dollars for men and women to get a proper education to work in the restaurant industry, and for feeding the homeless. He was a host at the event, and that was enough to start filling the room. He committed to it for so many years. Tony was this kind of guy who looks like he doesn't give a shit. Tony was never the guy who will tell you that he gives a shit about things; he will always do things to help, in very silent, powerful ways.

DANIEL HALPERN: We had friendly talks, and about what I should be publishing. It goes back to the loyalty; once he liked you, or trusted or admired you, he'd do anything for you.

First he said, "You ought to publish [UK chef] Fergus Henderson," and I said, "Tony, people don't eat offal here." Nose-to-tail eating, back then, in 1999, 2000—but he said, "You have to publish it. Just publish it."

It was a really hard book to do, and the photographs were from above, half-eaten plates of offal, in black and white. Just ugly, ugly stuff. But the book did so well.

Then he said, "You have to do Ferran Adrià's book, the El Bulli book."

Those books were already produced. And they were $350 books. I thought, *How are we gonna sell those?* But he was relentless. He said, "You have to do it. Don't you want to go to El Bulli? If you buy the book, you'll get a table."

So basically, that's why I bought it, so I could eat at El Bulli. They're huge books. There's not a recipe you can make in it. There were four volumes, so we bought [the rights to] one. And it sold out immediately, at $350 apiece.

DAVE MCMILLAN: We're very hard workers, and we've cooked for a very long time. I have no problem saying that we're very good cooks. Tony was good at identifying those people.

FRED MORIN: Yeah, Roy Choi, Dave Chang, Ludo— All his friends, he was adamant about putting them together, in some context. He was a curator of people. He had little scenarios in his mind. He wanted to curate the situations and the soundtrack. He would have been a great restaurateur, because he had a dedication to creating restaurants, and dinners.

Going overboard for making meals was something we really connected in, you know?

DAVE MCMILLAN: Tony brought all his crew up at the same time, somewhat, [and] all of us maybe helped Tony in getting where he wanted to get.

FRED MORIN: It was very mutual.

DAVE MCMILLAN: And he had a humble sense of, *I'm proud of these guys, it's super great, but I know that I had something to do with helping these guys enrich themselves and their families.*

ROY CHOI: He really shepherded me with the CNN thing. I got the opportunity to do a little web show with CNN, called *Street Food*, and he was there every step of the way. I got to experience his wisdom on a professional level. He did an episode with us, and then he really helped with promotion. He did interviews about the show, and he had us piggyback on his press junket when he was promoting season 3 of *Parts Unknown*. He was always there when I needed him.

MIKE RUFFINO: He was always very generous. He certainly gave me a lot, that's for sure. The opportunity to suddenly be composing for someone with whom I basically shared a brain, musically, and in many other ways—that's just not usual for the documentary television world. I had a lot of say in how things sounded. It was an incredible opportunity, and one I probably could have parlayed into more things, but I didn't, because why ruin it, right?

PETER MEEHAN: When *Lucky Peach* magazine ended, he caught wind of it, after everything had gone south, and he asked me, "Do you want me to buy it? I'll buy it for you." It was the most amazing thing to have Tony Bourdain come out of the woodwork and be like, "Do you want me to go to bat for you? I'll go to bat for you."

Things were already so fucked at that point and it was so clear that it never would have happened, and I didn't want to put Tony on the peg for it; it was time for it to die. But that was a pretty amazing thing for him to come through and offer.

NARI KYE: If Tony hadn't been attached, I don't know if *Wasted!* would have gotten made.* The funders were obviously very keen on having Tony. Initially, I had written him about it, and he wrote me back and said, "This is a little too activist style for me. It's not really me. I wish you the best of luck. You're going to kill it."

He was very apologetic, and I was like, *Well, I guess we're not*

---

* *Nari Kye codirected, with Anna Chai, a 2017 documentary about food waste, called* Wasted!, *with Tony attached as executive producer. He also appeared in the film.*

making this movie. And then the next morning, I checked my inbox, and he'd written, "Actually, I changed my mind; I *will* be attached to it. Let me know how I can help." I was elated.

When he sat down in that interview chair, we had him for only two hours, but we could have made a whole series out of what he said. Because he is so good, such a good talker, so funny, and so knowledgeable, even about something like food waste. Of course, he knew a lot about that because he was in the kitchen for thirty years, but it was amazing that even something like food waste he could make thoroughly entertaining.

But what was really funny was when we'd be rolling, and I'd say, "Hey, Tony, can you say that exact same thing one more time?" And he would never say it the same way. We're like, "Can you just say it like how you said it before?" He would always change it a little bit. He was always trying to improve what he'd just said. He was always tweaking and editing in his mind. Or maybe he just wanted to drive us all crazy. It was thoroughly fascinating just watching him on camera, the things he would ask, and [his] follow-up questions.

MIKE RUFFINO: There was a big book event [when *Adios, Motherfucker* was published, in 2017], in which I was, not for the first time, a bit embarrassed by his public praise. I don't know—he always gave me a lot more confidence than I should rightly have had. Over and over again, I felt very protected by him. I always got paid on time.

I learned a hell of a lot with other musicians in various places, and even when I didn't travel, there was a lot of collaboration. I was absolutely in a bubble. I had no idea. If I had actually known what a composer was supposed to do, and what the compensation for that would be, I think I probably would have just gone back to working in a pizza place, you know what I mean? It certainly would have been more lucrative.

He had a lot of pull, and certainly more than he would really discuss. I just assumed that's how everything worked. I mean, my entire perspective on television, and my musical life, since meeting him, was all through the filter of Tony.

DAVE MCMILLAN: People whom he had deep affection for, we also had deep affection for; and the people who he knew who had deep affection for us, had told him that we were the good guys here. So it was like, "These are your friends in Montréal. When you're in Montréal, these are your friends." But Tony had a Fred and Dave in every fucking city.

It takes sixteen weeks to get a reservation at Joe Beef. It's been like that for ten years. And that's not because we're really good at cooking. There's a lot of guys who cook better than us. We have people coming here from Taiwan. That's because of Tony.

PETER MEEHAN: The bulk of my relationship with Tony was doing *Lucky Peach*. I was always anxious about emailing him or asking him to do anything, which is insane, because he never didn't get back to me immediately, and he never didn't say yes. He wrote great stuff; he turned in things *early*. Who turns in things *early*? The fact that he was so good and he was so Tony, and he was turning in copy that was generally pretty sparkling and early, was very offensive to me, as a failing writer. [*Laughs*]

JASON REZAIAN: When you're dealing with people who are very well known, and who travel a lot, your interactions with them are not necessarily very many, right? And so, there's a different quality to the moments that you do have together. Something that Kim [Witherspoon] told me, pretty early on, was, "Tony, he chooses people, and he sticks with them. He's loyal to some people, even when he shouldn't be. I've got no doubt that you and Yegi are deserving of his loyalty, but he's not going to turn his back on you." And he never did.

YEGANEH REZAIAN: He never stopped advocating for us, not even after we were released. Sometimes people cause you a problem and they totally want to disassociate themselves from you. Tony wasn't like that at all. He was the opposite. He wanted to make sure that, despite the fact that he didn't cause anything like this, he's still there for you, and it matters even more.

JARED ANDRUKANIS: Tony had an impact on everyone around him . . . and it came from somewhere else. There's no training for it or anything; it's a personality thing, but way deeper. He makes people look good. I've had to work with other hosts where you're really trying to rein it in and make them look good . . . but you didn't have to ever do that with him.

Tony would make *you* look good, his writing, how he talked in scene. And even when we knew things were bad, he still made you look OK. Even the "worst" episodes were better than most anything else out there.

PAULA FROELICH: He was insanely loyal. I remember he had a gazillion people wanting to be his agent. And he was like, "Nope, I'm with Kim." And when I had just gotten back from Afghanistan, he said, "Oh god, I want to go, but I can't get insurance for the crew." I actually have a good Afghan crew whom I used, whom Tony could have used, but he said, "I can't shoot without *my* crew."

FRED MORIN: And he's like, "Oh, yeah, I'm getting this show on CNN, and we're gonna go on a train trip, we're gonna go ice fishing. Do what you want."

We're like, "We can do what we want? We want an ice-fishing cabin, we want four cooks, we want no budget, we want four trucks—" They were unflinching. This ice-fishing scene, that's the only time I had as much fun for real on TV and enjoyed it as much as I appear to.

DAVE MCMILLAN: The highs were euphoric, like drug use. All the planets have to be in line—

FRED MORIN: Like, this is never gonna happen again, you know? People were playing hockey—

DAVE MCMILLAN:—there were snowflakes, and the sky was extra black, and the food was delicious, and everybody was happy. We were all comatose drunk. And that was an epic, for real—screw the TV— that was one of the most beautiful meals of my life in that ice-fishing cabin, you know. We drank well, we ate well.

The most fun thing was the steamship dinner at the Wolfsonian Museum [in Miami, for the South Beach Wine and Food Festival in 2014]. And, you know, Fred and I are from Montréal; we have Impostor syndrome.

So it was us, Daniel Boulud, Eric Ripert, François Payard, Andrew Carmellini—these are monster, legendary cooks from Manhattan, three-Michelin-star, everyone—

FRED MORIN: And Tony said, "Make sure you book a few extra days; we're gonna hang out at the Raleigh."

DAVE MCMILLAN: We're in the pool with Tony, Ottavia, the kids, Debi Mazar and her husband and kids, for a week. It was amazing. We just, like, every day watched Tony hide cigarettes from Ottavia. He goes, "Where's Ottavia? Is she going to the bathroom? I'm going for a smoke. Cough. Cough if she's coming back."

FRED MORIN: It was surreal, in retrospect, too, you know? He's this very faithful guy, where things like that make you realize you can't fuck that up, you know? The friendship, not the perks. We can afford the Raleigh.

DAVE MCMILLAN: He was a real friend. He said, "Tonight, I rented out Cheeseburger Baby. We're going to watch the UFC. Just us."

FRED MORIN: "We're going to a lesbian cheeseburger restaurant. They set up the big screen in the back. Make sure you come."

31

"HE WAS A MAN OF EXTREMES"

EILEEN OPATUT: I don't know what he believed about god, but I suppose this [life] isn't a greenroom for something else, and he went for it, and he was able to.

JOSÉ ANDRÉS: The first time I met Tony, what I sensed was this amazing big man, tall man, with a body to command respect—his charisma, and the way he was made, and dressed, and hair, and voice tone, and hand movement, and long, thin legs. He looked like the Marlboro Man. I saw a person with an amazing sense of respect for others, giving respect to legacies, the work of others, the opinion of others.

JOSH HOMME: Tony was a bit of a nerd. I could easily make the case that Tony was pursuing his passions at the speed of inspiration. And what reason is there to go half measures, or to stop, if you're loving it? What about a lust for life that takes you down dark paths, that it's your job to overcome? What's that quote—"Wisdom comes from experience; experience comes from bad decisions," right? It's interesting, admirable, and exciting to watch someone who's chasing his passions at a pace that you cannot do yourself.

For self-proclaimed atheists, we had a lot of deep conversations about being on a rock that spins around a star that's exploding. Why do you think he was searching the world, looking for something to believe in? And finding it. And losing it. Chasing its brake lights again. And going in that direction. It's this existential crisis on a grand level, and everyone gets to watch. I mean, that's what we talked about.

ANDERSON COOPER: I think people who are drawn to a lot of the places that he went, and that I've gone, tend to be drawn, it comes— I think it comes from a similar place. I always felt that about Tony.

It's hard for me to put this into words without sounding like an idiot or a jerk, but there are people who are attracted to the edges of the world. And at the edges of the world, a lot of stuff is stripped away, a lot of bullshit, a lot of falsehoods, a lot of the stuff that anybody deals with in his normal life. Things are more elemental, or feel more raw, or more alive in some ways. The desire to travel to those places, I totally understand the appeal. I also understand the pain associated with it, and that it comes from— Just as comedy often comes from a dark place, if you are entirely content, you don't spend two hundred days a year traveling the world. There's a certain restlessness I think that is inherent in that desire.

DAVE CHANG: He jumped into everything headfirst, full steam ahead. Heroin never was replaced, actually; he tried to fill the void with celebrity and fame, which he didn't necessarily want, but it was temporary, and the notoriety. He tried to fill it with travel. I think the travel made the addiction worse.

NANCY BOURDAIN: Tony is younger than I am, by about fourteen months. The last couple of years I'd think, *How the hell does he do it?* It was a hectic schedule. He'd complain when we were together, about the travel, and how taxing it was. I think travel was passing for his addiction for a while.

MIKE RUFFINO: He had about ten years on me, but we both went pretty dark, at about the same time in our lives, so we had a lot in common.

I remember him once asking, "Well, how much crack did you smoke when you were shooting heroin?" I said, "What? None. That's crazy!" And he said, "See, that's the difference between you and me."

I guess there was a danger to it; he was a little bit more eager to ride the edge. He didn't really do the half measures of anything.

He was very aware of his self-destructive impulses. I mean, that's one of the things we discussed pretty frequently. Just by discussing them, they just don't seem that dangerous themselves.

STEVEN TEMPEL: The last time I saw him was in 2012, at [the] Googa–Mooga [festival, in Brooklyn]. He seemed uncomfortable in his own skin. I gave him a Vicodin and he put it in his pocket. Later that day when I saw him again, he remembered he had it; he reached in his pocket and took it, and gave me a thumbs-up.

HELEN LANG: I absolutely see him as an addict. He was a fiend. He had a totally addictive personality.

TOM VITALE: Everything in moderation was not something Tony ever mastered.

BILL BUFORD: I think it's the addictive personality [that] now makes sense of his busyness. His busyness kept him from being an addict. If you're busy, you're not allowed to follow impulses to where you say, "Why stop?"—which is the addict's intensity. Because he was the busiest, most productive person I think I know. And I know I wasn't seeing all of it, but I was certainly seeing enough of it.

NARI KYE: Tony's always been, in one way or another, addicted to something. He gets obsessed with one thing, and he gets really into it. We saw that with jiu-jitsu. We see that with the duck press. I remember he was obsessed with that for a while. He saw it in France, and he was like, "I need to have that." Weird, little, quirky obsessions, he would get really into. And I think it was a way for him to keep his very, very running mind focused on something, because he always had so much going on. I don't think he really slept much, so I think things were always running through his head. I think these obsessions kind of honed things in for him.

JOSH HOMME: Certainly, he was a man of extremes. So maybe it's an *extremist* personality that's the trouble. I guess I think of *addictive* as a word of negativity, and maybe that's just semantics. Because, at the end of the day, there's this amalgam of reasons why things went wrong.

ROY CHOI: Even though he was famous, he was still mad at shit. I knew that he was still struggling. I remember little tics about him; he always drummed his fingers. I know, because I'm an addict, too; I've always connected to him, knowing that there's something else going on.

NANCY BOURDAIN: When he smoked, he *smoked*. I remember Tony would wake up sometimes in the middle of the night, and he'd light a cigarette. I would say, "What are you doing? You're gonna be asleep in five seconds."

DAVID CHOE, ARTIST: Whenever I would meet Tony, there was very little small talk. We would just get into it. I had never met anyone who had beat heroin addiction without a twelve-step program. The relapse rate is like 90-something percent, and so I'm like, *What can I learn from this guy? He's like a walking miracle. If he figured out a secret way to get out of heroin addiction, that's amazing.*

And a lot of his theories and ideas on how to beat [addiction] were very similar to what I had thought: just get out of the house, pull yourself up by your bootstraps.

NATHAN THORNBURGH: One of the things that was always shockingly great about Tony was that kind of teenage enthusiasm, just the way he could immerse himself in a moment. It was why he could make such great writing, and why it translated to television really well. He really *felt* things, on a level that must have been out of this world. He was living there, he was camped out. He was so immersed in the moment of the absolute. Maybe it's like having too strong a sense of smell. Maybe that wasn't survivable, at the end of the day, that kind of quick response to the moment.

I knew, even in my deepest cups with Tony, there was always so much daylight between who we were. I mean, I live in a small apartment with my wife, whom I met when I was eighteen, and my two kids, and a dog, and like, that is who I am, and that is who Tony could not have been, despite moments, I think, of wanting to have that.

ANDERSON COOPER: The more you travel, you come back home, and you feel like you don't speak the same language. You've had these interesting experiences, and for everybody else, it's just been another week that's passed. And maybe they went out to dinner, or saw a movie, or whatever it was they did during that week, but in that week, you've gone to, say, Kashmir, and you've shot all this stuff, and had all these interesting experiences. And there's a disconnect, and at certain times your friends kind of fall away, because you're never around, and then, when you come back, the stuff that they've been doing just seems mundane, and it's hard to connect.

But I don't think it's that the travel leads to discontentment. I think it certainly exacerbates it, or allows you to delay addressing it, but I think it's the discontentment that leads to being drawn to these places.

32

"DARKER, MORE TRANSGRESSIVE, AND MORE LURID"

ROADS & KINGDOMS

NATHAN THORNBURGH: I had a lot of jobs at *Time* magazine. I was the national political editor for a hot minute, which is one of the worst casting jobs I can imagine, and not long after that, they put me in an even worse job, which was to edit the celebrity profile right at the end of the magazine.

Somebody suggested we do Bourdain. This was in 2007. He took the subway [to the office], and he was just great. He spoke in complete paragraphs. It was when he was on his anti–Rachael Ray kick, and it was so delightful to hear him splattering her entrails across the interview room. He took all the time in the world to do the interview. He was super interested in the journalism that we were doing. We were talking about Iraq and the Baghdad bureau. It was, by a factor of ten, the most positive experience I had in that entire run.

A couple of years after that, [writer] Matt Goulding and I started talking about *Roads & Kingdoms*, and started putting together this web publication that would end up, editorially and emotionally, in a space that Tony had been heading to. He was coming from food to journalism, and Matt and I were coming in the other direction. Matt had met Tony in Catalonia [Spain], with José Andrés.

MATT GOULDING, EDITOR-WRITER; PARTNER IN *ROADS & KINGDOMS*: In the spring of 2011, Tony was filming the closing of El Bulli with José Andrés and Ferran Adrià, and I was doing a profile on José for the *Wall Street Journal* magazine, and they invited me out for what's called the *caragol lleida*, the big snail feast in the interior region of Catalonia, in the spring. Lots of wine, just a shitload of snails, good times, everyone kind of just cuts loose. Can't really think of a better scenario in which to meet Tony.

He likened the villa where we met to a place in *The Godfather: Part 2*, where Don Ciccio gets stabbed in the gut by an emerging Corleone, when he goes back to Sicily. I mean, it was the perfect kind of Bourdainian moment. I was obviously super nervous because I'm riding shotgun with my hero, but he was great. We had really good conversations about the food media world, trading little anecdotes and gossip. I may have mentioned to him that I was starting something with my partner, in the food and travel, culture and geopolitical space, that might be of interest to him. And I got his email address, for a couple of quotes for the José story, which was a tether that kind of allowed me to circle back and reach out to him.

NATHAN THORNBURGH: We spent that first year going to these different countries that had really good food stories and interesting political stories.

MATT GOULDING: We were in Copenhagen, and we had just had a big night of filming at Noma with René Redzepi and the crew, and sleeping in this tiny houseboat, which was all we could really afford on the *Roads & Kingdoms* budget. We woke up, and our phones were vibrating like crazy.

NATHAN THORNBURGH: Overnight, Tony had tweeted something like, "*Roads & Kingdoms* does consistently fine work." Which, for a man with a lot of words, was pretty austere, but it was great. I thought, *Maybe he's full of shit.* We were slightly disbelieving, but psyched.

Not long after that, Matt was sending me these ridiculous emails from [his research in] Japan, and I told him that he should write to Tony and pitch his experience as a book. Matt did, and Tony wrote back right away, and that's how it started. It was all very strange and unexpected.

MATT GOULDING: Tony basically said, "Anything that is an ongoing expression of *Roads & Kingdoms* and its ethos, I want to be a part of." I don't want to overuse the phrase, but it truly was life changing.

NATHAN THORNBURGH: Tony invested $400,000 in *Roads & Kingdoms*, in the form of cash and services. He wasn't a private equity guy; this was money that he worked for, and it felt finite, and it was also just enough money to be dangerous for us. It was not enough where we could really go after a thesis; it was enough money to get him skin in the game, so that we could be empowered to go and make more money.

He wasn't anticapitalist. He just, from my experience as his business partner, had lots of bright lines that he wouldn't have wanted us to cross for him, in making that money, and I think that's why we got along. It was really fun running a business with him, because he always had this outlaw mentality, which is very rare in business in general, and particularly from the investor side.

MATT GOULDING: Everything he brought to the table was much more valuable than the money itself.

There were no questions about *What are your traffic numbers; what's your model; how do you guys make money;* do *you make money; how do you see yourself making money in the future? How can I help you guys make more for all of us?* That never happened, not once. We shared a couple of tax returns with his accountants, and that was it. That was the extent of our conversations about the business of *Roads & Kingdoms.*

NATHAN THORNBURGH: We knew that Tony wasn't going to line edit or sit in editorial meetings, but we would send him things before publication, and every once in a while we'd have a back-and-forth about a piece. The one that sticks out in my mind is when he said, "Just remember to make it darker, more transgressive, and more lurid." As the investor, he's got to know that that's really bad financial advice—ain't no money in darker, more transgressive, and more lurid—but he gave us permission to not succumb to whatever weird bullshit we might have gotten into as a media company, in a race to get him his money back, in a race to have an audience that would match the size of his television audience.

MATT GOULDING: It's not surprising that his favorite pieces were ones like "The Dog Thief Killings," about vigilante locals in Vietnam who were killing drug addicts who stole dogs to get their fix. That was a quintessential Bourdain story, so much so that when we went to CNN to pitch a television show, a *Roads & Kingdoms* TV show, *that* was the episode that had to get made. I remember [CNN executive] Amy Entelis kind of nervously shifting in her seat, being like, "Let's see."

NATHAN THORNBURGH: The last thing I wanted to do was be any kind of drag on him, because there was so much of that around. He had this obvious magnetism, amplified by the fame that he had, and I always tried to not need to be liked by him, because he was inscrutable and temperamental. Often he would be incredibly magnanimous in ways that surprised us, but I remember he was having a bad day, the day that we announced our launch, just a being-short-with-people kind of day. That taught me not to get wrapped up personally in shit. There wasn't any sense in having his reaction on any given day be a referendum on my relationship with him, or on the business.

MATT GOULDING: On a personal level, you were never quite sure where you stood with him, because of how he was. I don't think it was because of his fame or notoriety; I think just, deep down, there was a lot of shyness there, a lot of timidity. He wasn't a guy for chitchat. And when you tried, it didn't really move the needle. He wasn't gonna ask you, like, "How's your wife doing?"

And that's something that I still get anxiety dreams about—there's an assignment that I didn't quite deliver on, or, in one dream, I'm on a cruise with my dad and Tony, and I just keep on doing awkward things that make all of us very uncomfortable.

We'd started to work on something together with David Gelb and Brian McGinn, the *Chef's Table* guys, that was going to be a docuseries, bringing to life some of our more ambitious journalism;

that was still in the works when he died. That's one of the many really difficult things that we had to metabolize in the wake of his death. The first wave of it was that raw, searing pain of losing a friend, and someone you admired, and for me, losing my hero. That'll always be there.

We had built a business together that was, in 2018, about to go over the hump; all of that came to a crashing halt.

From a morale standpoint, it's really tough. This dream fell into our laps, in terms of being able to make media with the person who we thought did it best. And then suddenly to have that taken away from you—that voice, and that person, and that source of energy and strength and validation—that is a hole that you can't ever really fill.

NATHAN THORNBURGH: I think we had a lot more opportunity than we ever tapped into. It could have been a real business, and I find it hilarious, in hindsight, that Tony and Matt and I, collectively, had the business sense of a spotted owl.

33

"EVERYONE FELT THEY KNEW HIM"

CHARISMA AND RESERVE

NIGELLA LAWSON: His attachments with people—once he liked you and you were doing something together, there would be a very firm attachment. But it's not the same thing as just you both lying on a different sofa having a talk about nothing. Our friendship was very much based on being in the same place, at the same time, for a joint purpose. I was a close friend in the sense that I think we both felt very warmly about one another. But we didn't see each other outside those times. Which isn't to say that's a fake friendship at all. I think that was very much the pattern of his friendships.

ANDERSON COOPER: I was friendly with him, and I hugely admired him, and we got to hang out through work events. Our friendship, sadly, didn't really extend beyond that. But we would get together whenever he had a new season out, and have conversations that would end up being divided up and used to promote his series.

As somebody who was not an intimate friend in any sense, there was something about— Every time I was with him, I wanted it to go longer. And I wanted to be friends with him. I wanted him to really like me.

DEAN FERTITA: He was a great person to be around. You felt better when you were around him. The relationship I had with him, it was usually in a working environment. He was always motivated, always pushing forward. From my perspective, I forgot what was going on in my life when I was around him; I was able to lose myself in whatever project we were doing at the time.

NIGELLA LAWSON: I think there is something about those extraordinarily charismatic people, that everyone feels they're a close friend, you know, whether it's someone who's never met you, watches you on television, or whether it's all of us who knew him in our compartmentalized ways. I think that was very much part of his charisma. I also think that it's not entirely false, because I think he did make those connections like that with people.

HELEN CHO: He blended personal life with his work life. There were really no boundaries, honestly. He was a very private person, for sure. If we would go out to a restaurant, I would never put him in a place where I knew he would be a spectacle. You'd see it, the eyes on him in public, in certain cities and countries. It certainly felt like he was a spectacle. He couldn't be himself. Sometimes you'd see him in conversations in groups, and he'd command the table and go on these monologues. It was genuinely him, but it also seemed tiring.

DIANE SCHUTZ: I'm sure it's exhausting, to meet new people who want to ask the same questions, and you feel like you're putting on a dog and pony show for everybody. As his celebrity grew, he was pulled in so many more directions.

NIGELLA LAWSON: Everyone felt they knew him. That's what television does to you, and his particular form of television. I think it's very difficult, because you're dealing with a lot of people who need something from you, emotionally—they're coming to hear him speak, and for someone who was quite turned in on himself, as an introvert, he was, more than a lot of men, quite porous in the sense of feeling people's needs.

He wasn't like that with producers; he was quite capable of cordoning himself off and not really troubling himself about displeasing. But in terms of people who looked up to him, the sort of people who might come and hear him speak, I think he was very acutely sensitive to what they needed, and what he was going to give, which is why he always gave such a dazzling performance, with moments of showing vulnerability to people. That's why I think people responded to him.

JOSH HOMME: People knew who Tony was [*snaps fingers*] instantly, all over the world. That's an intense, unspoken relationship with people you don't know. And it can be challenging to navigate that. And in Tony's case, it got so ubiquitous, with him telling the right stories to the whole world. There are [questions of] how to manage that: *Am I doing too much? Am I working too much? Am I accidentally isolating myself because I don't want to be hit up for something?*

There's a psychological, mental health, and emotional price that comes with that, that you had no idea about. And when you're a workaholic, and you want to do a good job, and you don't want to let anyone down, it costs you your relationships at home, because it has to. And so you end up looking for people of a like mind who travel, gypsies.

Because of the nature of Tony's life, as his friend, you sort of existed in a vacuum. I didn't know if there were parallels to our relationship existing all over the place. "Does he have fifty friends this way? Four? How many boxes like this, and were their boxes like mine? Or was it a special box?" But I wish he would have unboxed some of it. It would have been more to his benefit.

ERIC RIPERT: The beauty of the relationship that we had was, I was extremely comfortable being with him in silence. And, hours together, half a day together, maybe most of the day, without exchanging a word, and not really uncomfortable. So he would be really himself, doing whatever he wants to do, and I will be daydreaming, or I will be myself, basically, and knowing that it was all good, and then, at night, we will have a fantastic evening, talking, and laughing, and drinking, and we will have a good time.

HELEN CHO: There were a lot of quiet moments, too, where not much was said. I remember us driving in LA, and he would just play music. And he would say, "My dad took me to this show," or something. I think about those quiet moments a lot. There was no pressure for him to be "on."

ROY CHOI: In LA, we spent a lot of time together, driving and talking, not being filmed. He was always fascinated with LA driving, the harmony of left turns in LA.

I could spend hours with Tony and not say a word. I had a relationship with Tony like, when you're young, with a friend playing video games and you don't talk for twelve hours, and the only thing you say to each other after maybe nine hours is, "You hungry?"

But, like, you're best friends, you know? That was the relationship I had with Tony: I felt I knew him, even though I didn't really talk to him that much, and I hope that's how he felt he knew me. It was almost as if we were both chefs together in a restaurant; we were very close, we had war stories together, but I never knew much about anything beyond that.

MIKE RUFFINO: Some of my fondest memories are days [at Chateau Marmont]; we'd just sit at the pool, and hang out, and read. And at some point, he'd get up and go, "OK, I'm taking a nap. Dinner at eight?" "Yup. See you." There was no need to even talk; you could just silently comment. It was just a good friendship that way.

ROY CHOI: There are certain friends he had in our industry where it would be about sitting for hours, drinking whiskey and debating, but me and Tony never had that relationship. I'm more like a dog, man. I like waking up and living and being excited, knowing I'm gonna see you. Maybe that's the side of Tony that I brought out: the generous, the good, the humorous, the simple, the kind, the caring and, like, brotherly, and always there for you. I know he and [Dave] Chang would always argue; I never got into political arguments with him.

I never really saw the dark side of Tony. I only saw Tony with a smile and open arms—that's how my whole experience of Tony was: every time I saw or emailed him or talked to him, he genuinely wanted to be there, too.

I knew Tony—I knew he had his darkness, but it didn't bother me; it wasn't something that I felt I needed to fix. It's not my business to know his darkness, and it's not his business to know my darkness, it's just to be together through that darkness.

34

"GET A BIG FUCKING BODY BAG"

FRUSTRATION AND ISOLATION IN THE FIELD

DIANE SCHUTZ: One thing Tony always valued was the camaraderie with the crew, but as time went on, our budgets increased, and you wanted to respect his time, so then he gets his own van to set, and the crew advances for an hour. Well, now he's just lost an hour in the van with the crew, and he's just there alone, with a local driver. That's something I wonder: In later years, was it a factor in maybe not enjoying the shoots as much? On the one hand, we're trying to make it easier for you, you don't have to be on set for five hours, but at the same time something is lost, not being around people whom you know and like, and who know and like you.

NIGELLA LAWSON: What is wonderful is crew life. If you work alone, crew life is great. The camaraderie of a crew whom you work very closely with over years and years and years makes a huge difference, because you have people to hang out with. But I'm not sure, if you're not feeling happy, that you're going to feel happy in a beautiful part of the world.

PAULA FROELICH: What people don't understand about him is, he was a serial monogamist. That kind of lifestyle, it's perfectly lonely and disoriented. Even if you travel with the same crew, those people work for you. You like them and they like you, if you work for a certain amount of time together, but there's still the employee-employer [dynamic].

PAT YOUNGE: I do also think we underestimated the impact of spending 200, 250 days a year on the road. I think that was really hard on him. I know he hated it more when he had a kid, but, as I look back, I do think, when you travel a lot, and you really think about airports, delays, reservation screwups, luggage not arriving, taxis to airports, all that stuff, it was quite hard; harder than I think I realized at the time.

We started introducing [episodes of *No Reservations*] with the best bits, where he would just have to film some scenes in New York, and we put together three or four scenes from other shows. But he hated doing those, because to him, it wasn't really the art of television; it was sort of commodified, like a tacky suit.

STEVEN TEMPEL: It had to have been 2009 or 2010, when I was down in Miami Beach with Tony. He said, "People think, 'Oh, you travel the world; you have the best life.' I don't want to do this anymore. I'm tired of traveling. I just want to do voice-overs."

JOSH FERRELL: I did the Ukraine episode of *No Reservations*. We went to Chernobyl. It was such a sad day, because it's fucking Chernobyl. At the end of the day we're like, "Well, that was terrible, let's all burn our clothes, and everybody take the night off." I called Tony and said, "Everybody's doing their own thing," and he said, "Let's go to McDonald's." So me and Tony went to McDonald's in Kiev, and had this little lonely meal, and talked about what a shitty day it had been. We both needed comfort food, and not to be alone, and to acknowledge that that was fucking heavy and terrible, over a Big Mac.

MATT WALSH: We did a show in Harbin, up in the cold northeast of China, that got weird at one point. We had a great location at this rustic restaurant, where everybody sits around a big wok with coal burning underneath, and they chuck in some broth, and a whole fish, and god knows what else, and it cooks in front of you. Sort of like hot pot, but not really. Everyone sits around this thing to stay warm. I think the food was terrible, but visually, it was a great scene. In those days, the working method was, the crew would set up whatever lights they needed and scope out the right table. I'd go back to the van to get Tony and brief him about the place—what am I eating here, what's important about this, what should I notice? I went out to the van to collect him, and I couldn't sense it at that time, but Tom [Vitale], who was on that shoot, told me later that something had happened while we left Tony in the van. He'd been on the phone to New York, and his mood flipped. He came in, and was very dark, and very uninterested, and the scene devolved. They kept trying to save it, and eventually they pulled me into it, which didn't help at all. He was just in a pissy mood. It was the kind of a thing I saw, in one way or another, on an increasing number of scenes, where I thought, *I get that you're the iconoclast, the anti–food show host, but, you know, think of the viewers. That's what you're here for. Do it. It's not hard.*

It's the greatest job in the world, just do it. He just sometimes didn't want to do it. And that was disappointing, and frustrating.

He grew increasingly tired, and he grew increasingly fed up with the process of making the shows. Tony was curious about the world, and just not so crazy about the process of making TV.

I saw that come to a head during filming *The Layover* in Hong Kong. He was really pissed off. We had moments of fun, but he was up to here with having a camera in his face twenty-four hours a day, which is the way *The Layover* was shot.

And it was June in Hong Kong, so it was hellishly hot, and he was an angry man. Watch the episode, you can see it.

ALEX LOWRY: He hated *The Layover*. He would call me and be like, "Why am I doing this?" and I'd say, "Dude, you tell me! You're the one who agreed to do it." He was desperately trying to get the number of days down that he had to be in a place.

He said it a few times, that he felt like a sausage being stuffed with food, but this was the back-and-forth. I said, "If you'd give me two or three days, then you don't have to do eight scenes a day." He was almost literally twenty-four hours in and out; he would come in the night before, maybe if we could get him to do a scene that night, he'd do a scene, and then it was all the scenes the next day, and then he would fly out.

JOSH FERRELL: I did a season of *The Layover*. That was terrible. Like most nonunion shows, it was a labor of love. It was just insane. I have never been a part of any show that worked like that. The show was thirty-six hours in whatever place, and it was literally filming with Tony for thirty-six hours. It was run and gun: "Is this gonna work, is this not gonna work? Let's overshoot it, because you don't know what scenes are gonna work, what scenes are not." So instead of doing two or three scenes a day, like you'd do with *Parts Unknown*, you'd do seven scenes. And there was so much food. Tony had to eat so much.

JARED ANDRUKANIS: The *Layover* years, when the Travel Channel years were coming to an end, Tony was overweight. He would do three or four scenes a day where he'd eat. But it was some of the funniest narration he's ever written; he was just angry at everybody.

I don't really know what was going on in his personal life, but we'd sit in the van in between scenes sometimes, and he would put the seat back and he was just breathing real weird. I could tell he was in pain. Really struggling. I would be like, "Dude, let's just cancel. We don't need to do another fucking food scene. You hate this shit. You don't need to strap on the feed bag."

But [he was] tied to the cart as much as everyone else. He wouldn't take the out. He didn't want to disappoint the guest.

JOSH FERRELL: I noticed that, with the humor that he would convey from *No Reservations* to *Layover* and then *Parts Unknown* to the end of *Parts Unknown*, the gag of like, "Oh this is terrible," it started getting a little more sincere, a little more— I would have him sitting at a whiskey bar in *Layover* and he'd be like, "Oh, I can't believe I have to sit here and drink this." And then we were somewhere for *Parts Unknown* and he would say, "I fucking hate this." And you would realize, "Oh, he's serious."

TODD LIEBLER: I think that when his expectations weren't met, it was a crushing blow for him. When he was getting angsty, he would definitely— Well, first of all, the dude was so funny, and when he got angsty, it would just turn darker, you know? Or he would just kind of be inside himself. It was, to a certain degree, obvious when he was in his dark place. He'd go inside himself.

SANDY ZWEIG: When we started *Parts Unknown* [in 2012], he was not in great shape, physically. He was a little overweight. He had been on a speaking tour just before we started, and we started shooting in November, which is very late, to get sixteen episodes done. It was a very tough season. There were a couple of back-to-back shoots. The Libya shoot was stressful for everybody; a lot of stuff went down there that was difficult to handle in the field. And then the Sicily shoot, at the very end of the season, where that fisherman had somebody throwing, basically, dead fish into the water for them to catch, there was a breaking point there. I got an email from him after that scene was shot, which started out with, "Is this what it's come to? After ten years on television?"

SALLY FREEMAN: Everyone asks, and used to ask him, "Which one was the disaster episode?" And it was one of mine, in Sicily. The story of that episode that's kind of gone down in folklore is not the true story. He kind of had a mental breakdown on that shoot. It's been played down and made into a funny story.

We took Tony fishing, and the chef who we got, in the middle of Sicily, was like, "Oh, come to this beautiful place. We'll go diving." And we realized, as Tony got into the water, there was another guy who came up on a boat, and was throwing dead squid and octopus and stuff into the water. And it was absolutely hilarious.

Tony was furious, in only that way that he can be. But it was so funny, because it was just— It's the exact worst thing that can happen during a scene, when you're trying to keep everything authentic and real, and this guy's, like, lobbing dead fish. Tony wrote about that in the narration for that episode, and he made it very funny.

He was so strong; some guy throwing fish at him in Sicily is not going to be the thing that sends him over the edge. But it was also his birthday, and he'd almost reached the age that his dad was when he died, and it got dark. He really went into a funk, and he said that he hadn't expected to live beyond that age. So, for me, whenever I hear somebody talk about this Sicily episode, and how the dead fish put him into a massive depression, it's like, well, I know that it was nothing to do with what we were filming.

We coped with a lot on that shoot. He was having breathing difficulties, which looking back, I don't know if they were breathing difficulties or whether he was suffering from anxiety, or something else. We got him an oxygen tank. We were texting him all night, every two hours, and if he didn't text back, we were gonna break the door in. We were truly worried about him; worried for his health, for his mental state. And there was a day when he just sat in the garden and he wouldn't film anything. That's when I asked him, "What's really going on here?" and he talked about his dad.

Nothing particularly bad came out of that episode or that situation, but if that had been a close friend of mine who was like that, I would have thought, *Yeah, he probably needs some help.*

JOSH FERRELL: We were in Budapest, at this little schnitzel place, like an hour outside the city. Giant schnitzel, as big as the table. This old man makes it in this little tin box of a place, and it's all steamy in there, and you drink the beer with it. So Tony eats it, and he was like, "Oh my god, that's disgusting."

We put him in his car, he heads back to his hotel, and we break everything down. Just before we leave, I say to my fixer, "You got the releases signed, right?"

And he says, "Oh, yeah, the old man said he needs to take a picture with Tony first, before he signs the release." And I was like, "Dude, Tony left like an hour ago. Can he just sign the release?" and he said no.

So I called Tony. "I'm so sorry; in order to get this guy to sign the release, he says he's got to take a picture with you," and he says, "Josh, I can *see* my hotel. I'm going to take the biggest shit of my life when I get there." I'm like, "I am so sorry, Tony," and he hangs up the phone.

A few minutes later the fixer tells me the driver just called, and they're turning back around. They drive an hour back. Tony gets out of his car, beelines it right toward the guy, and says to me, "Somebody better get a big fucking body bag." Takes the picture, gets back in the car, and takes off.

It was one of those moments where I'm like, *Is he fucking joking?* It was so intense. It was so intense, and so fucking funny. That was the relationship that Tony and I had; he could give me shit, and I could take it.

TOM VITALE: There was a sort of a sadistic element to the job and the relationship, but the way I looked at it, it relieved pressure from him, that someone else was suffering a bit, too, because it was a tough job for him.

ALISON MOSSHART, MUSICIAN: His impatience was fucking hilarious, entertaining to everybody. When you're a big figure like that, you're allowed to be impatient, because people will make it so you don't have to wait. Anytime you do have to wait, your brain explodes. A quick temper's not a great trait. He could always put a humorous spin on it, if people were listening, but you knew that he really wanted to get the fuck out of there.

I watched that whole thing happen again and again, the whole time we were filming [*Parts Unknown*] in Nashville. And then we did London, too. Jamie [Hince], my bandmate, was in [that episode]. I was there. It was fucking hysterical. Well, it's funny to the person who's not being yelled at, you know. You can get away with that for a long time, until that's exactly who you are. But he absolutely loved everyone who worked with him. That was his family.

JEFF ALLEN, PRODUCER: He would always stay in the nicest room, and that often meant he was isolated. It's probably depressing to be in the castle all alone. He would be in the palace, and we would be in the horse stables. That's literally where we stayed in Laos. Tony was in the Amantaka hotel, living in the villa, all alone, and the crew stayed in the former horse stables, which had been converted into a shitty little hotel.

We made a point to go over to Tony's room once in a while. It was a challenge, because the nature of the beast is constraints. We had budgets and time to deal with; we can't all afford to stay at the nice hotel with Tony, but we also can't afford to not get face time with him, because that's how we make the show—have a beer at the end of the day and talk to Tony about all the creative, and informing him who he's gonna meet the next day, and talking through ideas. And when we didn't get that, there were repercussions. He would get cranky, or come in pissed off about something.

ANDERSON COOPER: You spend a lot of time in hotel rooms alone by yourself, [and] it seems, from the outside, kind of glamorous, and sometimes they're really nice hotels, and sometimes they're not. But there is— It's just lonely. No one wants to hear anyone complaining about [it]. You're not working in a coal mine, and obviously it's fulfilling in a myriad of ways, but there is a real loneliness to it. It's like the old movie *The Loneliness of the Long Distance Runner*. And I think of that in relationship to Tony.

You have friends, and they love you, and you're loved by— Tony is loved by people around the world, but that doesn't really— In the end, when you're in a room by yourself, that's not necessarily what you feel.

JOSH FERRELL: We did a shoot in Tanzania, and we went to the Ngorongoro Crater, the crater of life. It's like fucking *Lion King*, all the animals in the kingdom are in this goddamn crater. We worked out a deal for Tony with &Beyond, which is the ultraluxe accommodation, cabins along the crater, all $2,000 a night, rose petal baths each night, that sort of thing. The rest of us were at the Econo Lodge on the other side of the crater.

The first night, Tony said, "OK, so we're all staying here?" and I said, "No, but we can come over here for dinner, or you can come over there for dinner." And he goes, "Why don't you just stay here?" And I said, "I can't stay here, there's no budget." And he says, "I'm gonna need you to stay here."

So I worked out a deal with the office and the hotel, and they let me stay at another cabin. Each night, at the end of each safari, Tony and I would have a literally candlelit dinner with, like, six butlers, and I would say, "How was your day?" and he'd say, "Eh, it was all right," and we'd just shoot the shit, talk about jiu-jitsu. He'd ask me about myself, we talked about shoots, and just have this lovely dinner together, each night.

JEFF ALLEN: In Indonesia, we had this nice hotel on the beach, and they're super pumped to have Tony there, and they put him in this isolated villa that's like a twenty-minute walk from where the crew is. So, every day, Tony was inviting the crew to hang out at his villa, because he's just sitting there alone after the shoot. All he wanted to do was send a PA out to get KFC and a bottle of Johnnie Walker, and drink and eat chicken and talk for hours. And it's challenging, as a producer or director, because you also have to get shit done. Hanging out with Tony is where the fun is, but I also have to manage a crew of twenty people who need to know what we're doing tomorrow, and how we're getting there, and what time. We hung out, but at great cost to our sanity and sleep.

In the Greece episode [of *Parts Unknown*], he asks a question in the voice-over, something to the effect of, "Is it worse to be in a bad place with people you like, or in a beautiful place all alone?" So much of his life was going to beautiful places and being all alone.

35

"TONY HAD A BURDEN OF LEADERSHIP THAT WAS REAL"

MARIA BUSTILLOS, JOURNALIST: I got the feeling talking to him—in the first part of our conversation [in February 2018], he was very polished, and very much the commercial product, but as time wore on, and we kept drinking, and he was letting his hair down more, I got a real sense of him having to manage his own admissions, or information. [We talked about] how he felt about Emeril, whom he had criticized so much, but then he came around, and the thing that he really identified with was that idea of having a big group of people who depended on him to look after them.

"I asked for the fame. I asked to be the big guy, and now I'm accountable to this huge group of people, and I have to do a really good job, and I have to be Anthony Bourdain all the time. I chose this, and this is the cost and the price." So that was the big vulnerability that I saw.

I said, "Is it worth it?" and he said, "Some days, yeah. Others, *eh*."

MIKE RUFFINO: When *No Reservations* still had a couple of seasons left, Tony was already like, "Ah, I'm all done."

His idea was that he was just going to be able to step back and not be on camera. But ultimately, there were a lot of people depending on him. And he wasn't gonna pull out of that.

MORGAN FALLON: I remember saying, "Why the fuck aren't you just slapping your name on a pizza box, dude? Sell the fuck out. Cash in. Stop. Don't be on the road 250 days a year anymore. It's one phone call, man. Who cares? None of the people who love you are gonna judge you for that."

I think he was so concerned, in some ways, about what his legacy would be. Here he is, this ex–heroin addict line cook and chef, who got away with the greatest fucking con job in the history of mankind, being paid to basically live out his personal fantasy. I think that became handcuffing, in a way. He had a lot of people depending on him.

TOM VITALE: I mean, he was a very successful writer. He could have dialed back the other thing and still been very comfortable, and flexed those creative muscles, everything good, and shaken off the bad parts. And yet, he just went after more and more intensity, those things that exacerbated the issues in his life.

FRED MORIN: We had a plan for Tony. He loved putting on tunes on the radio. We're like, "Sirius Radio, you have a show, you play music. The radio's the best, man."

DAVE MCMILLAN: "You never leave Manhattan. You'll be as big as Howard Stern. And you can interview everyone in the food world." He said he felt responsibility [to continue making television]. He was like, "I gotta fucking figure it out, but there's so many fucking people on the payroll." Tony had a burden of leadership that was real.

KIMBERLY WITHERSPOON: Tony shared with me his concern that he was floating the boat for a lot of other people. He felt tremendous responsibility for the team that he had assembled, in different areas of his life. He felt a lot of responsibility, for example, for his publisher, and for [production company] ZPZ. He never said that he felt responsible for me, but I always assumed that it was a 360-degree point of view. Even though I was making these deals for him, and for other clients, he also considered me part of his responsibility. I know he spoke to other people about the fact that he found that burden very heavy.

It colored his perspective, that he was supporting the people he was working with and had on his team. And, of course, financially, that was true. But the emotional dynamic was that he had a team of people who were invested in caring for him, not just because they worked with him, or for him, but because they were genuinely loyal and attached to him, as he was to them. He created this family of people, most of whom were initially assembled because they had work responsibilities. But, because he was so loyal, these relationships went on for years and years. And the familial component of it all became as important as the work relationship.

I think that the work aspect of it allowed Tony to have control over the emotional dynamic. Because we all worked with him, or all worked for him, he was able to establish and, to some degree, control how close people could get to him, what they could say to him, what he was willing to tolerate.

CHRISTOPHER BOURDAIN: It drove both me and Tony crazy that our mother just seemed convinced that "my son is now prestigious, and famous, and making a lot of money, so I deserve to have him give me all sorts of money." Where do you come off with that attitude?

There was always some story about why she was out a huge sum of money. She redid her apartment, and the contractor went flaky on her and left her in the lurch with a half-done job, and she was out $15,000. Every few years, something like that would go on, where she had the idea and the energy to get the thing going, but meanwhile wasn't attending properly to the financial details or protecting herself. And then Tony would get an email, like, "Oh, I need $50,000 in dental work, and I can't afford it, I have no money at all. Can you help?" And he did, at times.

There was one dinner we had where she presented the grand plan that Tony and I were going to bail her out, mostly Tony. I had found out a few months earlier that she had falsified my signature on a document, and had basically yanked our dad's ashes out of the place where we had them stored. She was technically still his wife; they never divorced. Even though she'd basically kicked him out, she had convinced herself, wrongly, that he had forgiven her, and they should have their ashes scattered together on Long Beach Island.

So just having her plop down that night at some restaurant and say, "This is what you're going to do for me: you'll buy my apartment, and, Tony, you'll give me a stipend," I think Tony's jaw dropped, and I went kind of ballistic about the ashes, which I very rarely do, and I said, "That's the shittiest thing you've ever done, you should be ashamed of yourself." She walked out in a huff, and Tony and I stayed and had dinner.

CHRIS COLLINS: We challenged Tony to dial back. Because I'm not convinced, necessarily—all that travel, as physically and emotionally and mentally draining as it can be—if it was the personal life that was more unstable, that he could not get right. He understood the road; that was, at the end of the day, the most grounded thing he was doing. We had everybody at this company surrounding him and trying to make things as good for him as humanly possible, you know?

PATRICK RADDEN KEEFE: Another of the big questions that I asked him about a half a dozen times over a year is, "What are you chasing? Why do you keep doing it? Why not slow down?"

He had shifting explanations, and honestly, I thought, for a guy who was so adept at diagnosing himself, none of his explanations were very persuasive. "Well, you go back to the same place you've already been before, but it's changed in the interim." Or, "Even if the places don't change, our filmmaking techniques do, and so we want to see it in another way."

We talked a bit about Iggy Pop in one of our conversations, because I think he saw the fact that Iggy was out there, and didn't quit, as inspiring.

To me, the most persuasive answer in the [*New Yorker*] piece came from Eric Ripert, when he said, "I think Tony keeps moving because he's afraid of what would happen if he stopped."

KIMBERLY WITHERSPOON: Even when he was on a shoot, he was also doing two or three other professional things, figuring them out, whether it was getting information on a book that he wanted to publish on his imprint, or getting ready to go on the road with a lecture series, or something else. I just always felt that Tony was studying harder and harder.

NIGELLA LAWSON: All that traveling—I remember asking him, was it another addiction? I asked him in a public space, by the way. I interviewed him at the South Beach Wine and Food [Festival]. He said, yes, in some sense, that was true, but he was worried about the dark space he would go into if he kept still for too long.

NICK BRIGDEN, DIRECTOR-CINEMATOGRAPHER-EDITOR: He was a guy who liked and embraced and invited change. I think he needed that. He wasn't in the same place for two weeks. He was a shark, always on the move. He had to move to survive.

36

"HE ALWAYS HAD TO PERFORM THE ROLE OF TONY"

KAREN RINALDI: Tony's persona got so huge; people thought he was a little scary or intimidating, and to me, he was always the opposite of that. I think he liked to push this persona forward, and it sort of kept people away. I can't psychoanalyze, but I think that conflation, that tension, probably got difficult.

NIGELLA LAWSON: There were two things running at the same time. He was very polished, and that side, never talking in a sentence that didn't end perfectly, and that would meander richly through many subclauses, all that was part of who he was. But, obviously, underneath that is something he didn't give much expression to, that thing of being so famous that everywhere he went, he would be approached by people.

He became that person he was on the television. He was a lot that person. He was wonderful, articulate, brilliant, funny, and really so enormously reflective, but so quickly and deeply reflective, which is an odd combination. But nevertheless, I think that it trapped him in a form of solitude.

Success is a great force for conservatism, because it's quite hard to break out of what you do to do something else, until it doesn't work. And I think that, for a restless person, that's a constraint.

KAREN RINALDI: I do think that these two sides of Tony—the shy, geeky, wounded side—maybe never reconciled with the level of fame and attention and how lauded he was. Maybe that's true for anyone with a conscience who gets famous. On one side, he's private, he holds himself close, and then he can just turn it on. He was performative, and that worked.

NIGELLA LAWSON: Tony had a way of talking about himself honestly without revealing himself, really. I mean, everything you read about him, he's not telling lies. He's hiding in plain sight.

HELEN CHO: The way he processed the world, it was almost too intense for him to keep up with the reality of what was going on. He was such a romantic, and had an ideal life in his mind, but the reality never lived up to it. And so, in my opinion, the way he was able to deal with how much he had seen, and how much he had experienced, was narratively.

He started doing his Instagram stories, these very similar pans of hotel rooms all over the world. If you just look at them, it was like, *Man, these are really fucking boring*, but if you really look at them, and you really listened to the music that he chose to play, if you really dissected them, I think you would find a theme and a story. He was telling people about himself through his experiences, wherever he was, through the music and film.

NIGELLA LAWSON: I feel that also, he always had to perform the role of Tony. So that performance was a form of protection, as well as a kind of punishment. I don't know that he could be in a room with someone and allow himself to be dull. Tony was never dull. But there's no such thing in the world as someone who sometimes doesn't feel muzzle brained or too low to have a conversation. I don't think he could put himself with anyone then.

DAVID CHOE: The first time I ever met him was at the Chateau Marmont. I was already meeting with Dave Chang, and he said, "Hey, can my friend join?" and then it was like, "Oh, shit, it's Anthony Bourdain."

The hotel has the reputation that celebrities can hang out there, because no one bothers you, but I will say that during that dinner, every single person, famous and not famous, stopped at our table, and it wasn't just for a quick picture. It was like, "I'm so sorry, but I just have to tell you, my son was this, my father did that . . ."

He was so nice and so graceful, and I was like, "Dude, is this your fucking life?" And he said, "In New York, I used to go down to the bodega to get something, and it would take five minutes. Now it takes an hour. I have to stop to take a picture with everyone."

I said, "I know we just met, but if you ever come back to LA and just want to have dinner at my mom's house, please do." So the next time, he came to my mom's house for dinner, and brought her Asian pears, which is a very Korean thing [*laughing*], and I was like, *This fuckin' guy*.

BILL BUFORD: Tony seemed like a person who had developed strategies for protecting himself. He would disappear. He would kind of hold himself back. He seemed to make sure that he had private moments. I got a feeling of a person who is on a really crazy schedule, and one of the difficulties of the schedule is that the content implicitly assumes a commitment to excess, which was a feature of his early shows. You know, out on the ice in Montréal, and everybody's eating and everybody's drinking. They're having their foie gras and their bottle of Sauterne. And it looked like he got into more politics and travel because they interested him, but there was a little bit of self-preservation there. He had enough of a history of being a person of excess to know he didn't want to make that his life. So he was careful. It was appealing.

PATRICK RADDEN KEEFE: What was daunting for me [as a writer] was that he'd been profiled a thousand times. It was a life that was very worked over already. Tony was such a pro, too; he gave a million interviews, but I think he was always very careful about what he showed to whom. I pretty quickly realized that there was an illusion with Tony, which was that he was an open book.

I think he was very attuned to these questions of who is the real guy, and who is the character that he's playing, and what are the slippages between those two. And I think part of the illusion with him was that he was so personable, and so open. You could be talking with him, or reading an interview with him, or watching an interview, and think that you're like, mainlining the guy in his entirety. But, of course, it was an illusion, right?

MICHAEL STEED: There's two Tony Bourdains in my mind: the real one, which is so close to the [other] one [whom] everyone saw on television. What's going to add to the mystique of Tony? You're sort of molding this character, as a director, adding more and more to this real-life person, and to the one on television.

PATRICK RADDEN KEEFE: I was always very aware of how he—it's almost a feature of his graciousness, combined with his awareness, as a writer, of what a writer needs. We had that amazing moment that's in the piece [in Vietnam] where he says to me, "Hey, come on. I'm gonna take the Vespa for a spin. Why don't you get up on the back?" And my internal monologue is like, *Yes, a scene.* And then, my *meta* internal monologue is like, *That's why he's doing this.*

I don't want any of this to sound cynical . . . I mean, I think he understood that there was a myth of Tony Bourdain, and he would attempt to burnish that myth. So maybe it was cynical in that respect, but I also think he was, at least in my experience, fundamentally a very obliging, accommodating— He came up in the hospitality business, right? So there's a sense in which he's like, "Patrick has come all the way to Vietnam. I know what this piece would need at this point, and it's a ride on the back of a Vespa around Hanoi."

In France, he has this weird near-death experience, and then goes back, and the first thing he does is write [a] letter to [Nancy]. That felt very revealing to me. The reporter in me is thinking, *This is gold*—and then, the person who has been hanging out with Tony long enough to know is thinking, *This didn't slip out under your expert questioning.*

NANCY BOURDAIN: I got mad at him when the *New Yorker* article mentioned the email. I remember when I got it, I felt very good. We had a nice little email conversation—and when the piece came out, I thought, *That was private. That was between us.* Why did he do it? Was it to publish it later? Everything was kind of grist. I don't want to be just grist for the mill.

RENNIK SOHOLT: He had his shtick, so to speak. He knew his story. I think that's important for famous people. They know their brand,

and they're able to articulate it and give people what they want, but then those stories sometimes become bigger than other stories that are just as important to the person and who he is, but don't necessarily sell the product. At a certain point, you become a product, so to speak, that ultimately needs to sell in a marketplace. I think Tony knew that very well. He knew his story, he knew himself as a product.

MARIA BUSTILLOS: When I read all his books, I had a strong feeling about his vulnerability; I got concerned that someone that vulnerable should be in the public eye the way that he was. Everybody wanted him to be perfect, and in the public eye he really was perfect, and he was really careful to say the things that sounded really good. For a person who had been through what he had been through, I thought, *This must be a huge strain.*

The more I read, the more evident it became to me that he was kind of constructing, I'm not saying a *false* persona, but communicating certain beliefs in a way that was suitable to the form. He had this reputation for extreme candor but . . . there were, like, ellipses in all these places. It was like he sprang fully formed from the head of Zeus at the age of forty-whatever, after *Kitchen Confidential* was published. He had this life before his forties that he wasn't super proud of. We know there was heroin in it, even though he talks about "my junkie past," and he makes jokes about it, but the details are scarce.

As an interview, he was telling you not what you wanted to hear, but what he thought would be useful to you in the context of what you were trying to achieve. I saw him being circumspect; it was as much self-preservation as it was also good manners, or sensitivity to all the different constituencies that we have to serve when we inform people. He had a really delicate, elegant, sensitive sensibility. At the same time, you knew there was this really renegade person with a lot to hide in his private life, who was willing to take a lot of risks, clearly.

It's weird, because, in his work, it's kind of the same, the good boy and the bad boy inhabiting the same person. It's a huge paradox: the really restrained, mannerly person who was raised to be that way by his mom—he condemned her, in my mind. That's my armchair psychology, anyway.

I think he was very lonely. But there were people around him who loved him and would do anything to be near him. And he had a close group of people. He did know who his friends were. He had lifelong friends, but I still think that he must have felt lonely.

37

"SUCH AN UNLIKELY PROGRAM FOR HIM"

THE TASTE

CHRIS COLLINS: There was a period in there where he was trending toward, "I don't know how much more I can do, I'm starting to feel wrung dry." And I think he did feel just completely weary and exhausted. He was trending toward dialing back.

LYDIA TENAGLIA: He was pushing us to come up with another construct that would take way less time to shoot, and we came up with a competition show called *Have Knife, Will Travel*.

We said, "Here, look, we can shoot the entire season in thirty days. We put time, money, effort, and work into trying to figure this out for you, because we get it."

CHRIS COLLINS: We built it to fit him, so he could slide into something that was not off-brand for him.

LYDIA TENAGLIA: We pitched it to everyone. We went to this meeting at CBS with Les Moonves; we're in this huge office, there's Les, and he says, "OK, I like this. I'm going to set you up with these two development people to push this forward."

Then he said, "Just so you know, this is CBS. This is the big time. Anything less than eight million viewers is going to be considered a failure."

We all shook hands, went out on the street. Tony—

CHRIS COLLINS: —lit two cigarettes at the same time—

LYDIA TENAGLIA: —And he said, "Eight million people? No way. I don't need that kind of pressure. I don't need someone up my ass like that all the time." He killed it.

We'd just spent time, $150,000 worth of development, traveled all over, went to LA, pitched everybody. We did exactly what he said he wanted, and he said, "Let's just keep doing what we're doing," so that's what we did. We kept doing what we were doing.

And then he made [the network cooking competition show] *The Taste.*

NIGELLA LAWSON: I really got to know Tony while doing *The Taste.* Such an unlikely program for him to be involved in. He'd been speaking to Kinetic, the production company, and the deal was, we would do it only if we were doing it together, and we were both EPs [executive producers]. Knowing that he was doing it, as far as I was concerned, guaranteed that it would have integrity.

I wasn't particularly comfortable doing it, but I loved doing it, because I liked hanging out with Tony and Ludo. We'd often go out eating in between times, but Tony really needed to be alone and in his trailer a lot. The only time I saw him outside was when he was still smoking. You'd be filming and there'd be a relight, and he'd be editing a book or finishing something, writing something. He didn't give himself that much time off, on purpose.

He was a very introverted person, which people misunderstood in a way, because of his facility with people, but he was always a slightly detached presence. Enormously friendly; he would look at you in a terribly warm way. And when he needed to pull back, I just felt there was something, like many introverts, he just needed a bit of space around him.

He was such a strange mixture between an extraordinarily measured person and sort of a manically obsessive person. I think that's why he was always so fascinating. I always used to describe him [as] something like Gary Cooper mixed with Keith Richards.

I loved being in his company. When you're young, what you want of people is that they're funny and clever. And then as you get older, you realize kindness is important. But it's not often that you meet people who are funny, clever, and kind. And he was.

Sometimes, as much as he could be, he was quite relaxed. I would like to think that he took for granted that he didn't have to perform in my company. I would say he was not a flirtatious person, but I also think I wasn't a woman he needed to win over.

We talked a lot about things other than ourselves. We'd talk about books. And he always wanted to add things to his life. He was never closed off to the recommendation of a book or a film.

He—as I did—he liked being in the Chateau Marmont for a month. I think it gave him a certain sense of stillness, but he was busy all the time; we had very early starts. I love being busy and not having time to think about myself or life. It's actually quite rare that you can do it away from home, but in a fixed place, for a month. It was quite a treat.

MIKE RUFFINO: Part of his deal with *The Taste*, you know, was he got September at the Chateau. So I would just clear the decks for September, and we would cram a lot in, including planning out most of the season for the show. A lot of dinners, and a lot of pool time, and a lot of whatever silliness we would get up to.

I think he was really riding the wave at that point. [With *Parts Unknown*], he really developed something that he could be proud of. And then, things like *The Taste*, he was just enjoying himself and getting a good run at the Chateau. There was nothing to complain about, you know? It seemed to me that that was about when he started to feel, at least, as much as he ever did, comfortable in his own skin, and with his own career, and his situation, instead of always having the feeling that it was too good to be true, that the rug could get pulled out at any minute.

PETER MEEHAN: I went to LA one September to interview him for an LA piece [for *Lucky Peach*]. There was something magical about walking up to the Chateau Marmont—you know, they give you that question like, "Who the fuck are you?" and I said, "I'm here to see Tony," and they're like, "Oh, sure." And then you were *in*. And going up to his room, and him answering the door barefoot and asking, "Do you want a beer?" and just sitting there on the balcony, smoking a pack of cigarettes and drinking all the beer in his fridge, until the sun set.

NIGELLA LAWSON: I remember saying to him—because he would have the spaghetti bolognese [at the hotel] most nights, or an In-N-Out Burger—"Tony, the food is so bad here." And he said, "If the food were good, it would ruin it. People would come here for the food. That's not why you come here."

I put my breakfast tray outside, and it would [stay there] longer and longer. And once it was up to about four trays, and I complained to him. He said, "Nigella, you're getting the Chateau all wrong. Obviously they can't do room service cleanup, but if you kill someone by accident, they will remove the body, no questions asked."

SAM GOLDMAN: At his speaking gig at the Pantages [Theatre, in Los Angeles], there was a Q&A, and somebody asked him about that terrible cooking competition [*The Taste*] he was doing, and Tony said, "I have nothing to say, except that my daughter is not going to community college."

TOM VITALE: I was with Tony and [cinematographer] Zach [Zamboni] in Paris, filming a scene for *The Layover,* and a couple of tourists came up to us and said, "Hey, aren't you that guy from *The Taste?*"

Zach and I had been devoting our lives and careers to Tony's shows, but we had nothing to do with *The Taste*, it being a studio show out in LA.

I was pissed at being interrupted while filming; not to mention that they knew Tony from a show I had nothing to do with. But the level to which Zach took it as a personal insult made the whole thing instantly funny, for me, at least.

38

"PUSH THE BOUNDARY REALLY HARD, REALLY FAST"

THE MOVE TO CNN

AMY ENTELIS, EXECUTIVE VICE PRESIDENT FOR TALENT AND CONTENT DEVELOPMENT, CNN WORLDWIDE: I came into CNN in January 2012. The prior year had been full of big breaking news stories—the Arab Spring, Fukushima and the earthquake in Japan, the tsunami, and I think there was a royal wedding that year—lots of big, driving stories that sort of kept people coming to CNN. But between those news stories, viewership totally dropped off. So it was a situation of peaks and valleys of viewership.

There was a recognition that something had to be created that would engage people, other than the headlines, because you could get headlines anywhere. The people who hired me had this idea that it should be original, long-form programming that was created by outsiders. The theory was that they had done a lot of interesting documentary-style programming at CNN over the years, but it was all done by the same people, more or less, from the same culture, who did the news, and therefore there was a sameness to it, if you will. Some of it was groundbreaking and award winning, but over multiple years, it seemed like it didn't break through. And I think there was a recognition that a great deal of money was spent on it, and it was not really returning anything.

They had this idea that if they took some of those resources and applied them in a different style, looking for outside directors, and producers, and creators, they would be developing programs that felt somewhat different from the normal fare at CNN, and would attract people, engage people, and would become, in the best of all worlds, appointment television. That was my mandate.

It happened very early on that we reached out to Tony. And one of the biggest challenges for us was to figure out how to make this programming fit into CNN, and make it organic to CNN, but also to distinguish it from what CNN did every day. That was a hard needle to thread, because it had to fit in the zeitgeist, but it also had to be special and different. We landed on the notion of Tony, because he was a storyteller, a brilliant writer, a world traveler, a thinker, and those elements seemed to add up to somebody who operated in the same universe and came out with a completely different product or vision, but not *too* different.

We called him, and had a secret room at the Time Warner Center to meet him. We just thought we should be a little bit quiet. He was within inches of re-signing with the Travel Channel. And so, our luck, timing, good fortune—everything just happened in a way that could never have been orchestrated.

It was capturing magic in a bottle, in terms of our coming together. He told me that CNN represented, to him, an ability to stretch and do things in his work that he wanted to do but didn't necessarily think he could do. Our view of the world, and our global reach, and our ability to get things done in crazy corners of the world, I think all those things helped fuel another level of his work.

EILEEN OPATUT: I'm so glad that Tony found a place that appreciated him, and allowed him to experiment even more, and recognized how much he wanted to explore, because he was so curious.

JEFF ZUCKER, PRESIDENT, CNN WORLDWIDE: I arrived in January 2013, officially. They took me through the plans for [*Parts Unknown*] in December 2012.

They had already bought the show, they were excited about it, and my job, frankly, was to come in and not screw it up. It was a whole new venture for CNN to move into original series, and Tony and *Parts Unknown* was the lynchpin of that whole idea. If it hadn't worked, I'm not sure the entire "CNN Original Series" thing would still be on the air today.

LIZZIE FOX, NETWORK EXECUTIVE: I was hired at CNN as director of original programming. What sealed the deal for me was that my first show was gonna be *Parts Unknown*. I thought, *Here's an opportunity that would be so stupid to not seize on.* So Tony actually changed the direction of my life.

CNN was zigging when everything else was zagging, and Tony was the face of that. He created the entire brand of that division, and everything kind of emanated from him and what he stood for.

ANDERSON COOPER: I was really kind of thrilled when he came, because I'd watched his show on other networks, and at the time, CNN was looking to try to diversify the range of storytelling that we were doing. I just thought it was a great fit.

He was a great storyteller. I knew that from the time I read *Kitchen Confidential*. To have a voice, and be able to write in your voice, and be able then to produce a television show that is completely in your voice, and is even shot in a way that complements, and is an extension of your voice, it's a real achievement. It's not an easy thing to do. Finding your voice as a writer is one thing. Making that into television is a completely other thing.

JEFF ZUCKER: *Parts Unknown* made a huge difference for CNN. First of all, it brought in a different audience than the one that watched CNN on a regular basis. Its ratings were incredibly strong, so it became the most-watched program on CNN. It attracted new advertisers. It really opened up a whole new world for us: new viewers, new advertisers, and a new way people started thinking about CNN.

CHRISTIANE AMANPOUR: Tony was a huge mountain in this landscape. And that's not to say that Tony was an angel, because he wasn't—he was profane, and really out there. He would say these things that people don't say in public. I couldn't believe it when CNN allowed him to take his writing into a realm that none of us in the news division, or in the documentary division—we'd never been allowed to go there, and none of us have been allowed since. He carved out this special place where he could use language and observation and push it to an extraordinary limit that nobody had heard before on mainstream television. And yet it wasn't insulting; he was very careful to be respectful, without being obsequious.

AMY ENTELIS: Certain people felt rather threatened by this new direction, and there was some backlash about Tony not being a journalist.

He called himself a storyteller, not a journalist, and to some people, that represented something at CNN that might threaten the natural order of things. It takes some education, or I guess the word now is *socializing*, across a very broad organization, that was successful at doing what it did and didn't see the need to do things any differently.

From our point of view, it was sixteen hours a year, you know? We weren't taking all of CNN and throwing it upside down. We saw it as completely additive and complementary. It was sort of two sides of the same coin.

You know, Anderson Cooper went to Libya to do the civil war, and covered that gigantic story that we were all riveted by. Tony went in several years later and did that story, but he did it from a different vantage point. He talked to people who lived through that, and actually said to them, "Where did you live? How did you live? What did you eat?"

Tony challenged us, and our systems, often. And he did get to do things that other people would not do, or didn't have to do. It wasn't that the standards were different, but they were necessitated by the kinds of stories he was telling and what he was trying to communicate.

JEFF ZUCKER: There were people who didn't think that we should be doing this type of programming. There were some people who, perhaps, didn't like Tony's brashness and language. And I completely defended it the whole way, and stood up for it, because I thought that we needed to evolve. Tony was a great face for CNN.

If you're going to hire Tony Bourdain, then you let Tony Bourdain be Tony Bourdain, and you don't try to water him down, and you don't try to change him, you know? We let him curse, and we let him have colorful language. We didn't hire Tony Bourdain to be somebody else.

CHRISTIANE AMANPOUR: I think he was a genius. I do. If you just go back and read *Kitchen Confidential* or watch *Parts Unknown* or listen to the interviews he does, I don't know how anybody puts those thoughts or words together and comes out with this just lacerating, and profound, and sympathetic, and eye-opening view of the world. It's extraordinary, the thoughts that come into his mind, and how he bunches them all together in this very unorthodox way.

LIZZIE FOX: In the beginning, I think he was really wary of all of us; he certainly wasn't an open book. He carried over a little PTSD from Travel Channel.

We realized pretty quickly that it wasn't about the food. ZPZ had it down, they knew how to do the food porn, and it was gorgeous, but you were always so much more interested in the conversation at the table. We wanted him in the journalistic mode, to make sense next to Anderson [Cooper] and Wolf [Blitzer]. Even though he never called himself a journalist, he was, so I think we always envisioned it in that way, and the food was the cherry on top.

SANDY ZWEIG: He was so much more engaged in *Parts Unknown*, engaged in the selection of locations, and just all around.

MORGAN FALLON: Immediately, we were all just making the show that we always wanted to make. We could really dig in on the cinematography, the identity issues, the global content. We had all the things that we could always fall back on, the food and the whole bag of tricks we had from *No Reservations* were always there, the world had just completely opened up, and that was awesome.

LIZZIE FOX: He wanted to push the boundary really hard, really fast. I never felt like I was duped by the locked cut, where I missed something and then he tried to sneak it in. He was like, "This is what I want, let's go from here," which I appreciated, because then you can sort of refine and position it. I always felt it was my duty to be the advocate for him, internally.

The first episode that I remember fondly was the Japan episode, because that was really pushing some boundaries. It was season 1; we were still figuring it all out. I loved him for it, but it was such a bizarre scenario. I remember standing in my office, late at night, on a phone call with standards and practices, saying, "So, the nipple pinch is not OK, but the spit in mouth you're good with?"

AMY ENTELIS: That particular episode, we had many, many, many rough cuts, and it went back and forth for a long time.

LIZZIE FOX: It's funny, because Tony was awkward, very socially awkward. That's where I give a lot of credit to not only Tony's capabilities, but also ZPZ's production of him and editing of the stories. If you let that live the way it was shot in the field, he wouldn't look nearly as charismatic as he did. He had it there, but that's editing and producing there, that combination.

TOM VITALE: He was just so good at being in front of the camera, partially probably because he was so uncomfortable with it. It kept him fresh. If he'd liked the attention more, I think he would have been less authentic. If he hadn't had those demons, it certainly wouldn't have lasted as long as it did. He hadn't crested yet.

AMY ENTELIS: There was a certain awkwardness to him. I think people at CNN were intimidated by him, and I think he was intimidated by the people at CNN, but I think there was a tremendous amount of mutual respect. Tony was sort of quiet and wide-eyed around

CNN, but I think it came from a great deal of respect, for knowing that he got to go around the world in a way of his own design. And the people whom he knew at CNN, and had known before he came, or got to know once he was there, I think he had a healthy understanding that they occupied the same terrain, but what was asked of them was completely different.

LIZZIE FOX: It felt like he was always a collaborator, even though he came to it with such a strong point of view. He knew what he wanted, but he also understood that someone with an outside perspective, who hadn't been in the trenches, might have a good idea or suggestion, and that we could work together to make sure it was the best it could be. It was the most gratifying time of my career.

PATRICK RADDEN KEEFE: The thing that was really striking to me [about his television work] was just the artistic ambition, frankly. Tony was aiming very high, and he surrounded himself with a lot of people who were really good at what they did, and who spoke a similar aesthetic language. When you watch the show, all that ambition is manifest on the screen.

LIZZIE FOX: You can get so stuck in the way you tell a story, especially in documentary, where you can do interview, archive, verité, interview, archive, verité. He was able to make minifilms out of these episodes, over and over, every single time, and prove that it can all exist under the banner of documentary.

That instilled in me a sense of, "Fight for the creative risks you want to take, because they're worth it."

JEFF ZUCKER: Tony Bourdain never wanted to be a company man, and yet he was always there for the company. He was always there whenever CNN needed him, whenever we called him for the upfronts—the annual presentation for advertisers—or when we needed him to do an event for us. You know, he could be a little prickly from time to time, but in the end, he always came through.

AMY ENTELIS: Tony always went along. We were always mindful of not asking him too much, because, if you know Tony, you know those are not his favorite things. I remember standing around with him at all those occasions, and he was not a glad-hander, by any means, but he knew the drill, and he pulled it off every time.

We never went with him anywhere. We had a very strong understanding that that wasn't the way he envisioned his work. There was no hanging around the set for CNN. We were fine with that, but when we were a couple of years in, we wanted to figure out some way to celebrate him. I remember looking at the shooting schedule, and I knew that we wanted Jeff [Zucker] to come, and I knew that we couldn't go halfway around the world and back in three days, so it was just sort of fortuitous that Havana was on the schedule.

We had arranged a dinner at a restaurant, in a sort of a dilapidated, beautiful mansion. It had a roof bar, so we went up on the roof to wait for Tony and his team. There was a band playing up there, and this beautiful sky, beautiful view of Havana, and Tony and the group sort of trudged up these long staircases to come to the roof. And I remember him looking around, and we were all drinking by then, and he saw Jeff, and he saw me and Lizzie, and he said, "Oh my god, am I getting whacked?"

And I think Jeff looked at him and said, "No, asshole, we're here to *celebrate* you." It was really a sweet moment.

So we drank on the roof, and then we went down into this magnificent dining room, and we had an incredibly wonderful dinner, and went out after that to a club and listened to music. And that was it; the next day, they went off to shoot, and we went sightseeing.

I think he was moved that we kind of picked ourselves up and went to Havana to say, "We love you, we appreciate you, and we thank you." I think he got it. And more than that, I think he probably appreciated that we didn't hang around after that.

39

"I REALLY WASN'T DOING IT FOR THE CRONUT"

TONY TRIES A TALK SHOW

On July 25, 2013, Tony sat in for Piers Morgan on his live evening broadcast on CNN.

AMY ENTELIS: It was definitely not an audition. I think we understood that what Tony did was completely different from what somebody who does a studio show does. It was more a matter of exposing him to our audience.

JEFF ZUCKER: [Having Tony guest host for Piers Morgan] was to increase his profile; he was still a relatively new face for the traditional CNN audience, and, look, I don't know that we thought it was a formal audition, but on the chance that it caught fire, you never know, right? At the end of the day, I think it was clear that Tony wasn't gonna give up his day job to do that on a full-time basis, and it turned out to just be a good promotional stunt.

DAVID SIMON: I know he couldn't say no to himself, in terms of adventures. He had me come up one time at CNN. He was filling in for Piers Morgan.

I get this call from Tony. He's like, "You've got to come. I need good guests. I want to show them that I can do this, because maybe I'll become a CNN anchor."

I said to Tony, "Motherfucker, you're doing the best journalism I've ever seen, traveling around and examining people and food. Why would you give up that gig, which is so beautiful, and so you, to be some dickhead talking head?"

He goes, "I just wanna try. You gotta come up."

I said, "I'm in Baltimore, I got nothing to sell."

He said, "I got Cronuts"—you know, these fucking Cronut things that everyone was chasing in New York. He goes, "Yeah, I got a box of them. I'll have them here for you."

I go, "All right, sold."

The planning period was rocky. At one point, Tony pushed back against the lighthearted nature of producer Shant Petrossian's suggestion for a Cronut-tasting segment, emailing him, "I may as well just go full Roker and put on a frilly apron, interview a guy dressed up as a seal, and fuck a rolling donut."

SHANT PETROSSIAN, PRODUCER: I do remember that email; I do remember the shock.

In hindsight, he was absolutely right. As producers, we think we know best. It's important to get the hosts to weigh in. He went to an extreme to prove a point. He knew what he wanted. In the end, he did enjoy himself, and we produced a good, solid hour of television.

We had four or five other guest hosts in for Piers that year. Every host came to the table with opinions. They all wanted to bring and do so much more than we could do. We had Rosie O'Donnell, Matthew Perry, Regis Philbin, Jane Lynch, and Harvey Weinstein, who threatened my family at a meeting across the boardroom table.

About Tony, I remember thinking that he was difficult, he was opinionated, all those things, but the day of the show, everything came together. And *Parts Unknown* was kind of a hero moment for CNN.

My favorite part of that day was when Tony interviewed Eric Ripert. Eric—there couldn't have been a nicer person on the planet, and everyone knew Tony was tough, and I was like, *How are these two guys best friends?*

DAVID SIMON: I really wasn't doing it for the Cronut. I couldn't say no to Tony. So I get up there, I walk into the greenroom and Eric Ripert and Mario Batali have their faces stuffed full of Cronuts, and they're just eating them, one after another. They're rushing, makeup, they put us onstage.

He had me on with [the late *New York Times* media columnist] David Carr. The way he got us both to talk about bullshit! I have no reason to do talking head stuff; I come out of my hole once every couple years to do publicity. If I'm not selling something, I don't want to be on CNN, doing two or three sentences about the NSA stuff that was going on. I'm like, *What the fuck am I doing here? This is what I got on an Amtrak for?*

I go back into the greenroom, and there's an empty box of Cronuts. And I go, "OK, where's the rest of the Cronuts?" And

Dominique Ansel goes, "We don't have enough. We promised the studio audience."

"What the fuck do you mean, you don't have enough?" So they bring out one Cronut, and we split it. I had actually been in an argument with David Carr before, over some column he wrote that I was in, but we actually bonded over being fucked out of our Cronut. It was probably the best moment I had with David Carr.

I get on the train and write this essay about betrayal. "Motherfucker, you owe me a Cronut." And Tony wrote back. He had no idea we were fucked out of the Cronuts. First he tried to blame the crew. And then, "I'll get 'em mailed to you." And then, "No, we can't mail them to Baltimore."

I never got the Cronut. In the end, never mind the stupid pastry; being able to banter for a whole day in prose writing with Tony Bourdain was the most fun I had all week. It was probably worth the trip to New York alone.

40

"MIDDLE-CLASS WHITE PEOPLE GOING TO POVERTY-STRICKEN PARTS OF THE WORLD . . . WITHOUT BEING DICKS ABOUT IT"

CHRISTIANE AMANPOUR: Maybe around 2015 or 2016, I suddenly had a whole epiphany about war, and about humanity and relationships and marriage and sex. This is something I've covered all my life, war and the consequences. I was always hearing terrible stories about all these Syrian refugees, from the raging war there, having to flee their homelands and come to refugee camps, and living cheek by jowl. Yes, they were being kept together body and soul, but what about their humanity? How do the women fare? How do they keep their marriages going when they're living in a tent with maybe five or six of their children, or in a metal container, with no privacy?

So that was the nugget of my exploration. I tried to persuade CNN and others to do it, and it took a long time.

One day I said, "Look at the way Tony Bourdain does essentially what I do: he's a foreign correspondent, he goes around the world, and tells his viewers stories, through the paradigm of food and community. I'm going to tell this story by going around the world and explaining what it means to be a woman."

So I took that concept to him. It was actually very informal; I wanted his advice. We sat at this beautiful bar at the Surrey hotel [in New York], the Pleiades, and talked for about two and a half hours. He loved the idea, and once he got behind it, I was able to take it back to CNN, and people had a new sort of respect for the idea, and knowing that his company wanted to produce it just gave it a whole new life.

AMY ENTELIS: There was Christiane pitching [*Sex and Love around the World*] to me, and then she said, "Oh, and by the way, Tony wants to do this with me." It was a fresh idea, it was a hard thing to do, but based on what Tony had done and accomplished so far, it felt like it was an obvious continuation of *Parts Unknown*.

CHRISTIANE AMANPOUR: We green-lit the series, and we did six parts, in six different cities around the world. I attribute the fact that it came to fruition to Tony and his belief in this, that he put his name to it. It was great to have that kind of validation and to know that he liked it.

MARIA BUSTILLOS: He was such a symbol of how Americans would maybe like to be better than they've been, vis-à-vis the rest of the world. Not just going to the George V [hotel, in Paris] and trotting in front of the Vermeers, but trying to understand the world. Learning how people live, in a place where they actually live; hanging out with people who live in that place.

SAM SIFTON: From the point of view of cultural journalism, which I think is really what he was doing, it's pretty revolutionary. He was performing a kind of reportage that allowed him to use his character to achieve a kind of mass success, but really what he was doing was reporting. And it really wasn't about the food, it was about the culture. And he was able to tell stories that I think others would have had a hard time telling, and he told stories that others haven't told, certainly not on TV.

I think there's a kind of travel that is embraced now that is curious about world culture, and curious about new flavors, and is both of those things without being disrespectful. And because of the mass appeal of his shows, he can be credited with some of that. I think middle-class white people going to poverty-stricken parts of the world and experiencing delicious food and incredible hospitality without being dicks about it, that's a testament to his work, if it's happening more, and I think it may be happening more.

CHRISTIANE AMANPOUR: He was an observer of the human condition, and he used food to be able to crystallize all that. By taking that notion around the world, and humanizing people around the world, particularly in this era where, in the West, the idea of the other, the foreigner, is suddenly so politically toxic—he, without being didactic or pedagogic, made people from all over the world and their culture and their food and their conversation and their traditions relatable. He showed a whole generation of Americans, and CNN's global viewers, that we're all essentially the same.

41

"IT WAS TOO MUCH OF A DREAM"

THE BOURDAIN MARKET

For a roughly five-year period, Tony and a small team of designers and investors worked toward building an international food hall in New York City. As Tony said to the food news website Eater, *"I've long felt that we should have the kind of delicious, diverse food centers that Singapore (for instance) enjoys. And, in fact, it is my hope that an important component of this project will be representatives of Straits hawker masters. My likes are pretty well known: dai pai dong in Hong Kong, Boqueria in Spain, hawker centers in Singapore, street tostadas in Ensenada. To the extent that I can help bring those things home to New York, along with a truly interesting collection of homegrown innovators, I will be very, very pleased."*

PATRICK RADDEN KEEFE: The market was actually part of my pitch to *The New Yorker*. I said, "Here's this guy who, presumably, could have put his name on restaurants a hundred times over, and never did."

ROBIN STANDEFER, DESIGNER, PARTNER, ROMAN AND WILLIAMS: For [partner] Stephen [Alesch] and me, the market represented something that we always wanted to achieve—this strange hybrid of a punk reality and a commercial and nurturing ability to be communicative and sort of public. Those things are often in conflict, and Tony merged them in the most extraordinary way.

PATRICK RADDEN KEEFE: I think his conception of himself as a chef, and where he sits in the universe, is a whole interesting theme of Tony. But, to me, the idea of the market was almost a hook for the piece. And then, over the time I spent writing, I felt as though, in slow motion, the idea kind of fell apart.

ROBIN STANDEFER: We had constant conversations about design— there's something about cinema and the theater of creating spaces that transport you that is really interesting, and that was a big part of our dialogue. Tony said, "Design is stupid, and it sucks, and I hate it." And I said, "I agree."

I felt that my most authentic self was engaged when I was with him, and that's a really beautiful, intoxicating way to feel. We talked about everything from Korean porn to Singaporean food—always such an engaged, awesome dialogue—we would talk and Stephen would draw. And also, he and I were raising money together, so we got up in front of [real estate investment trust] Vornado and [real estate developer] Stephen Ross; we put together this pretty epic presentation. We actually made a lot of them, for a lot of different spaces. I would never do that for anybody else, and I say that because, you know, we were barely getting paid. But it wasn't about that; it was about such a powerful vision.

There was some ambivalence from Tony about not being true to himself, about being in these meetings, and I heard that. The bubble of our world of creation was about an alternate universe, like *Blade Runner*. The collaboration between me and Stephen and Tony was almost fictitious, in a way, like we were making a movie. And we got close to almost making it, but then, somehow, it was too much of a dream, and I do think that ambivalence came from the fact that I just don't think money works that way outside the film business, where it truly is artistry. I think the mechanics of that, certainly in the United States, were too challenging to achieve, and I also think that there was a sense that it wasn't meant to be.

We worked on it for almost five years. We just kept going down the road, and it never ultimately made financial sense, and we ended up not being able to close the deal. It couldn't make the revenue everyone wanted it to, it was so complicated to operate, and Tony wanted real fire. There would have been health department issues, because the markets he loved were ones in places that have different rules and regulations and restrictions; they didn't have the requirements that new developments in New York City have.

But I always felt like it was a bigger issue than that. I always felt like these [financing] guys were sort of fearful of really doing something that true, in which money wasn't first. You need a partner who is brave enough—you need a crazy, I don't know, a Howard Hughes, an eccentric patron—and the world of development doesn't really have them anymore. When it comes down to it, those guys pray at the shrine of money, and it wasn't who Tony was, and it's not who I am or Stephen is—ultimately there wasn't a partner.

So this project became a dream. A dream of a reality of what markets are, and what gathering is, and what food is—the kind of gritty, fucked-up, aromatic, intense, compressed environment that he wanted to make would have scared the shit out of people.

PATRICK RADDEN KEEFE: I don't think that they could do it his way—he had these kind of outlandish— Even if you look at the stuff that he says in that piece, he's describing a vision that— I mean, it was obviously doubly difficult, or impossible, in Trump's America, but it wasn't gonna happen like that—a big butcher shop, with blood all over the place, and all these different vendors, whom you get visas for, and they come in . . . To me, there was kind of an interesting tension, where he was insisting on the only version of what he would have personally been cool with, which seemed to me to be a version that was almost impossible to realize.

I think part of the reason that people loved him as much as they did, and connected with him in the way that they still do, even now, was this sense that he wouldn't abide by any kind of adulteration, right? There was something just very unadulterated about who he was, the way he talked; he had this no-bullshit ethos. There was this sense that he wasn't willing to put his name on something that he privately felt was kind of crappy. Which isn't to say it never happened, but in the instances where it did, he would call it out himself.

That was the interesting question about the market; if they'd pulled it off, there was no way they'd have been able to do it in a way that he wouldn't have had his private misgivings about. It's not that the vision itself wasn't amazing; it's just that doing that in New York City in 2017 was tough.[*]

ROBIN STANDEFER: It never really ended. We weren't like, über close with Tony by any means, but I think he didn't want to let us down. I think we had a meaningful, creative connection, and I think that because Stephen and I just believed in him and the market so much that whatever version of it, whatever weirdo version in the ground floor of Tokyo Tower, or with those RXR [Realty] megadudes on the pier, whatever it was—certainly, the pier one fizzled out, but it wasn't super over. There was always this little secret area [of discussion] like, "Maybe someone else will come up with the money." Stephen and I created, with Tony, these vision books; and they *existed*, and the drawings existed, and the sketches existed and all the oratory existed, and so it was, "Why couldn't we put this incredible vision in another space?" There was always the hopefulness of that potential there.

---

* *In late 2017, Tony issued a press statement regarding the market's presumed home, at Manhattan's Pier 57: "Launching what is admittedly a very ambitious venture has proven to be challenging at every turn," he said. "It seems increasingly clear that in spite of my best efforts, the stars may not align at Pier 57, which is an especially complicated site for which we still do not have a lease. I promised a certain kind of market to New Yorkers and to potential vendors, and if that vision becomes clouded, diluted or compromised, it is no longer something that our city needs," he said. "I remain hopeful that New York will someday have such a market—I still passionately wish to create this resource that New Yorkers deserve."*

42

"YOU DON'T DIRECT TONY BOURDAIN"

LIFE ON THE ROAD WITH *PARTS UNKNOWN*

ERIC RIPERT: When Tony joined CNN, I went on with him in Peru; we did the French Alps; we went to Chengdu, in China. Where we really had a fantastic time was Marseille, in France. He was in a good place, mentally and physically. He was happy, and it shows. And we're having genuine fun, and we really go on a tangent a lot on that episode, and ZPZ just had to witness what was going on, and just film and put it together. It was like a vacation with cameras behind, which we didn't see anymore, because we wouldn't acknowledge them. When you see too many cameras, suddenly they become invisible.

Tony is, and he will admit himself, he was a barely OK skier. And I'm a pretty good skier. But, the way they edit the ski scenes in the Alps [episode], he looks like he's much better, and I'm much worse. And they make him actually win the competition. He wanted to compete, but he couldn't. He completely manipulated with ZPZ the outcome.

DARREN ARONOFSKY, FILM DIRECTOR: I was dating someone who was a big Tony fan, but I had never really watched the show yet. I noticed that he was following me [on Twitter], so I just followed back. I was really enjoying his feed, and I started to get to know his personality a bit through that. And then I had finished shooting [my film] *Noah*, and when you're in deep in post[production], you can get lost about what you're going to do next.

I wrote to him, saying, "Hey, do you ever have people tag along?" or something like that.

And he wrote back, "Where do you want to go?" And I kind of jokingly said, "Madagascar," because it was one of the farthest places in the world, and a place that is intriguing but very hard to get to. And he said, "When?" That kind of started a conversation.

It was coincidental that I had been doing jiu-jitsu at the same gym as him. I remember walking into the locker room and seeing Tony a couple of weeks before we were going to go, and I went up to him and introduced myself.

When I started to walk up to him, he had this look of—it wasn't quite confusion, or fear, but it was—I guess we were in a locker room, so it was a little weird to go up to him, half-dressed, and some guy, he had no idea who I was. I introduced myself, and he was like, "Oh, great, bring your *gi*. We'll do some jiu-jitsu on the trip."

The next time we met was in the airport in South Africa, before we took a shorter flight to Madagascar.

I could see when he was sort of shy about things, and it would take him a few minutes to kind of get into his storytelling mode. Then he would take control of the situation, as soon as he got comfortable. But before he was comfortable, he would be on the back foot a little bit.

I think he has a point of view when he starts, and he keeps pursuing it. In Madagascar, it was about ecotourism. He felt it was like a form of colonialism, a different type of colonialism, and that the service industry was an extension of that.

What happened on that trip, it was pretty interesting. And it was pretty sobering. We had a— I don't know, it was like an eighteen- to twenty-four-hour-long train ride. It was supposed to be like a nine- to twelve-hour ride, this whole French colonial ride to the coast. We were told that we were going to get food at this certain stop, and there had been some— It was a very strange train ride, because a lot of the train went through villages that had no road access.

JEFF ALLEN: That was such a perfect example of fixers promising, "In three hours we'll be at the food stop, and everybody will get to eat, and that'll be a great cultural moment for the show." We always send our fixers on a scout, they actually ride the train, and we have them take photos of detailed, time-stamped moments.

But sometimes you get there and there's no food stop. Sometimes there's not even a fucking train, you know? So what's supposed to be three hours ends up being like ten, because the train broke down.

DARREN ARONOFSKY: We'd held off from eating, and by the time we got to this one town, there was kind of a mad grab for the little food that was there, and there were also a lot of hungry children around. And it was almost, at a certain point, they were kind of surrounding Tony—because he had some food in his hands—begging for food.

And Tony was not comfortable with it and—at the moment, he got angry with the crew, because we were put in that situation.

JEFF ALLEN: There were a couple of European tourists on the train, and they had a basket of bananas and some rice packets that they started passing out, and this swarm of starving children start attacking Tony and Darren, too. It was a really bad scene, and really unexpected, and it shows how nothing ever goes as planned. What was supposed to be this kind of cute adventure ends up being a really kind of sad look at humanity.

Tony thought it was our fault, and it's true that production takes time; you have to ask people all the time to stop and start all the time, but we didn't have the power to stop and start the fucking train. He was pissed; he also was hungry.

DARREN ARONOFSKY: You saw this kind of weird colonialism that we were thrust in the middle of. I think Tony wanted to show that there's many ways to show a sequence like that on a travel show, where you could edit that out, or you could really show what was going on. Because the poverty in Madagascar was hard to fathom. And there seemed to be a lot of prostitution going on, and a lot of underage prostitution.

So there were some really dark things. And you're sitting there in your kind of incredible wealth, going, "What the hell's going on here?"

Really hard to understand. And it was impossible for you to ignore. And then the environmental destruction that was going on was just everywhere. You'd be riding a train, and you'd see the forest being burned down in the distance, these huge plumes of smoke. When we flew on a small plane from the coast back to the capital, you could just see the country burning. So, it was pretty bleak.

BEN SELKOW, DIRECTOR: There's very little turnover in the directing corps of *Parts Unknown*, but there was a year when they hired three of us to come in, and I directed an episode in Mississippi.

I remember first meeting Tony and trying to play it cool; he was this fucking huge guy with a giant head and a stoic poker face, and you don't know how he's perceiving you. I was intimidated, but it was underscored by the creative respect I had for him.

In the prep, he was a total mystery. There were a couple of emails exchanged, but the dynamic part of our working relationship happened in the field, and in post.

For the first scene we were shooting in Mississippi, I'd found a conscious hip-hop performer. We shot a music video with him, inspired by a Kanye West video, and then we were gonna have a chat with him and Tony at a community bar in Jackson. So we rigged it out, we did our lighting, made sure people were there—it was January, in the midst of an unprecedented cold spell, and people were not really trying to go out to a bar that night, but we got people there. Tony calls me right before the scene and says, "There were heavy winds out of Newark, I was a little late getting here. I ran into Mick Jagger's entourage in the lobby of our hotel, he invited me to a party, so I'm not coming to the scene tonight."

What are you gonna say? (A), it's Tony, and (B), it's fucking Mick Jagger. I pushed him a little bit, but he was like, "No, man, I gotta do this." So that was our kickoff: my first big scene with Tony, and he stands me up.

Two days later, we were due to do a scene on the Mississippi River, and go canoeing. At this point, this is pre–Tony quitting smoking, pre–Tony diving into jiu-jitsu. We get out on the river and it's windy, and there's a huge chop, and it's actually extremely strenuous. There's this island that we're paddling out to, and he's got to look cool paddling, but he's dying. Mo [Fallon] is looking at me like, *Oh man, this is kicking his ass; I don't think he's gonna make it.*

We're paddling alongside him, I'm taking pictures, and he's not mugging for the camera, but he did find a moment to give me the eyeball, and I'm like, *Oh, shit.*

Then we make it to the island, and we're OK. We've got all this meat: he's going to be grilling out with this Mississippi bluesman, outdoors guy, man of the river, and Tony says, "OK, this is heaven. I love to grill meat. Where are the beers?"

I was like, *Shit, I didn't bring any beers.* We're in the South, so there's all kinds of rules around church and alcohol, and it's a Sunday. I go to [producer] Jeff Allen, who never says no to anything, and delegate to him. I hear the motor start on our extra gear boat, and it tears off down the river. We start shooting the scene, and Tony's looking at me, looking real thirsty. It's going terribly.

And then, like the cavalry coming back, Jeff comes ripping up the river in the motorboat, dismounts into the water, and comes running up with a cold case of beer. Somehow, he'd made it into Arkansas, found an open liquor store, secured a case of beer, and crisis averted. So that was a big learn for me.

JEFF ALLEN: It took about two years for Tony to remember my name. I was the new guy. He never talked directly to me. I think it was in Borneo [in 2015] when he finally really acknowledged me.

It was fucking insane, getting a TV crew to go up the Skrang River, packing into these canoes with millions of dollars' worth of equipment and no support, in terms of PAs, because we didn't have a budget for it. The best shit comes out of chaos, and that was the most chaotic.

Paddling up the river with all the equipment in longboats took a lot longer than it was supposed to. "Oh, yeah, we'll be there in three hours." Ten hours later, it's sunset; we're arriving after dark. All the things we were supposed to film, we couldn't, because there's no lights, and we were in the middle of the jungle. We almost lost some gear on the way up. Tony was mad that it was taking so long. We have to stop and go, for TV. Things just never go according to plan.

What I'd walked into was, "You don't really let on to Tony how the sausage is made, because we need him to have an experience." We were just scrambling to pick up this insanity behind the scenes, left and right, and oftentimes that would become the story.

So, in Borneo, the whole idea was to have Tony spear this pig as part of a celebration, and he's standing down the river, getting furious, in a thunderstorm, and the pig isn't arriving on time, and it's out of our control. The tribe is supposed to bring the pig; we're just capturing the action. Meanwhile, in the thunderstorm, the pig got loose and it's running around the village, but Tony didn't know this, and he's just like, "Where's the fucking pig? I know it's production's fault!" He's standing there holding a spear, which is terrifying, and everyone was so scared of him anyway.

He demanded excellence, and he never settled for shit. I think he just wanted the show, and the experience, to be the greatest thing ever, all the time. And we all had that mentality, but it's not like it was a fucking vacation. It was insanely hard work, to think of creative new shit to do, to make every episode better than the last one, and then you had to impress Tony all the time. So you have this really demanding, powerful force who could get angry if shit wasn't going well, and it didn't go well all the time.

Anyway, he got to kill the pig, next to the chief of the village, and then we filmed the rice festival, which was three days of drinking and partying and insanity, and Tony ended up really loving how it all went down in the end. The last day, he was encouraging us to put the cameras down and stop filming. He said, "We got the story.

You need to live here for a moment and have an experience. Yes, we have a job to do, but life is short."

He'd said his favorite thing was to go down to the river and swim in the morning, because that's when the ladies of the village would go and clean clothes, and bathe with the kids, and it was a really joyful and peaceful time. The last morning, I walked down to the river, and there was no one else in the water except Tony, and he was clearly having a moment by himself, and I was like, *Oh, fuck, I'm not gonna interrupt Tony's moment.* And then he saw me and said, "Hey, come in! The water's amazing!"

We swam in the river for like an hour, just hanging out. It was a little awkward at first, but then we just started talking about stories, like he would do. You never really talked much *to* Tony; you listened a lot, and the dude was fucking funny, and had a lot to say. He asked me what were my plans after the season, because I was still a freelancer, and then he said, "It's good having you around. You should stay."

No one ever got compliments from Tony, and even that wasn't really a compliment, it was like, "Don't leave; you're useful," which was probably as big a compliment as you'd ever get from him.

ALISON MOSSHART: He was going to do a Nashville show; Dean Fertita, who's in Queens of the Stone Age—Tony had reached out to Dean and said, "Do you have any ideas?" Dean panicked and asked me, "Do you have any ideas?" I said, "I have a thousand ideas. I'm ready." I was just such a massive fan of all of Tony's work. I'd seen every single show. I'd read every single book.

It was a couple of months of working with the producers, writing emails full of things that I thought we should do. I met Tony for the first time at the part in the episode with the hot chicken, in the parking lot. I was a little nerved out by him. He was having this very heated discussion about jiu-jitsu [with the crew]. Then we sat down and filmed that chicken thing, and he had me laughing so much I was crying. He was exactly as I'd imagined him. We went for a ride in my car, and I was like, "We are gonna be friends forever, you know."

He really dug my car [a Dodge Challenger], and threatened to buy the same car. I wish he had done it, because it would have made him really happy. He loved that car.

So, working on that show was when I first got to know him. And then much more so when we did the party scene at my house. He wanted a scorpion tattoo, and I drew it for him. I was like, *Someone needs to explain to me if this is real life. I don't know if this is happening*—I was drawing Anthony Bourdain a tattoo that was going to be on his body forever, and I'd just met him, like, two days ago.

Tony seemed like he was floating. He was having so much fun. It really was the greatest week or two in Nashville.

After that, I went out on tour; Tony would write me almost every day. We became total pen pals. We wrote each other every single day, and the letters got longer and longer and longer and longer. We both just traveled for a living all the time, and we could relate to that on so many wonderful, spectacular, and bad levels.

JEFF ALLEN: Toward the end, dude had been fucking everywhere, probably more than any human being, and so to find a new, surprising thing about a country that you've been to four times already is, like, really fucking difficult. It's so easy to be jaded.

NARI KYE: On *Parts Unknown*, the production level had gone up dramatically since *No Reservations*. The amount of equipment, all the elements of production were drastically elevated. We wanted to push ourselves, do bigger and better things. And, Tony, the episodes he wanted to do were getting more and more adventurous. More dangerous.

TOM VITALE: Tony didn't want to be a high-maintenance host. He would usually rather be hungry than bother me [for a snack]—and it wasn't even a bother, because he would bother me for all kinds of shit that was so much harder to deal with, and he could punish you for things that weren't your fault. But he didn't want to be "the talent." He was very aware, I think, of his hunger needs. I don't think he was out of touch with that. I mean, emotional needs, he could be more out of touch with.

I guess some of it used to be funny, but the pressure was so much greater on all of us in the later years. I totally lost my sense of humor. The stakes were too high. We'd have a scene, and it would go really well, and especially if it was something that he hadn't been into in the first place. And then after a great scene, everybody was having a great time, and I'd say, "How'd that go? Are you happy?" And he'd totally change, and say, "Nothing to write home about. It was fine. Can we try to find something better next time, though?"

And I knew that he was doing that just as a game. He had very different relationships with different people. Tony was good at sizing people up very quickly, seeing what it was that they wanted. Then he'd either provide or withhold that resource in order to get whatever his end may have been. In my case, it was making the best show possible.

There was a lot of stress and pressure to get it right, in a very short amount of time. Even by the end, with what I presume are comparatively ample resources, it still wasn't enough. You could always use more time, or money, to make things happen. So I couldn't *not* take it really seriously. And I think maybe Tony had some fun with that.

MORGAN FALLON: Some of the most profound experiences, for me, and some of the most insightful ones into who Tony was, were the experiences surrounding the West Virginia [episode of *Parts Unknown*]. We went to McDowell County, a place that really just had the shit kicked out of it, in a really unfair way, for a very long time. And it's a place that has no restaurants.

I remember asking myself that question a lot: *How's he gonna respond to this place that's, on the surface, ideologically opposed to where he's at, though that's not true once you get under the surface? In a place where there's no food, none of the things that we normally get into. Is he gonna get this?*

The second day, we took him down into a coal mine, five thousand feet underground. We were hanging out with real coal miners, and not putting words in their mouths, and not trying to use it in a political way. We came back out; the crew and I went to film a homecoming parade, and Tony went back to the hotel. All of a sudden these tweets just started coming out; what he was expressing was exactly what I had hoped he would feel, and it was just this moment of, *Of course he gets it. How could you ever question that?*

That was the best of him, where he was able to strip down all the celebrity bullshit and connect with a group of people in a really openhearted, embracing, fearless, and empathetic way.

Later that week, we were in a high school, shooting a scene with all these football players. At the end of the scene, Tony made a beeline directly for me, in a very aggressive way, and grabbed me by the back of the neck. He said, "The fucking Secret Service wants to meet with me."

He had expressed his desire [to a TMZ reporter, who'd ambushed him in an airport parking lot with a video crew] to cook hemlock, a very Shakespearean entrée, for Trump and Kim Jong-un. I guess it's just a matter of protocol; the Secret Service had to make sure he wasn't serious.

We were supposed to go to the homecoming game at this big high school. Everyone knew we were going to this game, and there are some folks out there who take this shit seriously, so we ended up putting an armed off-duty cop right behind him in the scene, because I just couldn't take the risk that some wingnut—and, of course, everyone was lovely and amazing, and no one expressed anything but gratitude that we were there—but still.

NICK BRIGDEN: The one thing that I heard from a few folks was, "Don't make Tony wait. If he rolls up to a scene, and he has to sit there and wait for the crew to get their shit together, inevitably that is not going to turn out to be a good scene, no matter how great the sidekick is. When he waits, you start to see the kettle boiling."

I made superhuman efforts to make sure we were ready to roll as soon as he rolls up there. And I did that for every scene that we shot, because I learned the hard way once.

And it wasn't that he was being a dick, it was just— If he was sitting there with a sidekick, you want to get all the great, juicy conversation on camera, but he's sitting there silently, while the crew's trying to get their shit together. So it was avoiding that kind of awkwardness, making Tony as comfortable as possible, because this was his life. It wasn't like he was clocking in going to work; this was his life, day in and day out. And so if it's not fun, and if it's not comfortable, if it's not intriguing to him, he's gonna tell you, and it'll show up.

MICHAEL STEED: After wides is when you could get exactly the line you wanted.* So I would call wides, knowing that I wanted two things

* At the conclusion of shooting a scene, the director will call for wide shots, to establish the visual context of the area in which the subjects are speaking. On Tony's sets, this was generally understood to mean that enough dialogue had been captured. Tony would sometimes call for wides himself, when he felt he was done with a scene.

from him because . . . Tony didn't want us there, you know what I mean? Ever. Like, he would prefer that we weren't doing the show.

And that's what made the show fucking great, all the shit we had to do to make it seem like we weren't present. So if he thought you were *directing*, you know, he called it "stovepiping," he'd fucking murder you, you know what I mean, right then and there.

So you'd call wides but, right after wides, Tony's guard is down, he thinks it's over, so you can be like, [*whispers*] "Oh, can we just get this one more thing?" And I used that 100 percent of the time. Whatever he said after wides was always used.

TODD LIEBLER: Postdeath, everyone was saying, "Rest in peace," but Tony didn't enjoy peace, per se. He loved— I wouldn't say *conflict*, but energy. He was attracted to chaos. On set, he would even instill it.

As a camera guy, you want your actor to hit the marks and to be in the light. We gave our subjects as much room to breathe as possible, but there's certain things, like, you can't stand in the doorway with your back to us.

He would— I don't know if it was just him challenging us, or being passive-aggressive, but we'd say, "OK, Tony, just come from the door and stand right by this chair." And he'd walk from the door and go in the exact opposite direction.

If I really needed him to do something specific, 90 percent of the time, he would give it to me. But that's only because I asked for it maybe 10 percent of the time.

There was one time when he yelled at me and Zach [Zamboni], and Tom [Vitale]. I think we were in South America; I can't remember where. Essentially, we had a scene in this really big bar, and inevitably what would happen is, as we backed out of the scene to get our wide shots, all the fans would come in. So, often, we're running back in, to get people out of the shot.

At this bar, there were musicians who came in next to him, and all these other people, and I went in and said, "Guys, we gotta—" And Tony starts yelling at me, at everyone, that it's *his* experience that we're capturing, so we have to capture that as it is. Of course, it didn't play well for TV; it played well only for his experience.

NICK BRIGDEN: You don't direct Tony Bourdain. If a new director came on and tried to direct Tony, they would learn very quickly; Tony would throw a grenade into it. My job was, as a director, to direct the crew around him, and to lead the sidekick, or Tony, into areas of conversation that we really wanted to hit on. It was a lot of prep work, and once he walked into a scene, my approach was always just to let the cards fall where they will. But also, you had these veteran camerapeople who knew how to cover the scenes, and it wasn't so challenging to get really great stuff, because they just knew what to pick up.

Tom [Vitale] told me once, you know, if at all possible, if the scene calls for it, and if it's appropriate, if Tony walks on into the scene, and you can hand him a beer, sure as shit, things are gonna go a lot better.

MORGAN FALLON: Generally, I could get one question in, at the end of a scene. If that went really well, I could maybe get another one in, but that was it. It just wasn't gonna go down that way. He was gonna experience the adventure in the way that he wanted to, and the conversation was gonna go the way that he wanted it to.

And sometimes you're sitting there dying, because you spent all these resources, all this time, two months in preproduction; you have so much of your heart invested in these people and these scenes, and to listen to him fucking talk about *John Wick* for an hour, and then call for wides? And you go in, and you're like, "Dude, can we just talk about this one thing?" And he's like, "Ehhhh . . ."

At that moment, you wanted to grab him and say, "Mother-fucker, do you know how heavy this camera is? Just deliver a few lines. You want to talk about *John Wick*? That's great. We'll go to the bar and order a round of beers. When you're done with *John Wick*, call us and we'll shoot the scene. Trust me, this person is fucking important. I wouldn't have sat you here if he wasn't."

All these people [in scenes with Tony] were highly vetted. It's hours of conversations and research that goes into who those people are, why they're important to that story.

TODD LIEBLER: In Egypt, I think, we were filming, filming, filming, filming, and nothing. I mean, they're talking about rock and roll, or something that has nothing to do with what we're there for, and then finally we say, "OK, let's just pull back and go for the wides."

And then, as soon as we pull back, content comes out of his mouth. You know? So I don't know if that was his passive-aggressive nature. Sometimes it seemed like he was oblivious, which I guess he could have been, too.

MORGAN FALLON: He had these very reactionary moods that he was capable of. It made navigating the creative worlds with him very perilous. Everything was about how you phrased stuff, how you cor-roborated your evidence, how you presented things. He could shoot down really good ideas very quickly, based on some impression that he had, and basically those books were closed once they were closed.

DIANE SCHUTZ: He always wanted, going into a scene, as much info as possible, as much written info, any background that you could give,

but once the cameras were rolling, and once the scene was going—
he was fond of the expression "Stop stovepiping." We were shooting
at the Ganesh Temple in Queens, and I said to him, "Don't forget
to talk about *xyz*," and he got snarky about it, and said, on camera,
"Diane says we should talk about *xyz*."

MORGAN FALLON: We'd all send him bullet points for the scene and
hope that he hit those. You'd try to get the sidekick to get those in.
But if you were really pushing, that was "stovepiping," and that was a
quick shutdown. The problem, too, was once you got shut down like
that, it really fucked you. Once he said that word, you're not getting
another one in. You've spent all your bullets, for a couple of days.

You lose one of your major interviews because Tony's not into
it, your whole narrative comes crashing down. You've got to recon-
struct shit as you're going into the field. You'd see all of us in our
notebooks, moving scenes around, moving conclusions and shit
around, because Tony wasn't into it that day.

But all of that belies the fact that you had, probably, the greatest TV host that we're ever gonna see, and when he was good, the
conversations were so abundant that they became problematic in
post[production], right? You just were like, *I don't know what to cut
out of this, it's all great.* He was so far beyond where other people are
that that made it all worth it. And I think he kind of knew that.

BONNIE MCFARLANE: My husband and I did a segment on the New Jersey episode, in Atlantic City. I was actually really nervous about that,
because my husband [comic Rich Vos] is—he's very funny, and very
outspoken, and I was really scared that somehow he and Anthony
wouldn't mesh, but they got along great.

I've worked on a lot of television shows, and I fully expected to
be sat, and then be waiting, and then having Anthony come in, and

do it again, and then having us do an entry again—that's how TV is shot—but we walked in, we got our mics on, somebody got us a drink while we waited for Anthony, he walked in, we sat down and legitimately had dinner, did the show, and then we all left. Zero direction, zero notes. Nobody told us what to do or how to do it. There was no stopping. When someone knows what he's doing, and knows what he wants, it doesn't have to be as complicated as the industry sometimes makes things.

TOM VITALE: You couldn't win an argument with Tony; ultimately, he would always get what he wanted. My approach in the field was often to lead from behind. In the edit, on the other hand, the best strategy was sort of a war of attrition. If Tony disagreed about something I felt really strongly about, rather than try to reason with him—which usually just caused him to dig his heels in deeper—we'd address as many of his notes as possible and leave the thing that I liked. The hope was that his opinion would change, or that he wouldn't notice. It worked a lot of the time. In the field, though, getting what you wanted was much more complicated.

Everything happened so fast, and he would always say, "Just let it happen." But as the show got bigger, there were a lot more moving pieces. We had to worry about turnarounds, schedules, and setup times. "Just let it happen" was not a great business model. There had to be an element of—certainly not *fabrication*, but making sure that all the pieces were in place.

There was just so much less flexibility than there had been in the old days, when it was just one van. Back then, if something amazing started happening, someone could just pick up a camera and get the shot, you know? In the later days, the cameras were almost un-liftable, and it was important to adhere to things like turnarounds and the length of the day. Each different place around the world, there was a new set of rules, and no matter how much you plan, and learn, and preproduce, you can't really ever know what's gonna happen.

I don't know to what degree Tony was aware of the issues we dealt with. He seemed not to be, but he must have been, because he was rather omniscient.

NICK BRIGDEN: The process was, in post, before he wrote any narration, he would want to see the scenes in a very rough-cut state, even B-roll sequences, so he could write to picture. That was always a little challenging, because we had a finite amount of time to get these edits done. We would write some scratch, just some ideas about where we thought the narration should lead within the scene.

MUSTAFA BHAGAT: As an editor, you were just always trying to make Tony excited about the episode. It was always just about getting that first cut, the first thing that Tony sees. It was the most stressful and loaded delivery you were gonna have in an episode.

Sometimes I'd send act 1; sometimes I'd send acts 1 through 3, so he could see where we were going, never any more than that, because I could pretty much be guaranteed that he was gonna blow it up on the first cut. I think the best example of that was probably the Jamaica episode of *Parts Unknown*. I was working with Tom Vitale on the cut, and he sent it out to Tony, and Tony writes back and says, "This is a beautiful mess." And I was like, *Oh, shit, this sucks.* Tom said, "No, this is the highest compliment you can get, because he said the word 'beautiful.' You're already about sixty percent of the way there." Tony's reaction emails were always full of tough love, but what sucked for me and the director was he was always right, in the way he saw things and wanted to reorganize things.

NICK BRIGDEN: Sometimes he would stay on track, and sometimes he would take it in a completely different direction, which meant the edit would have to be recut. Sometimes he would cut shit out that I really loved, and I was banging my head against the keyboard, and then grudgingly recutting it as Tony saw it. But it was so wild, because he was always fucking right. Ten out of ten times, I wouldn't see it until I'd recut it. And then I'd recut it, and I'd be like, "Oh, of course."

If Tony loved something, he would tell you. And if he hated it, he would tell you that, too. He wouldn't dick around; he would give you a straight-up answer. And sometimes that would really sting, because it would be an uppercut. But those of us who stayed with it a long time, you would just know not to take anything personally. It was his life's work, and he never slacked. He would never miss a deadline. It would always be in your inbox that morning. He loved deadlines.

You hear from a lot of people who work with him, how harsh he was, how hard he was on folks, but if you hung around long enough, you just understood it was because he cared so much about the quality. And it wasn't even just the final show, it was, you know, people who would devote their time with him in conversation, or over a meal, or take a trip with him—he wouldn't want to let those people down. It was out of respect for the folks who would lend their time to him that he wanted each episode, each scene, to be the best it could be. And so, if you didn't raise your skill to that level, he would pick you up with a big wedgie and raise you up to that level.

I went to film school. Tony did not go to film school, but the expanse of his knowledge of film was just unreal. Half the directors of the films that he would talk about, before we would go into an episode, that he would want to pay some kind of homage to—half those directors I'd never even heard of. So it was almost like I went to graduate school, working with Tony. He would give us a list of films and we would go home and do our homework, and kind of absorb the style or the pacing of certain directors.

It was a language that we could communicate with, in an abstract and visual sense. We could talk about certain scenes, we could talk about certain shots within films that we would want to either completely steal from or lean into. We did an iteration of Fritz Lang's *Metropolis*, Maria's dance, in the Berlin episode, just for fun, over the credits.

But there was a certain pivotal point where, after years and years of working with him—he said something in the vein of, "At this point in your career, you don't need to borrow from anyone else. You are your own director. You have your own style now."

He saw something in me that I didn't even see. It was just a really wild moment.

TODD LIEBLER: At one point, Tony wanted to stop smoking, and he started taking Chantix, I think. And then he was being really sweet, which for him meant he would say to the crew, "Thanks, guys." He definitely loved us, but he wasn't the person who would give you positive reinforcement, you know?

But when he started taking Chantix, he didn't take us for granted as much, but that was short lived. That didn't sit well with him, that Chantix mellowed him out.

TOM VITALE: Tony had a saying: "Only pat the baby when it's sleeping." True, he could be tough in the field. He could be very tough in the edits, too, but when something was working, he could actually be quite complimentary.

MATT WALSH: In things I've read since Tony left us, he's been described as being quite hard on the crew. "Only pat the baby when he's sleeping." From my perspective, because I was an outsider, Tony was always very kind to me, very respectful to me. I think he made that distinction: insider or outsider. I would not flatter myself by think-ing it's because he liked me.

DARREN ARONOFSKY: In Bhutan [in December 2017], we spent a lot of time socializing. He was much more social than he'd been in Madagascar. And, of course, we really became very friendly. Ev-ery night, we'd hang out, and eat, and drink, and talk about what was going on in the world, which was pretty bleak. Then we flew back—I guess Tony never would eat the airplane food—and so we got to Bangkok. The layover was significant. We had several hours.

And I was like, "Let's go into town. Let's go get some real food."

He was resistant, and I kept pushing it. There seemed to be a pretty interesting place fifteen minutes from the airport.

I said, "Tony, let's hit this." He finally agreed to it. I found a guy to watch our bags, and then we jumped in a cab, and we went into this resort, mostly, I think, for Thai people, which had fake lakes, and giant golden idols, and waterfalls, and a huge, huge din-ing area with a big band playing kind of cheesy eighties songs—American eighties songs—with beer—the beer girls and boys walking around, selling them, wearing the different brands. And Tony was just thrilled with the menu, and we just ordered a feast, you know. And Tony dug deep, because he knew the cuisine really well. And then we went back to the airport, and we got foot mas-sages. And I was like, "All right, we're in Tokyo in seven hours. Perfect for another meal."

We were landing in the airport near the Tsukiji market, at, like, three or four a.m. I got him out. It was an amazing morning. We were leaving the airport, and you could see Mount Fuji from Tokyo, which is rare. We got to the market, and the main place was really crowded. There was this huge line outside. We just went around the corner and chose a random place that was empty, and had a great meal. It was a good moment.

43

"YOU WERE THAT GUY WHO GOT ARRESTED"

JASON AND YEGANEH REZAIAN IN IRAN

JASON REZAIAN: My first introduction to Tony was through television. *No Reservations* was the only show that provided that window into not only worlds that I could envision visiting, but also some places I had gone to. I was just getting started, postcollege, knowing that I wanted to write professionally, but also knowing that the traditional routes into journalism are fraught with all sorts of traps that can ensnare you in mediocrity forever.

I went back home to California, worked in the family rug business, and would take trips to Iran when I could. Watching Tony on TV was part of how I would pass the time when I wasn't traveling.

In 2007, I'd been going back and forth to Iran, I was starting to build up a body of work, and I knew the place really well. I built up the courage to cold-email Zero Point Zero, saying, "I would like to take Anthony Bourdain to Iran, and here's why he should go."

Six weeks later, I get an email back from a producer, Rennik Soholt, and he and I started a correspondence. We fleshed out a shooting plan, and everybody was really into it. They asked me to come see them the next time I was in New York. Lydia [Tenaglia] was really inquisitive, and kind of tough, you know: "Why do you think it's possible? How are we going to get into Iran? I've got Iranian friends, they tell me it's never gonna happen." Chris Collins was a little bit more like, "Tony really wants to do this."

I kept talking with Rennik for many months, and then he said, "Travel Channel's insurance—they're just not gonna take this risk." I let it go.

YEGANEH REZAIAN: I first watched a couple of episodes of Tony's show before I met Jason. One of the first episodes that I saw back then was the [2006] Lebanon war episode; Tony and his crew went, and they got stuck because of the war. That was a very powerful episode. I grew up during war [in Iran], and Lebanon and Israel and Palestine.

I remember watching that episode on one of the Farsi satellite channels, dubbed into Farsi, and I thought, *I have to find the English version and watch it again, because I'm sure the translations are not necessarily 100 percent correct.* So I was able to catch that episode a few months later, and it gave me a sense of freedom, of knowing what was happening in the outside world from a different perspective than I always heard in the news of my country.

JASON REZAIAN: In June 2014, I get an email from one of the producers at *Parts Unknown*, saying, "We're about to come shoot in Iran in a matter of days, and one of our contacts in Tehran said that you're a guy to talk to about where to find a good meal."

I was really in the habit at that time—I'd been in Iran for almost five years—I was really selfless about wanting to help any media organization that wanted to come do work in Iran. This is a massive country that's underreported. Anything that I can do to inform good coverage of this place, I'm gonna do. And being contacted by the *Parts Unknown* people was a feeling of arrival.

YEGANEH REZAIAN: Jason had this email, and he was reading it with so much joy, and he said, "Oh my god, you won't believe. Tony will come to Tehran in two weeks. This is unbelievable. I feel like all my efforts are finally bearing results." It was as if his mom were coming to Tehran, or his family members. So much excitement.

JASON REZAIAN: The last day they were in town, they called and said, "Would you and your wife be available to come shoot a segment with Tony?"

YEGANEH REZAIAN: The food at that restaurant was terrible. Jason was really nervous. He went and talked to the restaurant manager, saying, "You know who's coming here in a few minutes? Make sure you go and get good food from the next-door restaurant."

I don't think they had a good understanding. This restaurant had such a nice ambience, and not good food. Everything's so old and prepared, and they had plastic wraps on everything.

We sat down, and it took a while for Tony to come. Maybe we were there for an hour before Tony came. And at some point, I thought, *He's not going to show up.* Or, *He's gonna just come and see us for a couple of minutes.*

JASON REZAIAN: When he showed up, it was like, the wind starts blowing and a rock star walks in, you know? I assumed we'd sit there for fifteen or twenty minutes and then he'd disappear, but he lingered, and for an hour and a half, we had a really far-reaching, intense, friendly conversation.

The thing that I don't think most people realize is just how well versed this dude was, in so much. I can just imagine him in the eighties and nineties, exhausted from shifts in the kitchen, going home and reading for a couple of hours. So when I asked him about his knowledge of Iranians, Iranian food, US-Iran relations, he said, "I can't remember ever having much Iranian food before I arrived. I know some Iranians, and I know a little bit about Iranian-US history."

And then he dove into this whole thing about the hostage takers at the embassy, and how they had pieced together all the shredded documents. They had little kids coming in and literally piecing all of this stuff back together. He talked about the torture of the SAVAK, which was the Iranian secret police, under the shah. He knew a lot, right? But, characteristically, he was like, "I don't know shit, I know about as much as the average person."

YEGANEH REZAIAN: The depth of his perspective was really interesting to me. He was there [in Iran] for only four or five nights before we met him. But his eye caught things that local people don't pay attention to. Also, I have met other foreigners, other Americans who come to Iran, and they don't notice these things. On the surface, he's a famous chef, writer, traveler, but to me he sounded more like a foreign journalist who goes to a new place and observes and records everything, and when he's back, writes about all those things.

JASON REZAIAN: At the end of shooting, [director] Tom [Vitale] said, "Tony never sits around that long. He obviously likes you guys." Tony gave me his email address and said, "Let's stay in touch."

This was really special for me, but also for so many people in Iran. Most Iranians didn't know who he was, but people who were dual nationals, or connected to the outside world, did. And it went along really nicely with this idea that Iran was starting to maybe open the door just a little bit. It was, for me, a validation of the years of work that I'd been doing. Yegi and I rode that high until a few weeks later, when we got arrested.

Our participation in *Parts Unknown* never came up in our interrogations, until I brought it up, after I'd been in prison for three or four weeks. I was trying to do everything I could to rationalize with my captors.

I said, "Look, right before you guys arrested us, we were on this TV show that millions upon millions of people see, and we're talking in glowing tones about this country. You're gonna look like fucking idiots. This is not gonna work out for you. This is one more example of how and why your plan to take us hostage is gonna fail. You're gonna lose this public opinion battle."

YEGANEH REZAIAN: At some point, Jason and I were permitted to see each other in prison, toward the end of my imprisonment. In the very few seconds that Jason and I had together in prison, Jason conveyed the message to me that when you go out, no one should stop the premiere of the show because of our situation. It's more important for the people around the world to see us in that show and know who we are.

JASON REZAIAN: I had this deep concern that, ultimately, CNN and ZPZ would end up not using that segment, because they would be worried that it would make things worse for us. And when I found out that we *had* appeared in the episode, and that they talked about our arrest, I just thought, *That's a good thing.*

YEGANEH REZAIAN: I got out, and a couple of nights later, I remember that Jason's brother called me and said he was going to be on Anderson Cooper's show, with Tony, that he wants to advocate for us.

And I can't believe that I sat on my bed in Tehran, watching Tony and my brother-in-law on Anderson Cooper's show. It was so emotional, and so meaningful for me.

JASON REZAIAN: I've had the opportunity to meet all sorts of famous people over the last ten or fifteen years, and some of them are huge disappointments. From that first encounter until the last one, which was an interview for my book, in December 2017, Tony was so much more than the expectations. Just our ultimate champion. He didn't have to do all the stuff that he did. From the moment we were arrested, he didn't have to talk about us, he didn't have to write about us, he didn't have to stay in communication with the government about how to edit that [*Parts Unknown*] scene.

There have been so many times over the last five years when Yegi and I have said to ourselves, or to other people, "Thank god for Anthony Bourdain." I get recognized more because of being on that show than anything else. Eight out of ten times, people say, "You were that guy who was on Bourdain's show who got arrested." And at least half of those times, people add, "You were arrested because you were on Bourdain's show."

I've seen it in print, and I've heard people say it on TV, and countless people have said it to me, and every single time, I take the opportunity to say, "Actually, no, it wasn't the reason that we were arrested, and, more than that, I look at it as the thing that made it impossible for us to be ignored."

So often, you have somebody who gets in trouble, or is missing on the other side of the world, and all you've got is a couple of grainy photographs of them, and the neighbors who say, "He was a quiet man, he didn't cause any problems," but we had the most beloved television personality of our generation sitting having a really cordial and affectionate conversation with us [on *Parts Unknown*], that got played over, and over, and over again.

YEGANEH REZAIAN: One of the people who appeared on the Russia episode was killed. And I saw people tweet at Tony saying, "Wherever you go, someone dies, someone who appeared on your show dies," or something like that. But that just broke my heart, because what happened to us had nothing to do with being on his show, or meeting him, nothing like that. I remember telling Jason that Tony was being harassed, being unfairly judged by random people on social media. Jason was really upset about it, and he was like, "Every chance you get, make sure you make it very clear that our situation has nothing to do with this."

And, honestly, the first time we saw him again in New York, a couple of months after we were released, that was the first thing he asked. He wanted to make sure that he was not responsible, that he didn't do anything to cause us a problem.

JASON REZAIAN: It was important to me that Tony knew that our being on his show wasn't something that we thought of as contributing to our arrest. [On a 2016 visit to New York], we met him in the front door of this restaurant, the yakitori place that he liked— quick hello, hugs, waiting for a table, "How you guys doing?"—and it was the first thing that I told him, and I just sensed his shoulders loosen a little bit, and he just relaxed, and the three of us had the loveliest encounter that we'd had with anybody since the last time we'd seen him.

He said, "If I were you, I would go somewhere very quiet for as long as you need to. Go hang out on a beach for a month, go to rural

Japan. Write a couple of travel articles. Don't even mention the imprisonment. Do something therapeutic for yourself; take the edge off a little bit."

People had been telling me that if I didn't take advantage of this now, my window would close, people would forget about me. I was interviewing agents; I did a whole thing at CAA [Creative Artists Agency]. They were gonna put us on *Dancing with the Stars*. It was just, like, the classic pitch: "We're gonna give you this, we're gonna give you that, does your wife wanna do this, does your wife wanna do that? There's gonna be action figures, and scholarships in your name." It just felt gross. We were already scheduled to do a couple of big TV interviews.

And Tony said, "You don't wanna do that. If you go on TV, all they're gonna try and do is bring up these really hard memories. They're gonna try and make you cry. You'll be on for a max of three to seven minutes, and that will be you, to the world, for the rest of your life. And you won't feel good about it."

This was permission from Anthony Bourdain to give a big middle finger to everybody. And that's all I needed. He was so certain about it.

Yegi and I said to ourselves, "There's a lot of people right now representing themselves as friends to us, who have some kind of ulterior motive, right? If we're honest with ourselves, there's nothing selfish in Anthony Bourdain telling us to take care of ourselves." His motive was caring for us.

When you come back from a situation like that, you're in uncharted waters. Your life is different from the one that you left behind. You're scarred, you're scared, you don't know the world that you live in anymore. And the opportunities that you have, and the decisions you're trying to make, are really different from the ones that you ever had to make before. It felt really foreign to be putting my trust into people whom I didn't know very well. But Tony showed up for us.

And I mean, look, I've read his books, I've read about him. Some people love him, some people don't. He showed up for us, right? I'm not here to think about anybody else's experiences. In that moment, this person made himself available. And there was a continuity to that, that lasted right up until his death.

YEGANEH REZAIAN: We went to see Tony speak in Boston, maybe five or six months after Jason was released. Sometimes we went to places and Jason got recognized. Most people had been really sweet and supportive to us. And we met with Tony behind the scenes, a few minutes before the show started. We talked about several different things, personal and professional. His speech was really fascinating and very exciting, really fun to listen to, even informative. When he opened it up to questions, the very first question was, "What happened to the couple whom you met in Iran, and they ended up in prison?"

I jumped out of my place. This was a question for Tony; it wasn't meant to be answered by me, assuming no one knew that we were there, but I was very excited, and I just stood up and said, "We are here! We are here!" Waving my hand in the air, and Tony stood there quietly, just staring at me, and I thought, *Oh my god, what did I do?* And then Tony said, "I didn't want to destroy their date night, but they are here, and they are doing well."

People started clapping, which was really sweet. But now I think, I really would have loved to hear his answer, without my getting involved. I never gave the guy the chance to say what he should have said.

44

"THIS IS JUST ANOTHER TRIBE"

BRAZILIAN JIU-JITSU

MORGAN FALLON: The fucking smoking, man, and the exhaustion, and the travel, really racked up a hefty line of credit over the years. There were times when we'd be out on a hike [on a shoot] and I'd be like, "Who has the defibrillator?" Because I had Tony on mic, and I could hear him wheezing; I could hear him coughing.

NARI KYE: When we made *No Reservations* in South Korea, we got to do a tae kwon do scene, which was hilarious. Tony, then, was probably the most not-athletic person I've ever met in my entire life. He was still smoking a pack of [Marlboro] Reds back then, and he would never exercise. He was rail thin. He wasn't overweight, so he didn't look unhealthy. But he was so out of shape, uncoordinated, out of breath. Not flexible. And he wasn't really doing tae kwon do, but we were at least trying to make this funny montage of him kicking my ass, and then another little girl kicking his ass. So we were trying to get him to kick, and Tony, not even joking, couldn't even get his foot past his knees. It was just comical how out of shape he was.

OTTAVIA BUSIA-BOURDAIN: I was writing a blog for *Fightland*, and I was trying to find ideas on what to write. I was like, *Maybe I should have my close friends and family try jiu-jitsu, and write about that.* And Tony tried it, and he really liked it. I didn't push him; he just started doing it, and he really wanted to do it.

ROY CHOI: We filmed an episode of [CNN web series] *Street Food* when he had just started jiu-jitsu; he was still smoking and complaining. I asked him between takes, "What are you doing with jiu-jitsu? Where are you thinking of going with this?" and he said, "I have no idea, but all I know is that I can't stop."

OTTAVIA BUSIA-BOURDAIN: He was always making sure, when he was going on shoots, that there was a gym and that he had time for training. If he couldn't train, he was not happy.

And in New York, he had his private [sessions]; he would set them up himself; and then he would take a class. And he competed. I think it was good for him. He was in great shape doing it.

ARIANE BUSIA-BOURDAIN: Well, for the time I was doing jiu-jitsu, I was pretty small back then, so I couldn't really train with him, but I'd always do something called an arm bar, or like a rear naked choke, on him.

DARREN ARONOFSKY: When we were [shooting *Parts Unknown*] in Madagascar, he was deep into the jiu-jitsu, really focused on that.

When we weren't shooting, he went to his room. And he was only drinking on camera and stuff like that. He never went out at night.

DEAN FERTITA: We did a Nashville episode of [*Parts Unknown*]. Doing jiu-jitsu was one of the prerequisites of participation, and to this day I still do jiu-jitsu, in honor of him. It was something I never had done before, but Tony's interest in it, and dedication to it, interested me enough to try it.

I think I was surprised about that aspect of his personality, because it is a highly competitive thing, but what isn't surprising, thinking back, is the dedication that's involved in something like that, how much he devoted himself to everything he did; even his time away from work was the same way.

SANDY ZWEIG: It became a real responsibility for whoever the producer was on the show, to find him somebody to work out with. I mean, it certainly did affect the show in terms of the shooting schedule, but ultimately, it put him in a much better mood, so it was sort of worth it. There was a lot of pressure on those guys, to kind of make that all work for him.

TOM VITALE: With jiu-jitsu, I had to make the decision, do we miss this really important scene to illustrate this thing he wants to do, because it happens only in the morning, you know, versus the jiu-jitsu? How do we make it all work? It was every day.

JARED ANDRUKANIS: The first time he meaningfully touched me beyond a handshake was when he put me in an arm bar on a rooftop. That's when I knew he actually cared about me. It was in Shanghai, and we had just wrapped, so he was ecstatic, and he was going home to jiu-jitsu, and he was excited to see his daughter, and he just went up behind me like *whoop*. That was his sign of love and endearment. It was that weird moment where I realized, *He cares enough about me to try to break my neck.*

JOSH FERRELL: I was lean and mean when I started working with Tony, but working on the shows, I gained almost eighty pounds. In the midst of all that, Tony kept saying, "You gotta try jiu-jitsu." Finally, we were in Budapest, and I had rolled my ankle, and Tony was like, "Hey, man, this is tough love. Let me get your first few sessions," and then I did it, and I was hooked.

HELEN CHO: I was super interested in martial arts as a kid, but my parents couldn't afford to send me to a martial arts school. So I just kind of suppressed it; it was a childhood thing. And then, as an adult, I hear Tony and Ottavia obsessively talking about jiu-jitsu. I was really curious, and they showed me a couple of moves, and then Tony said, "Why don't you take an intro class? I'll set it up." I tried it, and I loved it immediately. It brought back something that I'd put away.

JOSH FERRELL: Being on shoots with Tony, he didn't have anybody to roll with, and he'd say, "Bring your *gi*," so, included in these crazy hectic shoot days, I'd go roll with Tony for an hour. Sometimes we'd go to gyms and there would be other people, but I remember in Senegal—there was no local jiu-jitsu club in Dakar in 2016—so in those cases it would be, "OK, let's just beat the shit out of each other until we're both exhausted." That would always get him in a really good mood. He was a very intense dude, and he did find the sport that matched his personality, his ability to go from zero to one hundred like that.

NICK BRIGDEN: There was a period where all he would talk about was jiu-jitsu. I actually started getting into it, being prompted by Tony to try it out. I was training for maybe four months, and we were all in Nashville together, and we decided to all train together. We went to this little academy, getting instruction, and then it was time to roll with each other. And I had never rolled with Tony, but I had some wrestling in my background, as a kid, so I kind of knew my way around the mat, and I had a few different moves that I had learned from jiu-jitsu. So Tony and I started sparring, and immediately I got him into this arm bar, and he tapped out on me, and I couldn't believe it, that I fucking tapped out Tony. And he got pissed about it, too.

In the next minute of that round, he went at me hard. He had his gangly legs wrapped around me, and he got me into this move called "the scorpion." At the time, I didn't know when to tap, before a limb is busted. And I didn't—he had got me in this move, and I didn't tap, and all of a sudden we hear a *tuk, tuk, pop*. And my knee had hyperextended. And he stops, and I stop, and he looked at me and said, "Oh, fuck."

I walked on it a little bit, and it felt funky, but it didn't feel horrible. So we finish off the session, and then we all piled into the van, and my knee just blew up. I had torn something. Tony did not feel good about that; he felt horrible about it. We finished that shoot, and then Tony gave me this great orthopedic surgeon back in Manhattan who fixed me up. I never blamed Tony. I think Ottavia came down hard on him about it. But we went at each other really hard. I think a lot of pent-up frustration through the years came out in that two minutes of sparring together.

MORGAN FALLON: There was this incredible relief as he began to get healthy: he quit smoking, he was doing jiu-jitsu every day, he was on a good diet, and he really popped to life. He had these two years that were just fantastic. It was like, *OK, he's gonna be all right. This is good.*

ERIC RIPERT: He had to have the trainer in the morning, anywhere he was, his victims. He said it would be good for me to do it. And I said, "Absolutely not, it's not even one percent chance of [me] doing it. It doesn't appeal to me." And, I know for him, it was very good for his mental [health], and it changed him—he lost a lot of weight, built a lot of muscles. It was good for his cardio. He stopped smoking, he stopped a lot of things. He started to eat better, and so on, and be more cautious. So, for him, it was a great experience.

And I saw him actually—in Marseille, one morning, he said, "You know, you have never seen me doing it. Come, come watch, come see it." And I went two mornings in a row, at six a.m., to see him. And he was with a guy who was very good, actually, and they would sweat on top of each other, and it was disgusting. And you could smell the body odor and so on, from far away. And I was like, *What are they doing? It's disgusting.*

TOM VITALE: He gave me the hard sell on jiu-jitsu. He offered me a jiu-jitsu training membership for a year, but I refused to even pretend to be interested in it. If, for some insane reason, I was ever going to get into jiu-jitsu, I would have done it secretly, and certainly not have told Tony. I didn't want to give him that satisfaction.

NIGELLA LAWSON: I worried about him when he started going so completely obsessive about jiu-jitsu. He got too thin. I said, "You always look gorgeous. You absolutely are wonderful, but you don't want to go into scrawny old man, you just don't." And he said, "I have to be this thin, because otherwise I'll get beaten." The way he was about winning.

DAVID CHOE: Every jiu-jitsu person I've ever met was like, "Tony came by my place and worked out three times in one day."

JOEL ROSE: He said, "The same way I used to wait on line to score heroin, I'll be at the dojo, waiting for it to open." He had the same feeling; he said he was trying to use that kind of addiction mentality for something else. I think that when you do have that kind of personality, it's all encompassing, and it reaches into every nook and cranny of your being.

MORGAN FALLON: It was fucking insufferable. I would try to telegraph to him, over the course of these hundreds of conversations about jiu-jitsu, like, "Brother, I have no fucking idea what you're talking about; I have no interest in what you're talking about; I will never know anything about what you're talking about; this is purely an endeavor of you telling me the same stories that you've told to everyone else."

He was a lifelong addict, man. If it wasn't heroin, it was work. If it wasn't work, it was jiu-jitsu. If it wasn't jiu-jitsu, it was relationships, or any number of other things. The way that Tony's power went out to the world was largely through his various addictions, and I think he very clearly understood that he was never gonna be someone who was free from those addictions.

The jiu-jitsu was good, because largely it was a positive addiction, and so, as much as it was fucking insufferable to sit there and listen to him talk about something that I knew nothing about, over and over and over again, I wasn't worried about him. I wasn't worried that he was gonna collapse, or have a heart attack, or die of emphysema.

OTTAVIA BUSIA-BOURDAIN: It's like he was getting maybe a high from doing it, you know.

People do become addicted to jiu-jitsu in a way. I mean, he had addiction problems. And I'm not saying being addicted to jiu-jitsu is a problem, but he tended to become addicted to things. I think that's what happened with jiu-jitsu.

NARI KYE: When we were in Korea for *Parts Unknown*, he was training, and he would tell us about all kinds of gruesome injuries. Like, his penis turned black. I was like, how does that even happen? It was crazy.

OTTAVIA BUSIA-BOURDAIN: I mean, he did get injured. And everybody gets injured. There's people way older than him doing it, so I wasn't super worried.

We trained together. He would have this burst of energy, where he would give it his all, and if he couldn't submit me, then he had to take a breather. He was super intense. And very competitive. And he was becoming really good.

PATRICK RADDEN KEEFE: The whole jiu-jitsu thing—on the one hand, it seems like just a hobby, but it was a pretty fucking serious hobby there.

I think part of the reason I wanted to write about him, aside from the fact that he lived an interesting life and seemed like a fascinating guy, was that I've always had a little debate in my head about the capacity for reinvention. To what extent is the die cast at a fairly early point? To what degree is the person you are when you're forty the person you're going to be for the rest of your life?

Part of what was so intriguing to me about Tony is that he'd lived a certain life until he was older than I was when I was writing about him, and then he changed in pretty radical ways, and lived this whole other life. What was fascinating to me about jiu-jitsu was—there's Tony until *Kitchen Confidential*, and then there's Tony on the other side of *Kitchen Confidential*, who has a certain persona he's cultivating, and then jiu-jitsu actually sort of upended a lot of that.

The idea that you'd be approaching sixty, and do that with the conviction that he did, and the obsession that he did, and as success-fully as he did . . . it's a corny word, but it was inspiring.

He has this Rabelaisian persona, where he goes out, and he eats anything, and he drinks anything, and it's abundance in all things, no filter on the stuff that's coming out of his mouth, or going into it. And there was always a little bit of an illusion there, because, as I discovered pretty quickly, he was really disciplined about all kinds of things, clearly, long before jiu-jitsu.

It was quite surprising to me to hang out with him and realize that he's kind of playing a character on TV, who has a big bowl of pasta and knocks back shots till all hours, not mentioning the fact that he's up at seven in the morning, sweating it out, and is becoming much more careful about what he consumes, and is thinking about consequences in a way that he hadn't before, and in a way that Tony Bourdain the character isn't supposed to.

I get in [to Renzo Gracie Academy, where Tony trained in New York], and I realize, like, this is just another tribe. It's just another subculture. This is the kitchen all over again. What he wants is to be the newbie, who's initiated roughly into a kind of marginal, secre-tive, obsessive priesthood. The camaraderie, and the way he related to everyone, a lot of that seemed to me to have pretty strong reso-nances of the kitchen.

When we went to spar at a random gym in Hanoi, he did acknowledge that it's very similar to the kitchen . . . it's a shared-language thing. So, suddenly, he has this mode that he can relate to total strangers anywhere around the world. He has to find them. They're not everywhere. He's gotta do some homework and fig-ure out what rock they're living under. But when he does that, he doesn't have to speak the same language, they can have nothing in common.... To me, that, that just felt very linked to everything that had come before.

MICHAEL STEED: There was this peak period where he seemed happy. That addictive personality was just all focused on jiu-jitsu. He wasn't asking about my family or anything, but he looked great; he had all this energy. At one point, at the end of a scene, he almost hugged me, and I was kind of like, "What the hell?"

And then fucking what's-her-name enters his life, and he starts smoking again, and it just sort of got back into that negative energy that fit this weird fantasy character that he felt he was, and needed a counterpart to.

MORGAN FALLON: He wanted to be a rock star again, and all of a sudden, it was right back to smoking, and not just smoking, but smoking *on camera*, which was totally unheard of. That moment in the Puglia [episode of *Parts Unknown*] when he lights up in scene: that was pretty intense, and kind of a really depressing signifier of him, in some ways, being like, *Fuck it*.

OTTAVIA BUSIA-BOURDAIN: I think he went back a little bit to old vices. You know, he went back to smoking every day, and maybe drinking more than he was when he was at home with us. Those things don't really make you feel like going training in the morning.

He never really quit. He had moments when he was like, "I'm really getting back into it. I really want to get my purple belt."

[At the beginning of] the summer he actually died is when he told me, "The goal for this summer is for me to get the purple belt." So it was always in the back of his head: "I better go back to training, like, seriously." But he had other things in his life that kind of kept him away from that.

45

"MAYBE YOU'LL FIND ANOTHER CHANCE AT LOVE"

THE END OF THE MARRIAGE

PATRICK RADDEN KEEFE: I probably talked to Tony for twenty hours, over the course of the year [2016]. And that was the year in which his marriage fell apart, and his show was kind of coming into its own.

Initially, I was gonna talk to both him and Ottavia together; that was something that he said very certainly was going to happen, in the early going. He really wanted me to meet her, and I did, too. I kept pushing for the three of us to hang out. At the time, I figured, *Oh, they're busy, it's tricky with schedules.* It felt to me as though, at the beginning of that year, it was important for him to project an image that this was a relationship that was really working.

OTTAVIA BUSIA-BOURDAIN: I mean, the fact that we had a kid, and got married, in a few months of meeting, in that sense, yeah, he was impulsive. But while we were together, and things were going well, I thought he was actually very levelheaded, and he really had always thought about the well-being of Ariane, or my well-being, before deciding to do something or not.

As a dad, he was always the good cop. I think it was fair, because he was around so little, so when he was home, there was no enforcing homework, there was no discipline. He was 100 percent fun dad, and he called himself "Silly Dada," 'cause that's what he was doing.

ARIANE BUSIA-BOURDAIN: I watched *Archer* with my dad, which I found pretty funny, even as a little kid. Of course, I still watched the regular kid TV shows, but I wasn't hearing about anyone else who was playing *Grand Theft Auto* with their parents. And I kind of realized when I was younger that, *Oh, not a lot of kids fall asleep to* Dexter.

I remember him struggling to put my Barbie DreamHouse together. Or I'd pretend that he was in a barbershop, and he wouldn't let me cut it, but I'd just put random soap on his hair. He played with me all the time; he went with it. If I was like, "Hey, let's pretend to do this," he'd pretty much do it all the time.

We had this tradition where we'd go to the Palisades, in New Jersey, and we'd climb up all the way to the top of this little mountain. There are perfect stairs, but we decided to just go through the trees and branches and stuff, which you're not supposed to do. And after that, we'd go to Hiram's, which is this very low-key spot for hot dogs, that's their specialty there, and I used to go there all the time with him. We'd go there on Father's Day. And he's been going there since he was younger so, of course, he's very familiar with the place. Every time we'd go to the Hamptons, we'd go to this place called

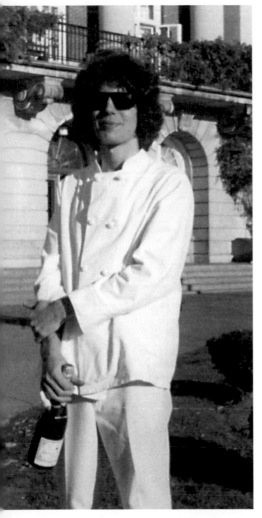

Tony on his graduation day from the
Culinary Institute of America, November 1978.

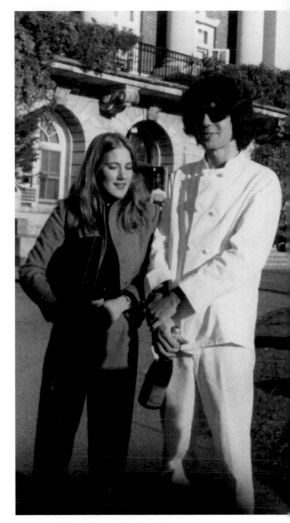

Nancy Bourdain (née Putkoski) and
Tony on his graduation day at the CIA,
November 1978.

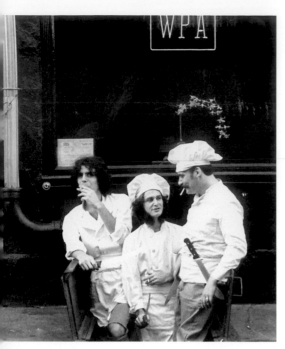

Tony, Sam Goldman, and Alex Getmanov outside the restaurant WPA, New York City, 1980. (Courtesy of Nancy Bourdain)

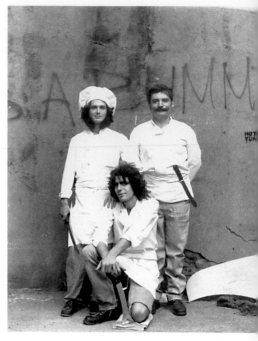

Sam, Tony, Alex, NYC, 1980. (Courtesy of Nancy Bourdain)

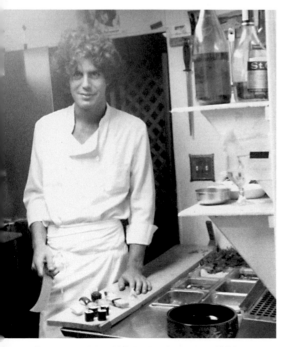

Tony in the Hotel Wales kitchen, circa 1988, New York City. (Courtesy of Nancy Bourdain)

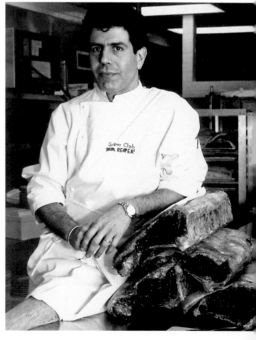

Tony at the Supper Club, circa 1995, New York City.

420 RIVERSIDE DR. #6B
N.Y. N.Y.
(212) 865-2071

Jan. '85

Dear Editors,

Having just read and been wildly impressed
by your publication, I enclose these two
short samples of my work-in-progress from
Zat Magazine.
    To put it to you quite simply; my lust
for print knows no bounds and I am
hopeful that you might be interested in
printing some other fragment of my current
project. It's called Chef's Night Out
and concerns itself with the familiar
themes of hard-drugs, haute-cuisine
and the occasional cathartic (but tasteful)
bloodletting.
    Though I do not reside on the Lower
East, I have in the recent past enjoyed
an intimate though debilitating familiarity
with its points of interest. It is my hope
that my prose contains some of its flavor.
                        Sincerely,
                        Anthony Bourdain—

Correspondence from Tony to Joel
Rose, who was then the editor at
Between C & D, a downtown literary
magazine. Joel would become a
lifelong friend, mentor, and writing
partner to Tony. (Courtesy of
the archive at Fales Library,
New York University)

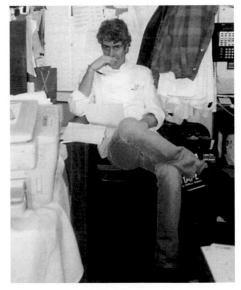

Tony in his office at Les Halles,
circa 1999, New York City.
(Courtesy of Nancy Bourdain)

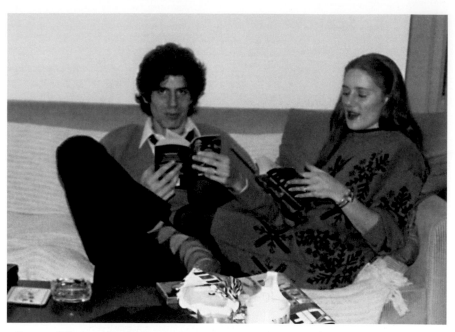
Tony and Nancy at the Larchmont home of Chris and Jennifer Bourdain, in the mid-1980s.

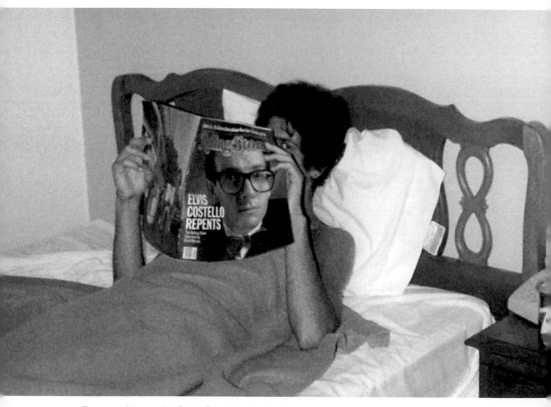
Tony reading at the Great Bay Hotel in St. Maarten, during his first visit to the island, with Nancy, in 1982. (Courtesy of Nancy Bourdain)

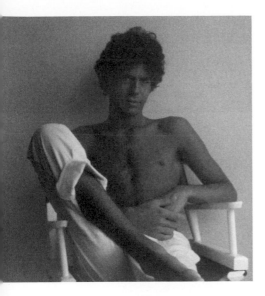

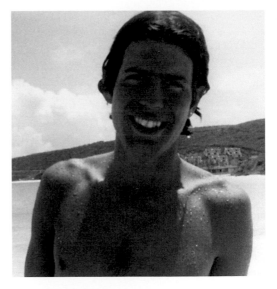

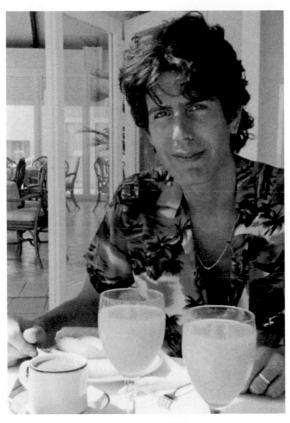

St. Maarten, 1982.

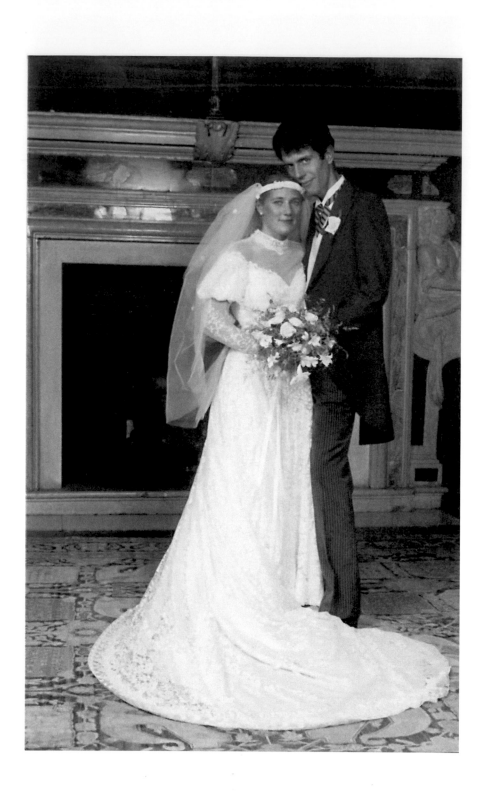

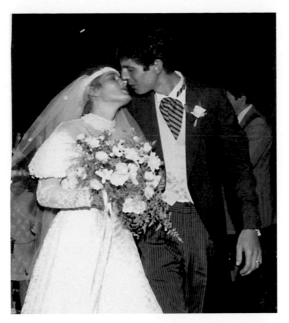

Nancy and Tony's wedding day, September 3, 1985, New York City. As befits a busy chef on a budget, the wedding was held on a Tuesday morning, followed by a brunch reception. (Courtesy of Nancy Bourdain)

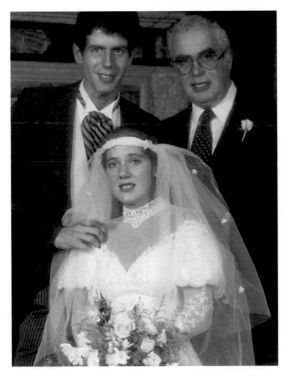

Tony, Nancy, and Pierre Bourdain at his son's wedding. (Courtesy of Nancy Bourdain)

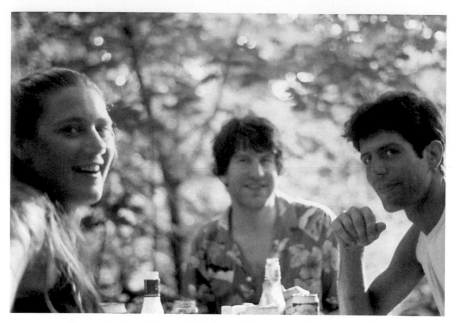

Nancy, Chris, and Tony at the home of Chris and Jennifer Bourdain,
Larchmont, New York, mid-1980s.

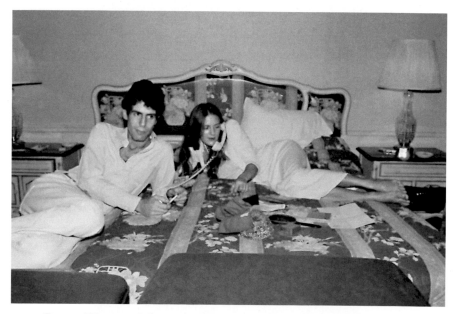

Tony and Nancy at their post-wedding party, at the St. Regis Hotel, New York.
(Courtesy of Nancy Bourdain)

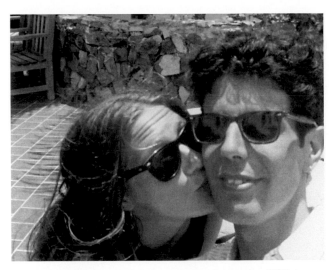

Tony and Nancy on their honeymoon, September 1985, in
St. Maarten, at the Oyster Pond Hotel and Yacht Club.
(Courtesy of Nancy Bourdain)

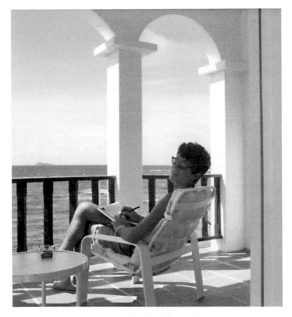

Tony at the Oyster Pond Hotel.
(Courtesy of Nancy Bourdain)

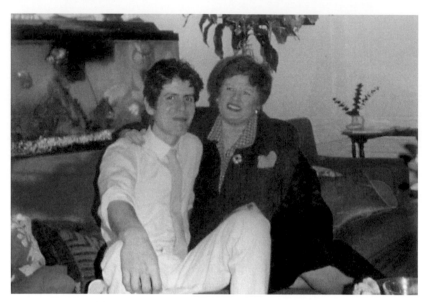

Tony at home with his mother, Gladys, mid-1980s.
(Courtesy of Nancy Bourdain)

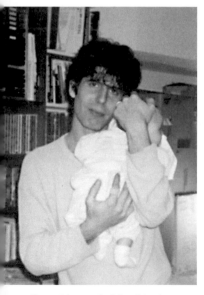

Tony at home, holding his niece,
Isabelle Bourdain, late 1990.

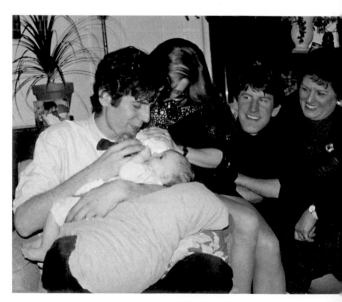

Tony at home with baby Isabelle, Nancy,
Chris, and Gladys, late 1990.

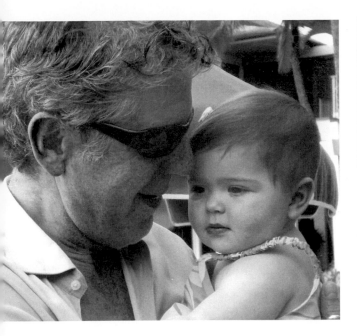

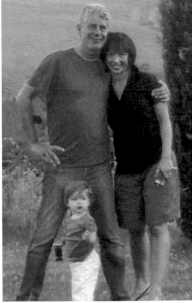

Tony, Ariane, and Ottavia in
Tuscany, summer 2008.

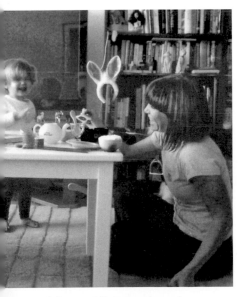

Ariane and Ottavia at home in
New York, 2009.

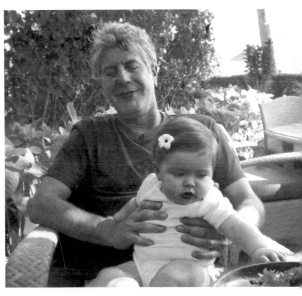

Tony and his daughter, Ariane, fall 2007.

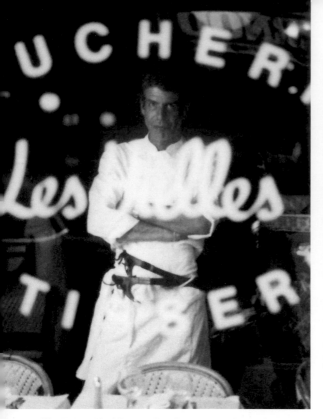

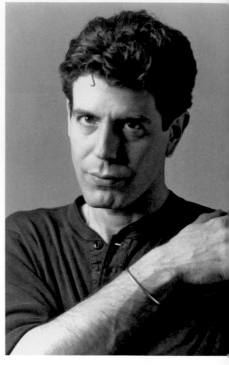

The Polaroid of Tony, taken for a promotion at Les Halles, that his editor and friend Karen Rinaldi would claim for the cover of *Kitchen Confidential*, asking, "Don't you want to hear what this guy has to say?"

Tony's author headshot, 1995, for his first novel, *Bone in the Throat*.

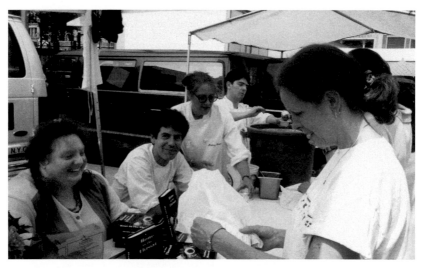

Tony signing copies of *Bone in the Throat* at the Union Square Greenmarket, 1995, assisted by Nancy Bourdain (in a chef's coat) and a trusted cook, Orlando Preciado, serving gazpacho to passersby. In the foreground is Maggie Topkis, the owner of Partners & Crime, a Manhattan bookstore, now closed.

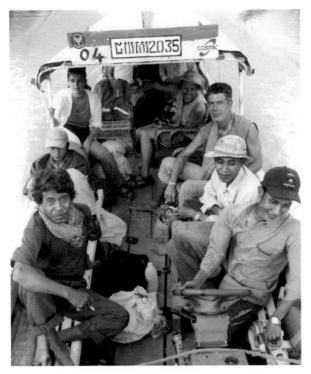

Tony, Chris, Lydia, and local crew on the Sangkae River in
Cambodia, headed to Battambang, for *A Cook's Tour*.
(Courtesy of Ottavia Busia-Bourdain)

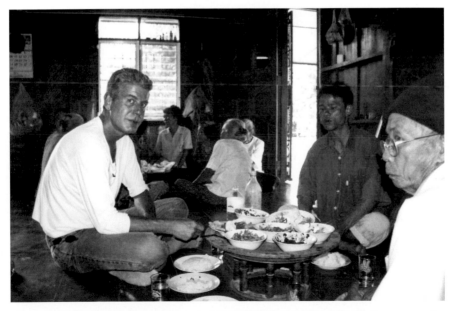

Tony and hosts shooting a meal scene in Chiang Mai, Thailand, for *A Cook's Tour*, season 2,
2002. "Tony's awkwardness was in full swing," recalls Chris Collins. "He just wasn't able to
engage with the folks we were eating with—thus the look on his face."
(Courtesy of Ottavia Busia-Bourdain)

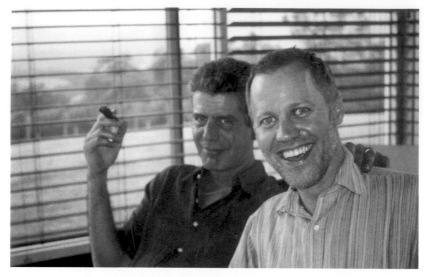

Tony and Chris Collins in Melbourne, Australia, for *A Cook's Tour*, season 2, 2002.
(Courtesy of Ottavia Busia-Bourdain)

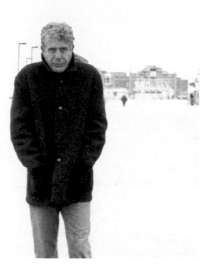

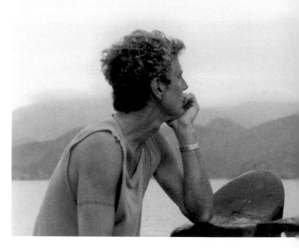

Tony during his first, formative
visit to Vietnam, for *A Cook's Tour*.
(Courtesy of Ottavia Busia-Bourdain)

On the Jersey Shore
boardwalk in winter, late 2000s.
(Courtesy of Ottavia Busia-Bourdain)

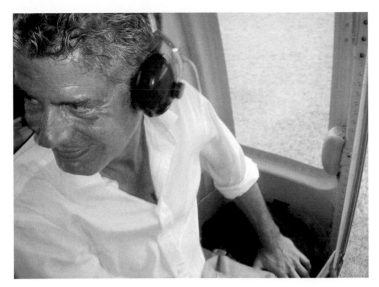

Tony in a helicopter on a 2006 shoot in Ghana,
for *No Reservations*, season 3. (Courtesy of Rennik Soholt)

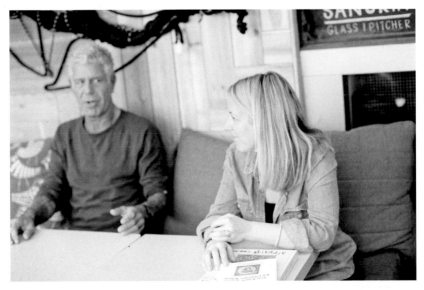

Tony and the author, Laurie Woolever, in 2016, at a day of interviews in Toronto,
promoting their cookbook, *Appetites*. (Courtesy of Philippa Croft)

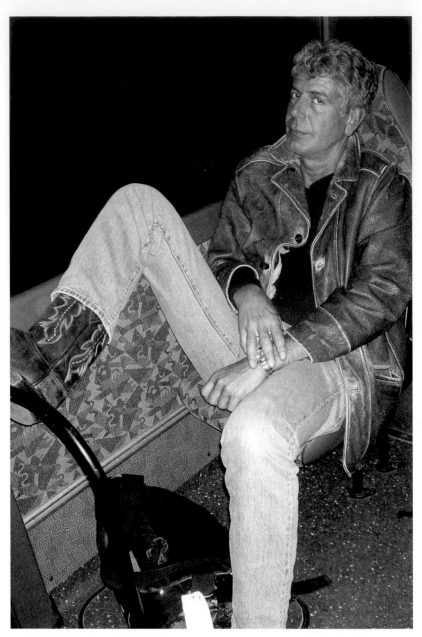

A weary but game Tony in a *No Reservations* crew van. In the early years, Tony would fly to locations and ride in the van with the crew. "We all fit in one van, and we went everywhere together," recalls producer Nari Kye. "[Tony] would play music. He would always be DJ, and we would always tell jokes and be gross and silly." As the shows became more demanding, Tony would become more isolated. "One thing Tony always valued was the camaraderie with the crew," says producer Diane Schutz. "But as time went on, our budgets increased, and you wanted to respect his time, so then he gets his own van to set, and the crew advances for an hour. Well, now he's just lost an hour in the van with the crew, and he's just there alone."
(Courtesy of Rennik Soholt)

Sip'n Soda, and we'd both always have lime rickeys there. Those two places were our favorites.

In New York, he would usually take me to one of those restaurants, like fast food, that my mom doesn't approve of. I think my mom knew, but he would make it seem like we were on this mission.

He would say, "All right, let's tell your mom that we're going to get the newspaper downstairs, but we're actually going to go to Papaya King." We'd get a hot dog and a papaya shake and we'd eat it in this little garden. Then we'd come back and say, "That was an interesting newspaper . . . yeah." I'm sure my mom knew. Why would it take us twenty minutes to get the newspaper?

OTTAVIA BUSIA-BOURDAIN: He really liked making breakfast for Ariane, and then, when she was a little bit older, they started cooking together. And especially in the summer, when we would rent a house in the Hamptons for a month, and they were really cooking together, and spending so much time together, and going to the beach together.

ARIANE BUSIA-BOURDAIN: I always cooked with him. We'd always cook ratatouille, from the movie *Ratatouille*, and we made it exactly like they made it. We'd cook schnitzel; he'd make little stations: one of them has the breading, one has the flour, one has the eggs, and my dad put it in the pan. He'd cook omelets for me all the time, and I'd help him flip it. He would let me sprinkle chocolate chips or blueberries into pancakes, and then he'd let me flip the pancake a little. When we were in the Hamptons, he'd cook dinner, cook breakfast, so that's when he really cooked for me.

He taught me how to cut things and not chop off my fingers, to curl my fingers under. He gave me my own little knife, and I still have it, and still use it.

OTTAVIA BUSIA-BOURDAIN: He was a great dad. And he was silly. He was like an overgrown child. They would make videos together. And play silly games, and he would tell her crazy stories, and he always said that we were a family of weirdos, but that was great, you know.

ARIANE BUSIA-BOURDAIN: We had this little thing called the Weirdo Club. And I don't really know what it was about, it was just us being weird. And I really liked it. He encouraged weirdness. He pretty much encouraged every single thing I wanted to do in my life, and gave me the information to back it up.

I just started drawing by myself, and I did very much get inspired by his drawings. I'd seen him draw before, and I don't think I really liked them back then, because they are very sketchy, you know, very his style, and then as I grew older, I kind of learned to like that style. So a lot of my artwork, you know, comes from his. And he might not really see that right away but it does; I do think of his style when I draw.

I was singing for a long time, and I still am. In order to be in my camp, where I do rock music, I also need to play an instrument. And I was thinking, *Oh, what instrument should I play?* My dad was like, "You know, the bass is, like, really cool. You're just in the back, you're just grooving, and it could also be the lead instrument of the song, it could just kind of put the song together." That sounded perfect for me, because I don't really like being in the spotlight all the time, so being on the bass, it's my thing. I play bass pretty much because of him.

OTTAVIA BUSIA-BOURDAIN: He really felt this responsibility to be healthy. He started actually getting checkups, and going to the doctor, and he had a CAT scan of his lungs, and turns out that they were totally fine. He was making an effort to be healthy, because he wanted to be around for Ariane.

But then, once he moved out, he seemed to be really impulsive.

Definitely for the last two years of his life, he made many impulsive decisions.

When he told me that he wanted to move out, there was not a big shock. For quite some time, we were basically friends. We didn't work out as a married couple, but we would get along so well, there was no reason for either of us to move out or change the way things were. Like I said, we didn't work out as a married couple, but we were doing very well as a family.

But then he fell in love, and his girlfriend told him that she didn't want to be a weekend lover, so he decided it was the best thing for his relationship to move out. And because of the relationship we had, I couldn't say, "Oh no, you have to stay with us." You know, it was his prerogative; he was a grown man, and we didn't have that kind of relationship anymore.

I was worried about Ariane, but I was happy for him, because it was like, "Maybe you'll find another chance at love," and I was like, "Go for it," you know.

He told me, "Nothing is gonna change. I'll be there every morning to take her to school, and I'll be there for dinner, and I'll still sleep over a lot of nights." And for a bit, it really seemed like things were gonna work out, but then everything changed. And that's not the way things went.

I feel like, for him, it was very important to have the kind of stability that he had at home. Even if our marriage didn't work out, there was still routine, and there were people who really cared about him. And Tony, he had this image of, you know, this bad boy, no fucks given, but he was actually really sensitive, and really fragile. And I really think he needed a stable environment around him.

When he left, he didn't have that anymore. It's weird to say nobody was protecting him, because he was a grown-ass man, but still—I feel like he needed, if not protection, at least stability.

46

"TONY'S CHANGED; TONY'S VERY DIFFERENT NOW"

LYDIA TENAGLIA: [Over the years] Tony's demeanor shifted; he went from, "I can't believe my luck, getting out of hot kitchens to do this," and you see, almost, a vibrating crazy energy. Then you see, in the middle of *No Reservations*, somebody coming into his own: truly, deeply understanding how the visual medium could be an extension of his own thoughts or writing, and how he could play with that. Toward the end, I just see someone who was getting really tired, just kind of weary, not just about traveling and things he saw and was exposed to.

DANIEL HALPERN: I started to notice it before *Appetites* [the cookbook he published with Ecco in 2016]. He seemed even more distant. He seemed not to have that same kind of energy. He just seemed to be carrying a greater weight in every way on his shoulders. And he didn't seem to be getting enough joy out of life.

He was, in some ways, breaking down, even physically, although he was in amazing shape. Something wasn't exactly right. He got tired. And I think all of the flights. Very few people could deal with that. He seemed to, but the last couple of years, he looked worn out. And not really happy. Very thin. He looked in some ways like he was suffering in a psychological way.

MICHAEL RUHLMAN: I made shows with him in Napa Valley, two in Las Vegas, New York City, Cleveland, and the Hudson valley. As the years went on, he seemed to have increasingly less fun, seemed to be increasingly less joyful.

AMY ENTELIS: I would say that, in the last couple of years, I worried a little bit more about whether he was gonna want to move on, in the sense that the work was becoming a little routine.

The two-hundred-plus days a year on the road, and the constant travel—I'm not privy to what was going on in his head, but we all used to wonder, How does Tony do this?

This looks like the greatest job in the world, but we were up close enough to it to know that it was really wearing. It would be wearing on anybody. And this was many, many years of it, not just at CNN.

I think the shows were as good as they ever were, but in terms of him, and how he approached them or what he wanted to do, I felt like there was some kind of a shift. I couldn't quite put my finger on it, but in terms of enthusiasm, it was waning a little bit. Whether that was the case or not is still unknown to me, but some of the energy and enthusiasm seemed to lag a bit.

LIZZIE FOX: In the last round of negotiations, we thought, *Well, maybe it will be only a year*, and we had asked for three. And, with enthusiasm, he signed on for more.

TODD LIEBLER: I think the big changes with Tony were his relation-ships. Like, as he was getting married, or having a child, seeing a new girlfriend, those were the times when you saw the biggest change in him. Ultimately, the last big change was not a good one. It always would be these intense women who had this effect on him. And that's when we really noticed the big changes.

KIMBERLY WITHERSPOON: He was devastated by the end of the relation-ship [with Ottavia], and it left him vulnerable to Asia.*

SANDY ZWEIG: In terms of the last couple of years, there was a turn-ing point that I saw, and it had to do with Asia. He was supposed to meet her in France.†

He had gotten shingles, and a lot of stuff had happened. I just remember him sitting in my office, and he— We weren't close, you know? We had a professional relationship, but he just sort of opened up about how horrible it was, and how he'd passed out on the street.‡

ASHA GILL: I remember when he was in France [in summer 2016]. I got a call then, and he was just not in a good space. So we had, over a week, quite a few conversations. And then he'd have a go at me. "Stop trying to make me feel better." Whatever was happening then, that was the first time that I really was concerned and worried, in fifteen years.

---

* *Tony met the Italian actress and director Asia Argento in Rome, on the set of* Parts Unknown, *in April 2016. They went public with their romance in February 2017.*
† *Argento canceled plans to meet him in France, shortly before the July 2016 trip.*
‡ *Tony relayed the episode to Patrick Radden Keefe, in the* New Yorker *profile, in which he'd had too much to drink, combined with some prescription drugs, while in France in July 2016. He lost consciousness just outside a bar and woke up speaking, as he recalled, perfect French.*

KIMBERLY WITHERSPOON: When anyone had misgivings, or just an issue with Tony, it would often land in my lap, and it was up to me to speak with him about it. And he was generally receptive to hearing it, and interested. But I'm not sure how much he could hear the increasing apprehension that we felt for his safety, his judgment, and his emotional and psychological well-being in his romantic relationships.

I was trying to get him to see that he had as many life choices as any of us have, and that his choices weren't as limited as he seemed to think they were. Once he became involved with Asia, many of us were voicing our worry directly about that relationship. And while he was engaged by it—I never felt that he shut me down when I was conveying the concerns—he thought the positive outweighed the negative.

SANDY ZWEIG: Looking back, it gave some insight into what that relationship might end up being. There were certainly highs. In the beginning, he seemed very happy. Toward the end, it seemed like he just was thinner, and probably not taking care of himself as well.

PETER MEEHAN: I saw him in August 2016. I was writing something about him for an Australian magazine, so I went out to [his] Southampton [rental house]. There were a bunch of ZPZ guys there, showing him footage from the Rome episode [of *Parts Unknown*]; he was crazy, talking about the cameras and Fellini and the whole thing.

Then Tony and I went out to the front porch to smoke cigarettes, and that's when he told me about Asia. She had sent him a picture of some kind of Japanese-style tattoo, which was like a broken-up yakuza girlfriend–style tattoo; it was some kind of message etched in her skin that was like, "Fuck off," and you could tell it just set Tony's heart on fire, and he was like, "I'm gonna do this." It seemed romantic at the time.

DAVE CHANG: The things that Tony used to love were disappearing, and he couldn't fill that heroin void anymore, and then a relationship came in at the right place, at just the right time for him. Something new, and dangerous, and foreign—all the same things that travel presented to him. It was inaccessible; the same thing that fine dining had been to him. Same shit. It was like, "I can't get access to this, and it's impossible to know."

ROY CHOI: When I saw him with *People* magazine [for a September 2016 shoot at the Chateau Marmont, to promote *Appetites*], I felt something weird about him that day. It was a larger impatience toward something. I just felt like everything was the same, but they turned the music up. I just felt like the volume of everything was louder. There was still the same Tony, but just with this impatience.

ADAM EPSTEIN: On that last speaking tour [in October and November 2016], he was in great shape, physically, but he did seem very darkly reflective, moody; you would rarely see him grin.

ALISON MOSSHART: I remember when we were talking a lot was when he was on that last speaking tour. And I remember that he was just not loving it. I don't know how anyone *could*, to be totally fair. [But] he didn't seem miserable. He seemed OK.

ROBIN STANDEFER: I could see Tony starting to morph a little bit, for sure; embracing a darker side. He was doing the *New Yorker* story, and we were part of that story, because of the market, and he asked us to come out to a Korean restaurant, and then to a club, and we were out all night with him and the writer [Patrick Radden Keefe]. We were talking about history and writing and reading, and then we sort of meandered down to this crazy Korean karaoke club, and

singing and doing shots for hours, till like six in the morning—and
it was that night that I started to feel a shift; I just felt like there was,
in Tony, a need to follow the demons a little more than there had
been for the previous three years. I felt it.

MICHAEL RUHLMAN: The last time I saw him was at the opening of the
Wasted! documentary [in the spring of 2017]. There was a palpable
depression to him. I thought, *It's just got to be fatigue.* His travel
schedule was fucking insane. But he seemed demonstrably sad.

KAREN RINALDI: One of the last times Tony and I talked, he said, "I've
never been happier in my life." It was at the *Grape, Olive, Pig* book
party, in May 2017.* I just wanted him to be happy. I remember
thinking that it was Tony letting all the noise out for a minute. It
was an incredibly intimate, wonderful moment. He showed me his
new carp tattoo.

MICHAEL RUHLMAN: He was a great correspondent. One of his last
emails was in response to my inviting him to my wedding reception.
He said, "I've fallen in love, too." He briefly described it, and the last
words I have from him are "love abounds," which was so uncynical
and so— I was surprised by the just heart-wide-openness of it all. He
truly was a romantic. It was part of what was so great about him—he
was a cynic who loved the world and always expected the best.

MORGAN FALLON: Even though we were familiar on set, getting to really know him personally didn't come until I was directing. I saw
what was really going on under the surface [of] someone who had

---

* Grape, Olive, Pig *is a book about the culinary culture of Spain, written by Matt
Goulding and published by Tony's imprint at Ecco.*

great reverence for the quiet places, big, open places where he could feel small and anonymous, like Oman, in the Empty Quarter [of the Arabian Peninsula], or West Texas, Big Bend, and those deep canyons. I saw in him this desire to be somehow swept away into the oblivion. Maybe that was his attempt to mitigate the kind of trauma he was experiencing as his celebrity grew, and his ability to walk down the street, or go to places that he loved, or have a normal conversation with someone, or just be left the fuck alone, kind of evaporated.

There was less looking for an acute sensory experience, and more of a slower, longer burn of searching for something that was bigger than himself. The other thing I saw change in him was that, frankly, he'd started to cry more. I had never seen the facade of control crack, but in multiple scenes, you started seeing him get choked up, not necessarily in sad ways, but in very connected, very empathic ways. I saw it in Antarctica, I saw it in Texas, in Florence. He was connecting with someone else, and really understanding his or her experience. I mean, we all know that Tony was, in some ways, a pathological narcissist, and I think that in those moments, that was broken down. There were certain people who were able to scale that wall and access him in a way that opened that up.

LIZZIE FOX: I think that he was a volatile person, in his ups and downs. At the end, there were a lot of ups. I remember he wrote me an email totally out of the blue. It was like, "Thank you so much for all the opportunities and really believing in me." It was so sweet, and I never think of Tony Bourdain as sweet. I thought, *He must be in a good place*. But then it's always, with an addict in particular, the shoe is gonna drop sometime, so if it's a high high, it's gonna come down to a low low. My brother's an addict, so I grew up, from a young age, observing that sort of behavior.

I think just in reading [*Kitchen Confidential*] and understanding where he came from—if you have an addictive personality, it's one thing or the other, whether it's food and booze, whether it's jiu-jitsu, whether it's cigarettes. Sometimes that can be a really wonderful thing, and a special gift, because it makes you take risks more than others might, but then it's also that feeling of, *When's it all going to crash down again?*

With addicts in particular, you want them to be happy, because you've seen them in such a dark place. You want to believe that it's all gonna work out, this is it, we've gotten over the hump. You're not even looking for something that might be a little off, because you want it as badly as they do.

ROBIN STANDEFER: It wasn't a surprise to me that he connected with someone erotically, that he could not disconnect from the intensity of that. When he talked, I still recognized it as him, but he was embracing another part of him. He was looking for something to give him that high again.

There were other moments when he—it's not like he *disappeared*, not in the psychological way that he did with Asia; that was a seismic change—but in that five-year period [of Bourdain Market planning], there were times when Kim and the investors and everybody was trying to put the deal together, and we wouldn't talk for a year, and then suddenly it would be, "Oh, we're gonna present, let's talk, let's do it." So I didn't know enough to know that this wasn't one of those times. It was clear to me he was going through some shit, but there are guys who get involved with some freaky person and come out of it.

CHRISTOPHER BOURDAIN: In the last couple of years, we all knew him well enough to know that, OK, you're in that intense, burning phase of your love obsession at this moment, so I should not expect to see you very much, because every spare minute that you have, you're spending with this woman. But I would have liked it if he'd just have shot me an email here and there.

It's funny, because Tony and our mom had not had a particularly good or productive relationship, but he was emailing with her much more than with me in the last couple of years. They were in communication more than he was with me, and I said, "What the hell? He doesn't even really like her. She's always a pain in the ass. I'm not," you know?

NANCY BOURDAIN: I didn't like the way he looked in the last couple of years. He looked like he was being ridden hard and put away wet. I hadn't seen him look so haggard, so tired. Overnight gray. I mean, he was always salt-and-pepper, but this was stark. And he seemed to not care about being tan anymore.

Joel Rose told me that he'd started getting one-word answers to emails. Tony was effusive; he was not a one-word-answer guy.

JOEL ROSE: In the last few years, and as close as we were, I felt emotional distance from him. Not necessarily intellectual, because we would work together all the time. I felt emotional distance from him. We didn't spend as much time together. He was busy and harried so much. In retrospect, I realize how tired he was; I didn't realize it at the time.

SAM GOLDMAN: Our emails had gotten less frequent and shorter. I'd tell him when someone died, or when something really good had happened to somebody, but by then we were really out of touch. I would say the last year and a half or so of his life, we didn't have any contact at all.

DAVE MCMILLAN: We didn't even want to go to Newfoundland, when Tony asked us to go [for *Parts Unknown*, in September 2017]. I was tired of the attention. We'd already said we were never gonna do TV or media ever again, and we'd figured that Tony was never gonna ask us to do anything ever again anyway, because we'd already done so much. We did five events with him over ten years, which is a huge amount.

FRED MORIN: The center of [our relationship with Tony] was a joie de vivre, and we had to express it through a massive amount of food, luxury food, and wine. And at first, the first show, I had no questions about it. I was like, great, you know? By the last show, I felt bad. I started to be more conscious about the—not the image, but the message.

MUSTAFA BHAGAT: The Newfoundland episode was supposed to be a double episode, but it just wasn't there. There was a classic failed hunting scene in which Tony was sitting out in the rain for four hours; he was supposed to get a moose. He was complaining the whole time. It was meant to be a grandiose episode with Fred and Dave, and they did have one grand meal, but it was clear that it was all a little bit boring for him. It just wasn't happening.

DAVE MCMILLAN: There was something going on there [in Newfoundland]. You could sense it. It was like, *Oh, Tony's changed; Tony's very different now. There's a vibe here. The camera crew's scared. They're no longer a happy family of gypsies making shows on the road.* There was a new element. Tony was exhausted. He didn't know that he was exhausted.

FRED MORIN: But as much as we were a bit tired of portraying that heavy-drinking fucking joie de vivre—smoking, swearing, whatever—

we were also wondering if there was any other avenue for us to live. Can we continue in that world of restaurants, without drinking? We thought that was the only thing.

I can only imagine how Tony must have felt about the lameness of civilian life, you know? Like, not constantly upping the ante, and going to further, further, more remote, more . . . And I had the feeling on that trip that he felt—not *responsible*, but he seemed to have changed his outlook about promoting that using culture, and that bro vibe. You could feel that was heavy for him to deal with.

NARI KYE: It was during [promotional activities for the documentary film] *Wasted!* that I started seeing the difference. All he'd talk about was Asia, and he was spending a lot of his time in Italy with her and her family. It felt like his physical body was here, but his mind was just with her, thinking about her.

WHITNEY WARD, FRIEND: Tony, Asia, Joe [Coleman], and I were all together in New York, just before the *New Yorker* article came out.* It was the beginning of the whole #MeToo business. He was very defensive of [Asia], and very supportive. He was the most eloquent and sincere supporter of women that one could ever aspire to be.

JOE COLEMAN, ARTIST, TV SIDEKICK: It was a scary time, you know, particularly for Asia. He was there for her, and I think it was important to have someone as powerful as Tony behind Asia, and defending

---

* *Asia Argento was one of several women who spoke to Ronan Farrow for an October 2017 article, published in the* New Yorker, *about their experiences of being sexually assaulted by the film producer Harvey Weinstein. She was in New York at that time and had recently introduced Tony to her friends Joe Coleman, an artist, and his wife, Whitney Ward.*

her against the powers that tried to silence her. It changed the world as we know it. I was the one who played Harvey Weinstein in Asia's [2000] movie [*Scarlet Diva*], so it was something that I was concerned about, too, that she was protected. She was fearful of what Harvey Weinstein could do to her. When *Scarlet Diva* first came out, [Weinstein] recognized himself.

NARI KYE: I remember when we had our theatrical premiere [for *Wasted!*] in October 2017; we were at Alamo Drafthouse [in New York], and he was there briefly, and he did an intro. And all he was talking about before he went on was Harvey Weinstein.

It was a few days before the news broke. And he was just fixated on that. And he even ended the speech—his intro speech was like, "*Wasted! Wasted!* Food waste," and then, "Fuck you, Harvey Weinstein." And we were all just like, "What is he talking about?" Because we didn't even know what was going on yet. Then the news broke, and we understood later.

CHRISTIANE AMANPOUR: I did notice that when it came to promoting *Sex and Love around the World* in 2018, I noticed that he was tired, and he looked older, and that he was slightly different than I had seen him months earlier. I wonder whether he needed to step back and take some time for himself and to surround himself with the people who really loved him. I think his friends feel very sorry that he might have been sort of led astray in his personal life, toward the end. This is all speculation, but I know what I saw, and I saw a very tired man.

OTTAVIA BUSIA-BOURDAIN: Tony would joke about everything, but he was much darker in the last year or so of his life. I stopped watching the shows toward the end because I could not really recognize him as the person— I don't know, it was just really strange seeing him. Like he was not the same person anymore.

47

"HE WAS ATTRACTED TO CHAOS"

JOSH HOMME: The last year of Tony's life was really tough for me to watch, because he was saying this thing that was like, "You know, I've put myself way out there, and I could totally be destroyed by tomorrow." I was worried.

ALISON MOSSHART: He did say, describing this relationship that he was in, "It's gonna end so badly." This was at the beginning of the relationship. He was smart enough to know he was in a dangerous place.

He could have been just sailing at that point in his life, had his brain allowed him to do that. I don't know if that was just Tony not emotionally maturing beyond a certain time, when you just want what you want when you want it. He was attracted to chaos. And there's something so beautiful and baroque about that.

KIMBERLY WITHERSPOON: I think he genuinely heard from me, and from [others], that her behavior seemed to me, and others, to be dysfunctional, and disruptive, and destabilizing. But I think he thought it was manageable.

Whenever I expressed doubt to Tony about his relationship, he would express tremendous empathy for *me*, and for *my* worry, and seek to reassure me that, yes, what I was saying was grounded in reality, that he understood, *really* understood, why I was concerned, and that on the surface, it did, in fact, seem dangerous. But he would also seek to reassure me that it was going to be fine, that he would be fine, that it would be painful, that things were going to end badly, but that he would be all right. He was unwilling to break it off. He wanted to see the relationship through. And I personally always thought that he was hanging on to this possibility that, by offering her unconditional love—because that is what he was offering her, just unconditionally supporting her—that love would, in fact, win the day.

Tony believed that he would be fine; that he was at a certain point in life, he was older, he had seen a lot, and that although this relationship was problematic, he was going to enjoy it while it lasted.

He said, "I hear you, I think you're probably right. This is going to end very, very badly, but it will have been a hell of a ride. And I will be fine."

ALISON MOSSHART: This is a sixty-year-old man making this choice. This is what he wanted. There's nothing else you can do other than say, "You're my friend. I love you. This is not a great situation."

I watched his personality change, I watched his letters change, I watched his reactions to things change very suddenly. I knew him for only like two and a half [years], but I know a lot of people who had known him for a really long time.

He had these moments of clarity, where it would be, like, twenty-six emails of brilliance. Funny, awesome, great phone calls. I'd see him at things with our friends, and it was fun, and we would talk all night, and I would think, *OK, everything's cool.*

I didn't know the depth of what was really going on. I knew that he had left his wife, I knew that he got a new apartment, I know that he made the whole thing [into] the Chateau Marmont. He was so proud of it.

DANIEL HALPERN: I guess if you're in that state, you're much more vulnerable to that kind of takeover by another strong personality, and it seems to me that he was taken over in a lot of ways. And I think five years ago, ten years ago, that wouldn't have happened. He was just—he was susceptible to that particular kind of emotional power play.

HELEN LANG: That's the thing about Tony: he had an incredible heart, and even though he was this tough guy, he could be very easily manipulated, I think.

LYDIA TENAGLIA: When Asia came along, it was like this shot of adrenaline. He had almost a frantic sense of desperation, like, "Keep her happy." He imposed it on all of us.

NANCY BOURDAIN: I felt kind of like a sibling to Tony. In the old days, if I didn't hear from him every couple of months, I'd check recent news, just to see what was up. And when it first started [with Argento], I thought, *Good for them,* although I did think it was odd when he went so public with so much. He wasn't that way, ever. He wouldn't deny his private life, but I thought that was a little odd. But people change, and things happen. I really don't know anything except what I can read online.

That's what drives me crazy, because Tony was a very smart guy, and if anybody knew how to milk the internet for information, that was Tony. So I kept thinking, his eyes were wide shut or open, however you want to put it. Part of me thinks, sometimes, he just wanted to go out in a blaze of something that he'd found fun.

MIKE RUFFINO: It's not like he didn't know what he was getting into there. It was, for lack of better words, a little bit of a junkie move.

SCOTT BRYAN: He had that junkie mentality; he was all in, or nothing.

JOE COLEMAN: There may have been a pathological side to the love, but nevertheless, it was love. And what are we here for, you know? If you go through this life and you don't really taste anything, you don't really embrace what life holds, then you're at a loss. You've missed out on something special. Tony gorged himself in being alive.

48

"THEY'RE GONNA TEAR YOU APART"

ALIENATING FRIENDS

JOSH HOMME: I was feeling lost in my life. The events at the Bataclan were weighing heavy on me, and I couldn't get rid of them.[*]

I started throwing myself into charity work, stuff like that. I played this Bataclan benefit, where I go and shake someone's hand, and, like, their arm is gone. A week later, I was playing a show, and I'm like, *I don't know how to understand what I'm feeling.*

Sometimes you go wild, and you scare an audience. And there's something magical in that, too. It's maybe a little lost in this society. I was kicking the lights off the stage. I even cut myself, bleeding

---

[*] *The band Eagles of Death Metal, for which Homme is the drummer, were playing at the Bataclan theater in Paris, France, on November 13, 2015, when ninety people were killed in a terrorist attack.*

up there. This camera comes up onstage, and it's dark, because I'd kicked the lights off. And so I just brush it with my foot, and I smile. I wasn't trying to hurt anybody. You know, it's like—if you've ever seen that shot of Johnny Cash giving the finger, or Iggy walking on the crowd—if you ask [rock photographers] Bob Gruen or Mick Rock if they've ever been bumped around to get the shot, that's part of it, for rock 'n' roll. That's it, right? I thought I was giving this person the shot of the night, really. But I looked, and I remember thinking, "Ah. She looks insulted."

She finished photographing the rest of the night. And all of a sudden, this woman's like, "Josh kicked me in the head." Now, there's a grand difference between brushing someone's camera away and kicking someone in the head. And to assert in front of a sold-out audience, I'm gonna just turn and kick this woman in the head—I tried to apologize via email, and text, and that got me nowhere; she wouldn't have it. There was nothing I could say. At first, it was put up with a "#MeToo." And I almost lost everything in a day, because, it was like, the mob burns the witch.

Everyone else called to see if I was OK, [but] I get a text from Tony. He was very rough with me. He says, "You need to do a full mea culpa, apologize. These people will come after you. They're gonna tear you apart, they're gonna tear apart the associations you have with me, and our friends. You can't say you were tired, or that you were drunk, you can't explain anything. Just fully throw yourself at the mercy of this."

My reputation is—I have my grandparents tattooed on my hands. My name means everything, respect means everything. So I went home and immediately filmed this thing, and put it up. It was my choice. I'm responsible for me. I always take responsibility for myself.

Tony had written something really negative about me [on Twitter], and had assumed that what he saw from the world, even though he knows about the press, was somehow true.[*]

DEAN FERTITA: With him not knowing the whole story, it was a conversation that those two should have had, and would have normally had, so I did think it was a little unusual that Josh and Tony didn't just talk. He didn't get a full understanding. At least talk to your friend, you know?

DARREN ARONOFSKY: In Bhutan, there was a lot of drama going on, because it was right during the week before Batali.[†]

So he was really freaked out about that. I think at the time, he was probably the most famous male that was completely engaged in the conversation. The Batali story was a big thing for him. He was done with him as a friend, he was clear. It was, like, unacceptable.

NARI KYE: He was always a feminist. Tony was all about equality for women and all that stuff, but never to this point. We were all just very much taken aback.

BILL BUFORD: It did seem like [his outspokenness on #MeToo] was informed by his relationship with Asia in a very powerful way, but a lot of people have come out and expressed indignation and horror

---

[*] *On December 10, 2017, Tony tweeted, in response to news reports of Homme having kicked the photographer: "Waking up in Bhutan to the Josh Homme @QOTSA shit and still in the WTF!!!??!! Phase. Senseless. And a weak ass apology."*

[†] *On December 12, 2017, news broke on the restaurant industry website* Eater, *and then in the* New York Times *and the* Washington Post, *about several women's allegations of sexual harassment by Mario Batali and Ken Friedman in the workplace. Tony, who had once considered Batali and Friedman friends and peers, had become a vocal supporter of the #MeToo movement, and was made aware in advance that the stories were in development.*

at some of the stories that emerged out of the kitchen. It felt like it wasn't incorrect, and it wasn't that surprising.

I never saw Tony ever be sexually abusive, and I think his relationship to women wouldn't even allow it. There was a high respect, there was an element of admiration, there was an element of fear. So he's got good credit. But [his outspokenness] was airborne by the fumes of a very intense relationship. And that, at least in the eyes of this beholder, seemed to discredit it a little bit. It doesn't say that it was wrong, or didn't deserve more, but it compromised it a little bit.

JOSH HOMME: I'm really leery of mob mentality, and so was Tony, always. And that he was kind of becoming the poster boy for this thing, it seemed odd to me. And then it quickly became him backtracking and saying to me, "I'm really sorry."

But I was like, "Man, we're friends. Will you do me a favor? Will you grab Tony and put him on the phone? Who the fuck are you right now?"

And he's like, "I'm sorry. It's just hard to be my friend right now." He was trying to make it right, but I was very upset.

When we made the California desert episode of *No Reservations* [in 2011], he and I got into this kind of physical altercation with a fan, a drunk, Palm Springs kind of golf-looking fan—just after we're done filming at Pappy and Harriet's, and we're excited like two kids—this guy comes up, very rudely interrupts us, and says, "My wife is drunk. She's a big fan. We go to all your shows, and watch your show, and we buy your books and stuff. Can you take a picture with her? She's outside, like, a hundred and fifty feet away."

Tony said, "Well, I'll take a picture with her," but I, to kind of protect Tony, I said, "Why don't you bring her in, you know? We're here. Like, come, bring her in. He'll take a photo."

He looks at me, he says, "Who the fuck are you?" And I said, "Well, you should ask around, and someone will tell you."

And Tony says to the guy, "That's my friend, you know. I don't want you to buy any more of my books, I don't want you to watch the show . . ." And the guy says to Tony, "Well, you know, technically, I pay your salary."

And I said, "You need to be careful about the next words that come out of your mouth, 'cause your life could totally change in, like, one word." And I'm smiling, he's looking at me, and he says, "Fuck you."

And I grabbed his hand, pulled him this way, and put my thumb underneath his chin. And I'm pushing him backward, to walk him toward the security guy. I was like, "You're done now." But over my shoulder is Tony, trying to grab this guy, going—"Don't you buy any books! That's my friend!"

You know what I took from that? No one's ever stood up for me before. It just wasn't necessary, right? But here was this guy whom I'd now known for five years, maybe, and he was standing up for me, like friends do. You don't know somebody until it all goes wrong. He literally had my back.

When you flash forward to the last year of his life, I was like, "Where's the guy who had my back? You believe something else, and write something, but you don't even call me?"

ALISON MOSSHART: It was really shocking and alienating for all of us when he did that. And all of us struggled with it, because we'd never seen anything like that from him. He was reacting to people whom he loved and trusted in different ways; that was shocking.

I didn't know then how much he was pushing people out. The Josh situation, that one hit home, because that's someone I know very well, and I know that he and Tony had been friends forever.

That's so not what Tony would have ever said or done one year before. None of us knew how to approach him after that. It was like, "You never even *asked* the other side. You *never* not ask the other side."

HELEN CHO: That was a huge red flag. We had dinner when he came back from Bhutan, and I said to him, "How could you do that to a friend of yours, and someone you've known so long, who has been so loyal, without checking in with him first?" I was very angry with him. I asked him, "If you do something like that, what kind of message do you think that also sends to all the people around you who have been loyal to you? People who have been working with you for more than a decade? Those who would drop everything to be there for you?"

And he was defensive, a little bit, and said he had no choice. But this is the thing with Tony, he would be open to being wrong, you know? He never had PR, he just followed his instincts, and his instincts were usually mostly right. But he knew he was wrong, and felt bad for what he had done. And he couldn't take it back, at least at the time, because of the manipulation and force of this woman—he just couldn't jeopardize that. He couldn't deal with that.

ALISON MOSSHART: I just thought, *Tony's going to get it together and apologize to Josh, and things will go back to normal.* But he had to alienate everyone else. And that's what he was in trouble about. That's what he knew. He was alienating the people who loved him the most, who cared about him, his family, his friends. You know, when you go that far, you don't feel like you can come back, and that is really, ultimately, what I think happened.

The trouble wasn't true trouble. The trouble wasn't going to prison, the trouble was, *I'm embarrassed and I can't turn around*, you know. *I can't face it.*

DEAN FERTITA: I could sense him trying to figure out where he was in his life, after his home life kind of dissolved. He was one of those guys—I never thought that he wouldn't figure it out. He was always funny, he had a decent perspective on whatever he was going through. I did feel like he was searching, trying to figure out, *What do I do at this stage of my life? What do I really want?*

LYDIA TENAGLIA: We thought, *We'll catch Tony when he falls, like we always have. Right now, he's fucking infatuated, knee deep.* This was a really extreme case of it, but it was like, *OK, he's doing this now, but we'll all be here to hold the big basket when he falls out of this thing.*

49

"HE WAS LIKE A YOUNG KID IN LOVE"

JARED ANDRUKANIS: Near the end, when he was in love, he would talk to me more about his personal life. Which he never did before. It was strange.

HELEN CHO: Tony would call me and Jon [Heindemause, Helen's partner] to have dinner much more frequently toward the end of his life. He wasn't in New York very often, but when he would come back, he'd text me: "Are you in the city? Do you guys want to have dinner?" It wasn't weird for him to ask if we wanted to have dinner, but the frequency, the intensity, did alarm me.

We would go and watch movies at his place. He was really proud of that apartment; he wanted it to look like a hotel, like the Chateau Marmont. But I also saw it to be a lonely place. He would say, after we would hang out, "Thanks for the company." He talked about how "a lot more people are asking me for pictures when I walk down the street."

But, obviously, his relationship with a very toxic person—everybody wanted to intervene in that, everyone who knew him. He spoke so effusively about her to everyone around him, because he was trying to convince himself it was OK. Everyone knew that that was toxic for him. He knew that, too, you know? But there was nothing that anyone could really do. I had spoken to him about it. I know other close people had, too. It was something that I just knew he wasn't gonna listen to. In fact, I knew he was gonna do the opposite, which is what he did.

DAVE CHANG: The last time I saw Tony was when Peter Meehan and I were getting "divorced" [over the fate of their business ventures]. Tony really mentored us, me and Pete. When we would have disagreements over the years, we'd always go to Tony, to be King David and to arbitrate.

It was spring 2017, right before *Lucky Peach* closed, and I remember he had just moved into the Time Warner Center, and we were trying to catch up for some time. We met at the Coliseum, which was a cook's bar late at night, and in the daytime it was pretty empty.

He ordered the fucking weirdest thing—curry fries. Then we go to Porter House New York [in the Time Warner Center] for dinner, and I was like, "Tony, you're living in a fucking prison."

I could see how fucking weird and plastic his life was becoming. We sat down, ordered an incredibly expensive bottle of wine, like way more than I thought we were gonna spend, and I just started to go into detail of everything that was happening, and just how fucking unhappy I was. Then he starts to tell me about his separation from Ottavia, and he said, "Well, I'm in love again." It was one of those moments where Tony's so euphoric in something that you know that it's irrational.

Man, he was fucking madly in love with her. Just the way he was talking about her, I was like, "Tony you sound like a fucking ninth grader! What's wrong with you?"

But I wasn't going to tell him anything. It was hard to criticize him, as a friend.

BILL BUFORD: My own take, just from glimpses, but they were kind of strange glimpses—Tony was insecure with women, and they brought out a kind of wild intimacy, brought out a kind of wild vulnerability in him, that his active, hyperactive, slightly-bordering-on-manic productivity would never suggest that he had. Tony kind of liked being an uncomfortable member of a male club. But, fundamentally, he had a very nervous relationship with women.

His relationship with [Nancy] seemed almost like she was his mother. When I met Ottavia, we were doing a library event, Tony, me, and Mario [Batali]. Tony was all excited by the event, and he was very excited about the fact, I think, that Ottavia was coming. I remember when he said, "I can't wait for Mario to see Ottavia."

And it was almost adolescent. It was certainly disjunctive. And connected to what I'd seen with his first wife, I thought, *This is a person who's got a complicated relationship to women*. And it doesn't surprise me that they split up, just for the simple reasons of Tony's life.

He was profoundly, darkly vulnerable. That was all I got from my little glimpses. None of those things are normal things.

NATHAN THORNBURGH: I remember when he first— We were in Catalonia, filming the [*Roads & Kingdoms*] series we did out there with him in February 2017. It was the first time he had talked to me about Asia. He started flipping through her Instagram and he was like,

"She's trouble." Matt [Goulding] and I were just kind of looking at each other like, *Are you fucking seventeen?* The foment around her, I would say that was a noticeable change in him, and I had been working with him long enough to know that that was unusual.

JOSÉ ANDRÉS: He was in love. He was like a young kid in love.

DAVE McMILLAN: He was an adult man who fell in love with a girl like a sixteen-year-old boy falls in love with the first girl who gives it up. That's how it felt. We were in the car; Fred [Morin] and I were, like, rolling our eyes, and he was going on and on in the front seat. I was like, "What are you? Sixteen?"

My ex asked me, "How is Tony? What's with that relationship?" Which, by that time, was all in the press.

I said, "I don't know, man, but it's fucking heavy. That relationship is so fucking intense, it reminds me of your first love of your life who really ripped your heart out of your chest."

LYDIA TENAGLIA: He was emotionally immature. In eighteen years, he didn't evolve much emotionally. He became this great cultural anthropologist whom everyone so loved, but fundamentally he was like a teenage boy with his emotional development. He'd get into these relationships and kind of become somebody else. His whole life he gravitated toward these extremes of high and low.

CHRIS COLLINS: He'd go all in. He was never going to have a consistent relationship. I mean, that's not the partners he chose; that's Tony. He wasn't capable of engaging in what is necessary.

HELEN CHO: He was the most brilliant person, but when it came to love, it seemed like he was just back to being a seventeen-year-old kid who just couldn't help himself and wasn't gonna listen. He pushed people away, people whom he had been loyal to for years. He left his base. He was not in his right mind.

He knew it, too. He was a smart guy. He knew what he was doing, and he couldn't help himself, and it was paralyzing to witness, and I felt very helpless.

I told him. I said, "You're playing with fire. You know that, right?" And he's like, "Yeah, I absolutely know, but what can I do? She loves me."

That was worth burning everything else to the ground.

ALISON MOSSHART: In Tony, you've got this person who is so in control, so opinionated, so quick, so sharp, so observant, and at the same time, someone who is a fifteen-year-old boy, who's so not observant of what everyone is receiving from you. This is extreme behavior. In a positive, it's beautiful behavior, but there has to be some sort of a balance. There wasn't.

Everybody's guilty of this a little bit, when you start dating someone and you're in love. You take on some things about that person; you sort of melt into one person. But there's got to be separation. You are two people, you've got two life histories. Some things started to vanish with him. I couldn't see him.

NARI KYE: The beautiful thing about Tony, he's very passionate about something, and he really gives it his all, you know, in his work, in his writing, in his shows, in everything. And I think that's what happened with this woman. He got obsessed, and the obsession got dark.

PAULA FROELICH: He needed and he liked being challenged in not-obvious ways. And he really appreciated and loved smart women.

But we can all get in a rut. You find yourself, perhaps, hanging out with the wrong crowd. And it has nothing to do with the crowd. It's really your masochism. There was a streak of masochism [in Tony], and it definitely plays into a long-standing trope of live fast, die young, that he would always claim to want, but then, if you dug deeper, he'd be like, "Yeah, I don't. I don't want that at all."

I wish that Tony had been mature enough to know that he needed to be careful. Because I think he had always just had it, in a fucked-up way, handed to him.

DAVID SIMON: My time for being a friend of Tony's where he could be a little intimate about what he was feeling personally was a very short window. I didn't know him when he got married. I didn't know him in earlier relationships. I knew this moment of him going to Italy and blowing up his life and falling head over heels. It felt like a glorious midlife misadventure. I wasn't judging it. I get it. The power of the new romance is relentless. And it's always there. And that it happened, it didn't seem inevitable that it happened, but it didn't seem implausible, either.

He said, "This is the best thing that's ever happened to me in life. This is everything. She's perfect." I was hearing the power of new.

MARIA BUSTILLOS: The way he was in love, and described being in love, I would have been concerned if I'd been one of his friends. And I'm not saying that in retrospect; I thought it then [in February 2018], for sure. He didn't go for five minutes without saying, "Asia thinks this" and "Asia thinks that." He sounded like a person who was deeply infatuated, obsessed, even, and it struck me as a vulnerability in him.

Just the way that the idea of who he was when he was alone was so bound up with this lady, that was concerning. I would have been concerned.

DAVID SIMON: The new romance—all the places where you've shit the bed in life, those get scrubbed clean, and you get to start over and be charming and be charmed by the new person. I experienced Tony going through that with Asia, though I never met her.

She was the new person with him, and it was powerful, and it was kid-like, in a way that we're all kid-like at that moment. Show me an eighty-year-old widower who takes up with a seventy-five-year-old widow at the nursing home in Florida, and he's going through the same emotions while they play canasta in the community room. That's just who we are; it's what long-term relationships are battling all the time. You have familiarity and trust and history and love and shared sense of purpose, but you don't have new. And the new person, you get to start painting all over again. And so I saw him in that moment where he was painting all over again with somebody he was in love with.

ALISON MOSSHART: It's so strange. Tony—as Tony as he was in his work, and his actual personality, and what he's like with his friends—everything about that guy was like a fucking dream. And then there was 5 percent of him, his psyche, that was strangely not matching with anything else. He wanted to be loved so much, but in this insatiable kind of way. There was that need, or that addict part, that he just couldn't let go of, that came in to fuck up all the brilliant shit in his life, made it impossible for him to enjoy it.

Nobody's perfect, nobody makes the right decisions all the time. There was just this slight disconnect, and it fucked him.

DAVE CHANG: He told me, "I'm done. I can't carry the load for everyone; I have to make myself happy. I'm just going to disappear and move to Italy and grow old with Asia, and that's it. I'm gonna let the guys at ZPZ know. I'm done with it all."

50

"EVERY GOOD BAND EVENTUALLY BREAKS UP"

CHRIS COLLINS: In 2017, there was an epic, epic meeting between me, Lydia, and Tony. We went to some Irish bar. I'm sure at that moment, he was walking in to call it a day, and we were walking in with 100 percent clarity. Lydia and I stopped outside, looked at each other, and said, "If it's done, it's done. There's going to be no tears. It's going to be fine for all of us." Because it had reached a breaking point. We had, for the better part of that year, been avoiding him as much as possible.

LYDIA TENAGLIA: Because he was behaving really poorly.

CHRIS COLLINS: It was not productive for business and, mostly, the relationship. There was no talking about stuff; and it had just become too much; and Tony had enough people sucking up to him where he could get that. I don't think we ever fulfilled on that level, buying into the bullshit. Could we have been there for him more? Maybe, I don't know.

LYDIA TENAGLIA: Kim [Witherspoon] had even staged an intervention with us and Tony, before this meeting, because things had gotten so bad. And then we had that meeting in the bar; he became really dramatic.

His opening salvo was, "Look, guys, every good band eventually breaks up. They just come to the end of their run. It's just better to go our separate ways, and I think we've reached that point."

Then he launched into all the shit that we didn't do.

CHRIS COLLINS: It was just Tony unloading about stuff that wasn't done, and what he needed, and probably part of it was right. I'm not saying we were perfect, by no means. There was a fair amount of jealousy, on his part, that we, as a company, had grown. He had grown out his work world, and we were no longer the center of each other's worlds.

LYDIA TENAGLIA: This was somebody who, for whatever reason, was hurting emotionally in his own life, so it was, *Now I'm going to shit on the people who I know will always be there, regardless of how poorly I behave.*

So when he said, "We're done, it's over," Chris and I are like, "OK, got it."

CHRIS COLLINS: "We're good."

We had built this Tony thing together, and he built his Tony thing off to the side, and we built ZPZ into a bigger company. So when this came, we were ready for it, and I don't think he thought we were going to be ready. And we weren't bluffing when we said, "We got it, we hear you."

And then Lydia and Tony, in Lydia-and-Tony fashion, proceeded to argue and argue and argue. Tony said, "I just want to go away, live in Italy." Lydia said, "We support you. Put your jacket on, get up, and go." He stood up, put his jacket on, and stood there. They kept arguing.

LYDIA TENAGLIA: I said to him, "You're full of shit." The subtext was, *You're yelling at us that the nature of our business and what you're doing is preventing you from going to be happy now.* I said, "You're completely in command of your own destiny. If you really want to go, why are you standing here?"

CHRIS COLLINS: We're in the upstairs of this bar, and I'm pretty sure there's a couple listening, and some guys behind us, and I'm thinking, *This is gonna end up in the papers*, because he was wearing a jacket that said BOURDAIN on it, the navy jacket.

It got to the point where I was now uncomfortable with him standing in the middle of this bar and I said, "Sit the fuck down. Sit the fuck down, right now." And he did. Then he fell apart.

LYDIA TENAGLIA: I think Zero Point Zero, me and Chris, the people he went out with on all these shoots, we were the long-term relationship that he was able to sustain, even though he yelled at us, and this and that. I don't know if he was truly capable of having a relationship in which you actually have to attend, do the relationship, be present, deal with all the shit, all the good and the bad and everything in between.

We were, to him, like a surrogate family. He knew that when he was really hurting, or having a hard time, or angry about something, he could shit all over us. And he did, many times over the years. I mean angry, angry shit. Angry letters, angry phone calls, nasty lashing out, and it hurt at the time. It caused unbelievable stress and anxiety—almost like, *Do we really need this kind of stress?*—but somehow, we knew we were Tony's family. We'd been together almost two decades, and who are you going to lash out to? You're going to lash out to the people you feel closest to.

I think he always realized when he had behaved badly or pushed it too far, and he would be conciliatory, in his way. It was never, "Hey, I'm sorry I was a dick," but he always came around in a different way. I don't think he was good at self-reflection, but [he knew], *There's only so much shit I can put my friends and loved ones through; I'd better say something.*

CHRIS COLLINS: There was a certain level of self-awareness; it didn't necessarily mean he was gonna change how he acted, but it gave him a moment of pause. More times than not, he would—not so much apologize as acknowledge poor behavior.

I saw it countless times in the field with him—he shows up an hour later, sort of contrite, just to you, not in front of anybody else, and says, "I fucked up." Doesn't mean he's not gonna do it again and again and again, but there was that sort of reflection.

Frankly, for me, it was part of his beautiful charm, that douchebaggery that manifested itself, that he could see through it, and apologize in his own way, which might be by sending a stupid fucking gift basket with fruit in it. He truly enjoyed that stuff. He liked the swag that came with some of what he did. He loved *flowers*. He wanted to do a gardening show. Maybe we should have done a gardening show; maybe we'd still be doing that gardening show.

51

"EMBRACING THE CHAOS"

ROME AND PUGLIA

Tony and Asia first worked together on the Rome episode of Parts
Unknown. *The following year, they collaborated on the Puglia
episode. After that, Asia directed and appeared in the Hong Kong
episode, and she was central to a shoot in Florence, three weeks before
Tony's death, that was never edited into an episode. She was also
slated to participate in a* Parts Unknown *shoot in India, in late
June 2018.*

JEFF ALLEN: The Rome and Puglia episodes were two totally different
experiences of making TV with Tony and Asia. In Rome [in 2016],
it was really challenging. It was our most ambitious episode to date.
I mean, every episode ended up being that, so it's not really saying
anything, but it truly was. We had gotten all the specialty cameras,
the biggest crew, and the most money we had ever invested in making the look of the show, with this Panavision kit, and grip trucks,

and dolly tracks, and storyboarding out shots, and really going for the boldest look ever, and that was so exciting.

Asia was supposed to be our fixer on that episode, but the reality is, a lot of the time, the people who have the best ideas might not have the best tools to execute those ideas practically. And that was the case in Rome. She had incredible access to characters and locations and ideas of what to shoot. Tony wanted her to give that to us, and then also expected of her, maybe naively, to find out how to do it, but she didn't offer that. She didn't know us, or trust us yet, so she was being very kind of standoffish about volunteering information or people to help us out, and that made it incredibly challenging.

We ended up planning a whole backup show, in the event that all her ideas just might not work, because they weren't happening, going into it. We bent over backward to make it all work, but we were terrified of her.

She is a fucking ballbuster. She's very strongly opinionated, and Tony knew she was really special, and we had to treat her like royalty. So not only were we supposed to rely on her for all this stuff to make the show, we also had Tony screaming, asking for updates, because we had to make it perfect for her. And the real world doesn't work like that when you're planning a travel show, with all the insane shit we do. In the end, we made it work, but it came at great cost. To Asia's credit, she ended up pulling together some amazing shit for us.

By contrast, Puglia [in 2017] was this magical experience. She was, like, our best friend, she was happy the whole time, and of course, Tony was in love and overjoyed that they were making a show together. And all that reverberated in our experience of making the episode. Puglia was insane for other reasons—southern Italy is extremely difficult to film in, because people aren't on time, and nothing's really planned until it happens, and we were filming with Francis Ford Coppola and his people, so the stakes were even higher.

But Asia was supportive, and when shit would go wrong, she'd say, "Don't worry. It's gonna be fine. We'll figure it out." And Tony was supportive of us.

And shit went *wrong*. I mean, in all of my days of being a producer and director, I'd never lost a filming day until Puglia, because the fixer had promised us to film in this *masseria*. We get there, and we had the whole Italian film crew setting up dolly tracks, prepping lighting, and Zach is building an insane lighting grid for this epic feast we're gonna have. We had invited fifty people to come, and everybody's cooking food, and planning, and there's dancers, and music. Guests are starting to show up, and then that shit gets shut down by the Italian equivalent of the FBI, because, apparently, the fixers had not brokered the right means of permission with the Italian government, and we had to cancel the whole thing.

I mean, we have only eight days to film an episode. Losing a whole day is insane, let alone a supercomplicated huge party, with fifty people, and guests, and food, and music. It was the scariest moment. It was fucking terrifying, and Asia and Tony were like, "This is hilarious. This is the best story ever. Don't worry, we'll figure it out."

Like, who are these people? Tony should have been furious at us, but they were incredibly supportive, and embracing the chaos, in a weird way that we had never seen before.

So that was different, for him to say, "Don't worry. You've had the worst day of your entire life in production? It's gonna be fine."

We ended up pulling it together, at about two in the morning, at a different *masseria*, and people showed up, and it was fucking magical. That was the last time I worked with Tony and Asia together. I know things changed, but from my perspective, we went out on top.

52

"WE BOLSTERED EACH OTHER'S INCORRECT ASSERTION THAT ASKING FOR HELP IS SOMEHOW A MISTAKE"

PATRICK RADDEN KEEFE: Tony always struck me as very, very—as far as people I've interviewed go—very self-aware. To this day, I don't know how much therapy he'd done.

JOSH HOMME: Oh, fuck. The amount of times we made fun of getting help in various ways. Talking about psychology together, like, "You're a stranger, right? Can I give you some money? Will you listen to this? Do you have any training whatsoever? No? I'm in." Taking potshots, to make each other laugh, that are categorically incorrect, without a single right thing, necessarily.

I had this discussion with him about therapy. I had a bad experience as a young man with a therapist, and it's terrified me from then on. He and I had talked about that. And we're making fun of it. We bolstered each other's incorrect assertion that asking for help is somehow a mistake.

Our hardships were strikingly similar, about feeling down and getting stuck in the molasses of depression. I'm glad I had this kind of existential relationship with him. And I miss it. And I also don't think, in this context, he took any of my advice, because look what happened.

ALISON MOSSHART: How old was he when he became famous? He was quite old [forty-four]. So you're always stuck in that time when you weren't famous yet. You're always stuck in whatever disaster of a life you had before that. That's just who you think you are. You don't just wake up and go, *It's all sorted out.* It's not. It's even cloudier, because you've got all this, and everybody thinks you're so great, and it's just like, *This is what kind of made me good, made me cool: having problems, having something to push against and fight against.* You know: being broke, being high, being in a bad relationship, something. So there's a tendency to repeat that, because you know that that works to get you to the next place.

PAULA FROELICH: I saw him a couple of years before he died, at an event, and he was just cordoned off by himself. Like, literally, they put him behind a velvet rope by himself. It was like he became the zoo animal, and he was so uncomfortable with it.

Being on CNN heightened his fame to a certain level where it became oppressive. I'm not blaming CNN. I'm quite thankful that he had the opportunity. But it *is* oppressive. Who the hell are you going to meet, you know? Like, how do you meet someone?

And then you had depressive tendencies, and you live a certain lifestyle that, to the outside, is everyone's dream, and you can't bitch about that, because they're like, *Oh my god, what do you mean?* Your brand is being adventurous and super cool—you can't ever let anyone not see that.

And then you're traveling, you don't even know what country you're in half the time, you know. You know shit because you get the information packet the day before. And you try to prep by reading certain books, but then you're traveling so much, you forget which book you've read. And have to be *on*. And being on is exhausting.

So, after shooting, you're just exhausted, because you've just been filming for eight hours. And then you just want to go and have a cuddle or touch base with someone, and have comfort.

What was great about Nancy, and me, and Ottavia, was that he had a home base to come home to. If you don't have that—we all absorb the energy around us, and who we choose to hang out with.

DAVID CHOE: I've done a lot of work on myself, and I'm not trying to be a detective, but it's very clear to me what happened. He was very depressed; he told me he was depressed and miserable.

I don't know very many people who are in the entertainment business, no matter how cool they are—and Tony's up there with the coolest—who aren't sick. You have to sort of be sick to be in this business. There's a lot of narcissism, there's a lot of ego, there's a lot of "not enough."

Is Tony, "the most interesting man in the world," allowed to ask for help? Because the place he was at, when he died, he was pretty much a god. Is a god allowed to come down to the mortals and say, "Hey, guys, I'm like you, I need help"? That takes a lot of surrender.

MIKE RUFFINO: There was a brutal moment, in the last year or so, when Tony just outright said, "I have no friends." And it just killed me.

I know what he meant, that he just didn't have the opportunity for normal friendships. It just made me think about how much he did for me, how many people he was protecting and helping; that also is gonna alter any relationship at least a little bit.

It's been a strange realization, to recognize how much normal friendship, that thing that didn't fit, just got kinda chucked off to the side. These things that are interfering with a normal life, you just accept them, but they have this impact that you can't change or predict.

People around him, myself included, would like to think that that's exactly where we could have helped, but how?

DAVE CHANG: I was at a crossroads in my life. I told Tony I wanted to figure out how to start a family, I would love to be a father, all these things. I was asking him advice, and—it's hard to even say—he said to me, "You're going to be a horrible father. You're going to fuck it up just like I did." It was fucking hard.

I know he didn't say that to hurt me. I know that it was him projecting, but it just crushed me. Then he went right back to talking about Asia, and I'm like, *What the fuck is happening?*

I don't really remember too much after that. He didn't know that he had hurt me, and I just tried not to show it. I think he was really talking about himself.

After that, he sent me an email, right when I got home, that said, "Be a fool for love, for yourself, what you think might possibly make you happy, even for a little while, whatever the cost or the consequence might be."

All I ever wanted was his approval. And as Tony's life got more and more insane, all I ever wanted was for him to be happy and to pursue what he wanted to do.

53

"CALL IT IMPOSTOR SYNDROME, IF YOU WANT, BUT TONY DEFINITELY HAD IT"

ALISON MOSSHART: Tony was like me or you, with real-life worries and issues and sadness. The guy who can figure out everything and is so incredibly observant can't come across like he's not, and like he doesn't know what he's doing.

It was incredible what he did for people. I always tried to explain to him what a gift he was giving, making people understand other people, other cultures; how important that was, the work he was doing. There was part of him that didn't understand what I was saying. He didn't feel any of that. He would change the subject. He wouldn't want to talk about that. He couldn't accept it. I think it was absolutely impossible for him to see it. I don't think that's totally unusual, but it was pretty extreme.

DAVID SIMON: I will say this: Tony did not believe, fully, any praise that was delivered to him unequivocally. I don't think he ever heard me say how good a writer he was, and I told it to him routinely, when he would turn in work, or after he would come up with ideas, or after I'd thank him for this last season of this and that storyline.

I don't believe it when people compliment me. It's part of being a writer. You know your bag of tricks, and you know what you've done before, and you know what you can't do or what you didn't reach. You sit down at the computer and you start typing and what you come out with is 85 percent of your intention, because nobody can get everything. And deadlines—even good writing is abandoned at a certain point.

And so you're not being grandiosely self-effacing when people are telling you you're a frigging genius, you're the best writer, this is the greatest—I love you, I love you, I love you. You're saying, *Calm the fuck down.* Call it Impostor syndrome, if you want, but Tony definitely had it. Even when he was at the top of his game, he'd be like, "Ah, that was a shitty episode." Which is how you have to be if you're going to get better, or stay on your game.

I never got a sense of any level of self-loathing that I took seriously. I have all kinds of memories of beautiful and comically delivered self-loathing, and "I'm so full of shit, but nobody will catch me now," laughing-at-himself sort of stuff, and I'd be lying if I said now I'm hearing it with a different ear because of his suicide. I don't think so. It was delivered in such a way that it seemed like the very wit of mental health.

JOHN LURIE, ARTIST: I don't think he knew really what he had. He did sort of seem to have a low self-esteem. Like, *I don't deserve this thing that I got.* He had a thing—I wouldn't call it self-hatred, but it was more like he felt he wasn't so important. There was something else, almost a saintliness, and I think that was why he was so beloved. I didn't see it until I met him in person, but I think others just felt it off the TV. And what is weird, or unfortunate, is that I don't think that he knew he had that. I can't think of hardly anybody I'd rather have in my corner than him.

The last thing I ever said to Tony was, "It's such a relief for me not to be famous anymore. I didn't know I hated it when I had it, but it's worse than drugs. It gives you this buoyancy that's false, but you can't explore your own soul and your own psychology." And he said, "Oh, I know, I'm completely agoraphobic. I don't like leaving the house."

We were talking about going out to eat. And I said, "I don't really want to go anywhere where I know anybody." He said, "I don't want to, either." There was a pain behind the eyes, but I didn't know him well enough to *really* see it.

He could have just disappeared for a couple of years. I'm sure he was polite to every fucking person who approached him, and that's just exhausting. Each one of those fans—it takes a little tiny chunk of your soul. It gives you very little back, and takes something from you. And some sick thing in you wants more of it.

54

"WE SHOULD DO SOMETHING TOGETHER"

KENYA WITH W. KAMAU BELL

W. KAMAU BELL, HOST OF *UNITED SHADES OF AMERICA* ON CNN: I was a comedian, not very successful, so there was a lot of sitting around, watching TV. I stumbled into that cable universe of *No Reservations*, *Dirty Jobs*, *MythBusters*—the kinds of shows that basically used to play on PBS, but the personalities are better, the hosts are better. They're allowing themselves to have fun with it. I remember thinking, *I'd like to have a show like that someday.*

Years later, I'm sitting in the CNN offices, having a general meeting, and my agent said, "They have an idea for a show for you." And that's when they told me about the show *United Shades of America*. I remember thinking, *Bourdain can pull this off.* Like, it didn't make him softer.

So I had the show at CNN, and I got nominated for an Emmy

the first year [2016]. I was just happy to be there, because I'd never put *that* in my dream journal. At the Emmy after-party, I thought, *I have to try and meet Tony.*

People think there's a CNN cafeteria where Don Lemon and Anderson Cooper and Erin Burnett and Tony and me are, like, you know, "Waffles are good today." It's not like that. I'd never run into him. And everything I had heard about him was that he doesn't suffer fools gladly. So I wanted to meet him, but I was prepared for him to not know who I am.

I looked over; he was talking to somebody. He looked my way, and his face lit up. He did the thing where I knew I was next in line. There was no, "Hi, my name is"—he knew me. He very quickly complimented the show and said, "We should do something together."

I just thought, *What a nice thing for him to say.* I've been around long enough in the business to know everything someone says to you, at some point, you have to realize it's just nice words.

My wife took a picture: you can see him looking like America's James Bond, and I look like I won a contest.

Months later, we did a cover shoot for the *Hollywood Reporter*, and again Tony said, "We should do something together."

[CNN executive] Amy [Entelis] was there, and she said, "Well, Kamau, where do you want to go?"

"I don't know, maybe we'll go to Oklahoma."

Amy said, "Remember, he goes all around the world."

I said, "Everyone's always told me I should go to Kenya," and to my immense surprise, Tony said, "I've never been to Kenya." It didn't seem like he had to be talked into it.

Then we had to wait until the schedules synced up. It took a whole year, you know—hurry up and wait.[*]

---

[*] *Tony and Kamau traveled to Kenya in February 2018 to shoot an episode of* Parts Unknown.

It was twenty-two hours of flying. I landed, went to the hotel, crashed, woke up in time for breakfast, and saw the crew—[director] Mo [Fallon]'s got a laptop and three phones working—and in the corner, Tony's by himself, smoking a cigarette. And it was like, *All right, I'll go say hello, but I'm not going to get in his space.* Hosting a show—sometimes there's too many people trying to get your time.

But he said, "Hey, man. Sit down," and we were off to the races.

Tony and the crew made me feel like I was one of the guys. Mo went out of his way to let me know that I was doing well, whether he knew I needed that or not. Maybe he knows that us people on camera need that.

And Tony—one of the first things we shot was us walking down the street on our way to this restaurant. I told him I'd never been to Africa. He said, "I'm going to be teasing you relentlessly about this, by the way."

It was clear that if he liked you, you got his energy and time. And if he didn't have use for you, you didn't. So many of us are giving it away to everybody, because that's the polite, societally acceptable thing to do. Maybe he had been like that his whole life. When he's done talking, he just sort of walks away; he's gone. He was protective of his time and energy.

When we went to see *Black Panther* in Nairobi, not for a scene, just for fun, it was such a big deal to me. "He wants to hang out!" One of the great pleasures of my life. They played the Kenyan national anthem before the film. And I'd already seen the movie, so I was, like, watching him watch it.

We discussed it afterward. He loved the race politics of *Black Panther*. He got it the same way that I got it, the same way that people in Oakland and all over the world—he totally got why this is a big thing. He's the example that other people need to follow. He used white privilege as a tool for good, not as a bludgeon.

We talked about our kids a lot; he talked about his daughter, how they were friends. He talked about Ottavia, bragged about how she was choking people out in jiu-jitsu. We talked a lot about our lives.

He was talking about being on a lecture tour. He said, "Some people have jokes, and I've sort of run out of jokes."

And I told him, "You don't actually need jokes. People just want to hear what you've done since the last time you were in that town." And I feel like he really took the note. I thought, *What am I doing, giving him a note?* But I do know a lot about live performance.

The thing that is so clear to me is that everyone was there in service of Tony. That was what they'd signed up for. They were in the Anthony Bourdain army. Didn't mean it was fun all the time, but they very much believed in the mission. The whole thing was in service of what Tony needed, in a way that on my show, it was not. I learned a lot.

Tony showed me that you can both leave it all on the court, so to speak, in a way that's healthy for you, but also have a line, and don't let people cross it. And if you are clear about it, other people will hold your line for you.

I would have paid for that—you know, master classes, Neil Gaiman teaches you how to write, or whatever? I would have paid to go to *Parts Unknown* camp and not even be in the show, just be around it. I didn't expect it to be that valuable.

He spent a lot of time on camera asking questions, and then sort of sitting back and waiting. When he sat down at those tables, he never sat at the head. He let the person in charge sit at the head, and he took a seat. And it's clear Tony had a huge ego. You can't work in TV, on camera, and not have an ego. But it was like, *My ego demands I know this. My ego demands I experience this*, and not, *My ego demands that you watch me do this.* He didn't need to prove to you how smart he was.

When he passed away, I thought about the [*Parts Unknown Kenya*] scene on the side of the hill, where we're looking out over the animals. I told myself when I went there, *I'm not going to be too cool for school that I don't tell this man how important he is to me.* I've lost people before. You have to let people who are important know it.

So we shot the scene on the side of the hill, and then he called for wides. We were still mic'ed, but they weren't looking for content from us. They'd pulled the cameras.

We were chugging gin and tonics for the shot. And I was like, *All right, I can feel my feelings now.* I told him how surreal it was for me to be sitting there after watching him on TV for years, and how it's pretty cool. Things are going OK for me.

He leaned in and said, "As soon as the cameras turn off, and the crew will be sitting around having a cocktail, I'll fucking pinch myself. I cannot fucking believe that I get to do this." And the way his voice was, it was beautiful. It was not the guy on TV. It was Tony.

55

"I KNEW *SOMEONE* WAS DOOMED"

HONG KONG

Shortly before the Hong Kong episode of Parts Unknown *aired on CNN, Tony published an essay in the* Hollywood Reporter *about the experience of making it:*

On *Parts Unknown*, we reference films frequently—and whenever possible, invite filmmakers I admire to talk about their work and the places that inform it. . . . I have long been particularly besotted with the work of Wong Kar Wai's frequent collaborator and director of photography, Christopher Doyle. For me, he was always the Big Kahuna. For years now, every time I visit Hong Kong, I can't look at it without thinking of his incredible work on such films as

Fallen Angels, Chungking Express and his masterpiece, *In the Mood for Love.*

My highest hope was that someday, just maybe, we could convince the man, known locally by his Mandarin name, Du Kefeng, to appear on camera, talk about the city he'd lived and worked in for 30 years, and tell us what he looked for when he looked at Hong Kong through his lens. Secretly, I hoped we might convince him to pick up a camera to shoot a few seconds of B-roll—just so I could tell people, "I worked with Christopher Doyle!"

To my surprise and eternal gratitude, after years of my reaching out, Doyle agreed to appear on my show. Plans were made, tickets bought, equipment packed. ["Anthony Bourdain: My 'Cinematic Dream' Filming with Asia Argento and Christopher Doyle (Guest Column)," *Hollywood Reporter*, June 2, 2018]

SANDY ZWEIG: I always felt like we had a relationship of mutual respect, one that was fairly straightforward and honest. I do think that that changed with Asia, because then I felt like there was really only one focus. Certainly, that Hong Kong episode [of *Parts Unknown*] was another turning point.

[Director] Michael Steed had to have his gallbladder removed, and we needed to replace him as a director on very short notice.

When Tony found out, it became an "It's my way or the highway" kind of thing. And that meant Asia directing. And the fact that that hadn't been our first thought, it really angered him. I got a call at eleven something at night, and when I talked to him—I mean, I'd never dealt with him when he was that angry.

I feel terrible saying this, but there did feel like there was some sort of desperation in his voice about, somehow, if she directed, that would kind of solidify something, or they would be collaborating again, and that somehow would make his life better.

NICK BRIGDEN: I think there was an obvious distraction in that final year, a vampiric kind of energy suck that, you know, Tony could be on the other side of the world, and still that cyclone would be sucking him in. Once it started bleeding into the work, it was surprising. There was a lot of confusion within the crew. There was a lot of concern.

LIZZIE FOX: When I sort of had a little alarm ring for me was when he shot Hong Kong, the one that Asia directed. That's when I was like, "There's an issue here," just because of what happened on that shoot, how that all went down. That was my first red flag.

MICHAEL STEED: I say this jokingly but, having to direct this Hong Kong episode, then me losing the gallbladder—I often blame my gallbladder as the sort of beginning of the end of Tony's life, weirdly.

The second that I knew that [Asia] was slated to direct, I knew it was doomed; I knew *someone* was doomed. I had already planned on how I was going to keep Tony's focus off of having [guest cinematographer] Christopher Doyle take over. I knew [cinematographer] Zach [Zamboni] was not going to be cool with it. But, man, once Asia took over, I was just like, *Oh boy.*

JARED ANDRUKANIS: When I met [Asia] the first time, it was in New York, at a VO [voice-over] session. She came in and was wrapped up in this shawl, or giant scarf thing, very quiet. She's, like, sitting there, and her presence was so—she could expand into this massive fiery thing, and also compress to this weird little dwarf.

Tony was in the booth and just rips through his lines like he always does, just blasts through four pages of narration. Does the whole thing in like fifteen minutes. He comes out of the VO booth and is bouncing around and asks her, "Hey what did you think?" She's like, "*That's* what you fucking complain about all the time?"

When I got to Hong Kong, I met with them in the hotel room that they shared.[*] I walk into the room, it's a nonsmoking hotel, and the room is a cloud of smoke. There's just papers everywhere, and she's full-tilt smoking, going through the schedule, tearing apart all the work that we did, which is fine, I mean she's directing the episode, and we're support for her, but . . . I didn't want to interact with her at all, because I knew it would just be dangerous for my career. It's a weird feeling, one I never had on any shoot before. She had snapped at me so many times that first meeting.

MATT WALSH: She was not rude to me, but her influence on the whole thing—it was Yoko Ono in a Beatles recording session. She didn't bring anything to the table.

Things got weirder once we got out to [the fishing village] Tai O. Asia felt that Zach was taking too long to set up the scene. That's, I think, that was where things broke.

But, Tony being such a fanboy of Christopher Doyle, there's no— He had extra-thick rose-colored glasses on for the whole experience.

JARED ANDRUKANIS: Tony changed. The way that she operated as a director, which was so opposite to the way the directors he liked to work with acted, showed me very clearly— Actually, in the show, when Asia and Christopher Doyle interrupted him, midscene, to

---

[*] *Andrukanis was one of two producers on the Hong Kong episode of* Parts Unknown.

move a fucking light and change the blocking of the scene—if I did that, if any of us did that, he would have wanted to murder us. [In that scene] he was talking to two literal refugees, but he goes, "No, no, fix the light."

I see now that the work thing went out the door, for her. And I was like, *Oh, shit, this is bad.* This is one of those kind of relationships that can push someone with a code like Tony's, like his top ten rules, she could blow that out in a second in front of the entire world. I didn't really know how to deal with that with him.

MATT WALSH: I understood her frustration with Zach.* Many of us got frustrated with Zach, because he's such a perfectionist. I love Zach, and I learned so much from him. But the deeper he got into feature film work, the more he carried that kind of work approach into the scenes for Tony, and we just weren't able to do that. I respect what he wanted to do, but we weren't building sets to work on, or spending tens of thousands of dollars to lock down a set, so you could spend six hours lighting it. The old run and gun [approach] was acceptable-enough quality. Losing patience with Zach the artiste is, I think, reasonable. And Asia lost patience with Zach on that.

JARED ANDRUKANIS: Tony called me a couple of times that night, drunk. He told me I had to send Zach home that night, and I could hear her in the background, just screaming, "It's me or him!" Pressuring this guy to [fire] one of his friends. Tony knew that this move . . . It's like, you can never see this person again, you have to fuck up his job, get him fired, and make him embarrassed for the rest of his life.

---

* *A few days into shooting the Hong Kong episode, tension over creative differences between the director, Asia Argento, and the director of photography, Zach Zamboni, came to a head.*

I said, "I'm not gonna send him home tonight. It's midnight, and I've had five beers. We're going to deal with it tomorrow; please don't do anything until we talk tomorrow morning," because I wanted them to sleep it off and maybe change their minds.

It sucks, because he was not operating logically, but he didn't want to upset her.

MATT WALSH: My heart was breaking for Zach. It wasn't nice to be around.

JARED ANDRUKANIS: I sat and talked with Zach for three hours in his hotel room, then I went to scene. I won't speak for him, but can you imagine what that felt like for him? In front of everybody? Zach was the senior DP [director of photography] on the Hong Kong shoot, and had brought on the AC [camera assistant] personally. And he ended up getting canned.*

Zach and the other DPs were responsible for how the world saw Tony as the show evolved. They had the burden of delivering on higher and higher demands, as the cinematic scope grew and grew. You'll hear that we all have pretty particular relationships at work, but Tony *loved* the camera guys. He knew they made him look good. Made us all look good, really. And Zach was one of three people who did that job, consistently, for over a decade. All untouchables, really. Or so I thought.

The only good part was that we clearly could figure out a way to utilize this newfound enjoyment of making television; as Tony had said on Twitter [about shooting in Hong Kong], "Making TV is fun again." Christopher Doyle shot Tony riding in the back of the Star Ferry. I mean, no one lives that life, and that's amazing. I'm happy

---

* *Zach Zamboni declined to be interviewed for this book.*

that he was happy. His happiness was also a wonderful thing for us to see.*

Shortly after Zach was fired, Asia wanted to walk Tony through a throng of tourists [for a shot] because it looked cool. Usually [with Tony] that's a "No, you're fucking crazy." You might even get fired if you suggest that at this point in his career. And he didn't know that this was coming up—another rule was "No surprises"—so he'd gone to his hotel for downtime. And another rule was, "Don't fuck with my downtime." I call him, ready for some pushback, and he answers right away, and I'm like, "Asia was wondering if you could maybe take a walk from your hotel?" He's like, "Yep, when do you need me there? I'll be ready."

We meet at the hotel; I'm there in five minutes, and he's already ready. We're walking under this underpass to get to where Asia is waiting for him. He turned to me and said, "I had to do it." It was the first time he had ever said anything like that to me; I knew what he was talking about, because clearly it's been on his mind, that he had to fire his DP whom he trusted for a good twelve years. Zach was one of the biggest heads you could go after. He's like, "I had no choice. I love her."

I told him, "I know you had to, and I understand why you did it . . . but it doesn't make it OK." He was like, "I know, I know, I know." But he didn't get mad at me for calling him out on that part.

We were all like family at that point, especially the people who

---

* *Tony closed the* Hollywood Reporter *essay with the following lines:*
   "It was the most intensely satisfying experience of my professional life and a show that I am giddily, ecstatically proud of. I plan to get a Du Kefeng tattoo, in the original Mandarin, as soon as possible. As you might have guessed, I already have an Asia Argento tattoo." ["Anthony Bourdain: My 'Cinematic Dream' Filming with Asia Argento and Christopher Doyle (Guest Column)," Hollywood Reporter, June 2, 2018.]

had been with him for so many years, but now we were all of a sudden expendable, if his girlfriend hates us.

He put a lot of everything in that basket—he shoveled his work life, his personal life, he shoveled his persona into his relationship, and that is a recipe for fucking disaster, no matter who you are.

MIKE RUFFINO: When he got back after Hong Kong, he came through LA, and he said, "I'm coming in. We're having dinner." It was during that dinner conversation that I got a little . . . I guess *worried* is the word. Because his take on what had happened in Hong Kong did not jibe with what I understood. He was thanking me for putting together the band [that appeared in the episode], along with arranging a couple of other things. I'm like, "What band? What are you talking about?" I had done none of it. It was all [producer] Helen [Cho].

Whatever work Helen had done, he thought *I* had done, because Asia, I guess—she was trying to kind of maneuver Helen out of her position with Tony. I'd never had that experience before, where he was not on top of it. I mean, there were times when he may have had people keeping information from him, for one reason or another. It was not serious then, or he just didn't give a shit, but never before was there a deliberate [attempt at] misinformation. He didn't understand it. And I didn't understand it. But, at the same time, his level of commitment [to her] seemed to be getting even deeper. So I was a little unsettled.

MICHAEL STEED: She had made her way into the inner circle, and now was being treated as a director—and she brought nothing to the fucking table. All the decisions that were made in that episode, I manipulated her into believing these decisions were hers and could be good. It was a whole game I played with both of them, to make sure the [Hong Kong] episode was something, because she was giving nothing. I put all the footage up and said, "Let me know; I wasn't there."

I was making sure that Tony saw that Asia had control, because there was no rational person in him at that point. I knew that my input was only going to be filtered through her, and I also wanted the episode to be good, and make sense.

56

"YOU CAN'T PUT YOUR ARMS AROUND A MEMORY"

NEW YORK, ASTURIAS, FLORENCE

The last few episodes of Parts Unknown *that Tony shot, in the spring of 2018, included Indonesia; West Texas; Asturias, Spain; and Florence, Italy. The final new episode to air on CNN was "Lower East Side," which used an experimental style to take a clear-eyed look at a fast-changing downtown Manhattan neighborhood where Tony spent time as a young man. It was shot in April 2018.*

MICHAEL STEED: I wanted to break the fucking show, you know? We're talking about an era in the Lower East Side, we wanted to stay true to that era, and try to make an art film that people needed to watch. All that music was chosen beforehand. The last track ["You Can't Put Your Arms around a Memory"] was something Tony [chose].

The walk-around scenes, through New York—he hated fucking doing those scenes. It's a trope. He walks as fast as he can, gets to Tompkins Square Park, we turn the cameras off, de-mic him, and he says to me, "Oh, I'm going to just walk over to Fourth [Street] and [Avenue] B and just look at my old spot, where I used to score shit," and I'm like, "All right, dick." And then, "Cameras, go."

That little moment at the beginning, where I'm kind of on camera, asking him questions and he's talking to me—that moment still really chokes me up. Once he freed himself from a mic, he was really just talking to me; it was true fucking vérité, that perfect sort of moment where he's just revealing and vulnerable. Just telling a story, like he would at a crew meal or something.

JOHN LURIE: I had a dream that me and Tony were on the radio, talking about how to curb your Twitter addiction. And I came downstairs, opened my email, half-awake, and I saw [an email from Tony]: "Would you like to be on *Parts Unknown*? We're doing the Lower East Side, nothing too sentimental." He must have been writing it at the exact same moment as I was having the dream.

I wasn't that hopeful . . . I didn't think I was gonna dislike him, but I just thought, *This'll be good for me, to be on the show. Maybe I can get my paintings in there.*

The crew was just— I hate having people in my apartment. There's always that one asshole who needs attention, [but] they were just the nicest. I was happy to have them here, which never happens. I thought, *Well, is that a trickle-down from Tony? Or has Tony lucked himself into this situation?* And then he just kind of walks in, and I liked him immediately. He was just so unassuming. And he's also kind of awkward, but kind of elegant at the same time, which I just love. And he has an apple juice. And then—he's got all these people here who are basically working for him, and I've got my assistant—and the motherfucker goes and washes his own glass.

ARIANE BUSIA-BOURDAIN: We were in this old Italian restaurant [John's of 12th Street], and I was at the table right behind him, and he was filming with this guy who painted with, like, one hair [Joe Coleman].*

JOE COLEMAN: We talked about the Lower East Side and danger; part of the thrill with copping drugs back then, too, was, you go into an abandoned building and the cops might arrest you, or you might get shot by someone who wants your money. And you can get a bag of poison that you go shoot up, instead of heroin. You have no idea what you're going to get, but that is part of the excitement of being addicted to drugs. We both went through a lot of the same experiences. We learned about life from a period of chaos.

ARIANE BUSIA-BOURDAIN: It was kind of chaos, because there were a bunch of people coming into the restaurant at once, and people filming outside. But it was fun, and I think he was happier that I was there. And then after that, he took me to this little place, Trash and Vaudeville, and bought me some really high platform boots, and checkered jeans, and these really cool spiky choker things. When we got home, I was expecting my mom to be mad, but she was like, "Oh, that's really cool." So I ended up wearing that to one of my concerts.

NICK BRIGDEN: Asturias [Spain], with José Andrés, was the last episode I did with Tony [in April 2018]. I didn't see it or notice it, until I got

---

* *Tony's daughter, Ariane Busia-Bourdain, visited him on the Lower East Side set one day, shortly before her eleventh birthday.*

back home and really was looking closely at the footage, but there was—weariness? There was a weight that—when we were shooting that episode, it just wasn't registering, because there was so much on my plate. It was a tricky episode to do, logistically. But looking back on it now—and I remember watching the footage and seeing—there was a weight. He was carrying something deep and internal. I think he was expending a lot of energy, just processing what was happening outside the shoot, in his life. And I didn't know at the time what that was, but now, knowing, the pieces come together.

Also, we had put together some jiu-jitsu sparring in Spain, and he had wrenched his back, because some guys went at him really hard, and he hadn't been training a lot. So, toward the end of the shoot, he was in physical pain, and certainly he needed to alleviate that physical pain with whatever he had on hand.

JOSÉ ANDRÉS: We were in this place where my father and mother [were] married, these beautiful lakes that are mythical in Asturias, where I was born. These beautiful lakes, and the sun was so high, and in the mountains, it is rare that the clouds and the blue sky all at once, and the cows. We were looking back at it all, but the cameramen wanted that view behind us, as we were talking to each other, so we were looking at the bathrooms. It's TV, I realize. Tony was like, "What the fuck are we doing? Why are we talking about how beautiful Asturias is, and we're looking at the ugly fucking bathrooms?"

NICK BRIGDEN: There were a lot of factors contributing to a heavy disposition on the Asturias shoot, but we had some great times, some really authentic, lovely, beautiful times. And Tony was never a physical guy, but he had a last scene with José, a big meal scene, we drank a lot, and it was just such a high note. We were getting him into the car to get to the airport, and he just gave me a big hug. That was the first hug I ever got from him, and that was the last time I saw him.

JARED ANDRUKANIS: The last time I saw Tony, he was really happy, I remember, because he was going to Florence in a few days.

SANDY ZWEIG: When we were getting ready to shoot the Florence episode [in May 2018], Tony asked what we could afford to pay Asia, and what did producers make? He was surprised, I think, at the number, how little that was. He then said he would supplement that, in order to pay her more. So I think he clearly was looking for ways for her to be involved, but I also think, ways for her to be gainfully employed.

MORGAN FALLON: I did not want to be on a show with Asia. I especially did not want to direct a show with her involved, because I knew it was basically her show. Tony had so empowered her that even shows that she wasn't involved in, I was getting notes from her.

The psych rock segment [on the *Parts Unknown* Nigeria episode] was a perfect example of it. We were not talking about the problems [in Nigeria] so much, but about the tremendous depth of potential. And then, plastered in the middle, is this archaic scene about Nigerian psych rock that didn't make a whole lot of sense in the context of the show, but it was a mandate that came down from Asia. And, by the way, it was super expensive to license [the music].

That whole genre of music was a reaction to the Biafran War, so we were able to make this narrative left turn into the fallout of the war, and a larger statement about antimilitary, antiestablishment [sentiment], and move that into the Kuti family. It happened on the fly; that whole scene came together in twenty-four hours, because we got a message from on high. And that proved the theorem that I didn't want to do a show with her.

Lo and behold, the next season, I got assigned a show with her, the Florence episode. I said, "This is your show; you just tell me what to do." That wasn't a hill to die on. I had no particular attachment to Florence.

She's super smart, and she's a good character, and Tony was just frankly really into it. And [at times], she came out with extraordinary venom, cutting down ideas, cutting down scenes that she had approved, characters that she had given the thumbs-up to, and was into, the day before. She was volatile, and that was really hard to navigate.

Luckily, my wife [Gillian Brown, who was the episode producer] and I ended up making this incredible show, the lost episode of *Parts Unknown*, which will never be seen.

At the end of the Florence shoot was the happiest I have ever seen Tony. That's what fucking hurts so much. I said goodbye to him on this gorgeous sunny spring day in Santa Maria Novella Square. He was fucking glowing, gave us huge hugs. He had talked to my wife the night before and said, "I love doing this with you. We're gonna do this many, many times again. I just signed for another three years." And that was it. That was the last time I ever saw him.

JOSH HOMME: The last conversation, we were on the mend. We ended up talking about being lonely on the road. I said, "You know what? We should take our daughters on the road and let them experience our lives." And he said, "Yeah, I'm gonna do that."

And then he said, "I know it's been difficult to be my friend lately. And the shoe will be on the other foot, I promise you, and I know you'll be there."

ALISON MOSSHART: The last email he sent me was like a week before he died, and it was really sweet. It was because Ariane came to my gig in Brooklyn, and then she went home, and she was really excited about it, and he said, "I've never seen my daughter so happy in my life." That was the last I heard from him. I hadn't heard from him in a number of months. Really, after the Josh [Homme] thing, I didn't hear from him again.

DAVID SIMON: I will say, in my last conversations with him, especially that one at [Coliseum], where we drank ourselves silly, he was head over heels for [Asia]. And if it didn't work out, it would put him in a trough, as it might have put anybody in a trough if you're in a relationship with somebody whom you really care about.

I also know that he was a tangle of emotions about his ex-wife and his daughter. He had upended a lot, and he was spinning. He was living life at a high rate of speed, and at some pretty acute vectors, bouncing around. Grafted onto all of that was the travel. He was living life in a metal cocoon, traveling from one part of the world to the next. All of that can unground an even very sensible person. But I'm speculating now, and I'm doing it in retrograde, because I didn't have any sense of it.

57

"ALL OK"

ALSACE

In the first week of June 2018, Tony and the ZPZ crew, along with Eric Ripert, went to Alsace, France, to shoot an episode of Parts Unknown, *directed by Michael Steed.*

MICHAEL STEED: The first day, he was fine. We shot a fairly benign scene with Eric [Ripert] and Tony, eating the pot-au-feu.

The next day, I was shooting Tony and Eric riding through wine country, getting wide shots of those guys riding this fucking tandem bike. I have a picture of it on my phone, and every time I see it, I think, *Oh my god, this must have been the final straw.* It's either crying or joking, right?

They had to wait, we had to set up cameras, go down the hill, stop, resets, resets, real big wides, so there was a lot of waiting and driving back to location. At a certain point, I see Tony, and he's so pissed. He comes up to me and says, "I just want to go back to the fucking hotel. I don't want to fucking miss lunch."

And I said, "Tony, we'll get you to fucking lunch, man. This is all you're doing today. All you gotta do is ride this fucking bike down to the bottom of the fucking hill."

LYDIA TENAGLIA: [Director] Mike [Steed] touched base with us right away, first or second day of the shoot. He said, "Something's off, Tony's off; he's in a kind of dark mood. I don't know what's going on." I texted him: "Hey, you doing OK, you wanna talk? If there's anything we can help with, please let us know."

He just wrote back, "All OK."

MICHAEL STEED: The next day, we're filming at this fourth-generation, five-star French restaurant where the grandma feeds bread to the geese every day. Before lunch, two beautiful women are giving these two old men [Tony and Eric] massages. It's everything he likes, with a guy he really digs, and he can go take a quick nap before we set up for lunch. And he's a grump. He said something to [producer] Big Josh [Ferrell] that was not jokey, kind of mean.

Then he has the meal, has a couple of drinks, and he's talking to Eric about French food, but also about shitty New York hot dogs, and choking to death on a hot dog. There's this conversation about death. Tony is being hyperbolic, crass Tony, and Eric is shocked. They're playing their parts. The vibe's not terrible, Tony's on, it's a funny conversation, and they have cheese. Tony goes out and smokes a cigarette, and he's on the phone for a while.

TODD LIEBLER: At one point, he went outside, probably to talk on the phone with Asia, and Eric turns to me and says, "What is wrong? What is going on here?"

And I said, "I don't know. I mean, he just had a massage, maybe bad things came out?" I was just very naive to what was going on.

MICHAEL STEED: He again says something kind of dickish to Josh, and I call Helen [Cho] and ask her, "Is there something up?" And she sends me the tabloid shit.*

HELEN CHO: Up to his very last few days, he was still posting Instagram stories of empty hotel rooms with soundtracks from films; he was telling about what had just happened, the [tabloid] pictures that came out. He posted a story with music from the film *Violent City*. It has a very ominous soundtrack. Essentially, it's a revenge film, a story about betrayal and revenge.

TODD LIEBLER: The crew had lunch afterward, and then the whole thing with Asia and the photographs came up, which made it a little more understandable. Although I did think that the paparazzi can turn the story into anything they want. And I was a little disappointed that Tony would get so swayed. My first thought was that Asia just couldn't handle that he was turning into this mushy little schoolboy, and she had to throw a wrench into the pot. Once I could see that the hurt was way more evident, I was more sympathetic to him.

Tony and Zach [Zamboni] had had a pretty good relationship. I felt that if Zach were there, he definitely would have reached out. But Zach wasn't there, and I felt compelled to reach out to Tony that evening. I texted, just saying, "Hey, it looked like you had a tough

---

* *While Tony was in Alsace, the Italian tabloid* Chi *published a series of romantically suggestive paparazzi photos of Asia with the French journalist Hugo Clement in Rome. The US tabloid* National Enquirer *informed Tony that it also intended to publish the photographs and asked for comment.*

day. I hope you're doing OK. Let me know if there's anything I can do." And I never heard back from him.

KIMBERLY WITHERSPOON: I still have the text. "I'll be OK." He wasn't picking up his telephone when I was calling him. He just kept saying he was coming home that Monday, and we would get together and talk about it when he got here, and that he was OK.

MICHAEL STEED: Next day, we're at this old French monastery and we're gonna shoot a meal and talk about the weirdness of Alsace. The meal is fine, and then—I remember it vividly—after the meal, he's looking over this valley; it's just idyllic, beautiful, and he's smoking a cigarette. I go out there and I say, "You all right, man? Are the tabloids just trying to fuck with y'all, or . . . ?"

He says to me, "A little fucking discretion. That's all I ask."

And I was just like, "Whoa, man, I just want to make sure you're—"

He says, "Not you. *Her.* I don't want to be on the fucking cover of these tabloids, and answer people's questions."

And that's all he said. That's the last I talked to him.

TODD LIEBLER: Friday morning, we were expecting Tony on set. We prepared the area, and we're waiting, and finally I just got up and started shooting B-roll. And I'm just double-checking where we set up all the flags, and stuff for the lights. And then I get this massive punch in my shoulder, and I turn around, and Mike Steed is already walking away, but gesturing for me to follow him. And he turned to me and said, "Tony hung himself."

And I asked, "Well, is he dead?" In that moment, I didn't know what that meant. And then when it was clear what had happened, we all just started walking around this location like fucking zombies, just completely lost and in shock. There was just disbelief and confusion. It was pretty fucking confusing.

CHRIS COLLINS: Mike called us [in New York] at three o'clock in the morning and said, "Tony's dead, and he hung himself."

JOSH FERRELL: We did HET [hazardous environment training] courses about kidnapping, about gunshot wounds, about getting sick, fires, catastrophes, monsoons—we talked about every single thing under the sun that could happen to us, as a crew, and this was the one thing we had never prepared for. That really fucked with me. I was always taking care of Tony, and that was on my shoot.

The day he died, the second scene we were supposed to do, and I had set this up—he had this thing about the Swiss, Switzerland; he feared them. So, with the permission of Mike [Steed], I organized a Swiss brass band to be playing music on the border, next to a bar in France where Eric and Tony were gonna be having a drink. They were going to be drowned out by the goddamn Swiss brass band. Wearing lederhosen. That was the second scene of that day. And Tony didn't know.

So there's all these little things I think about, like, *If he had only known.* Or, *Did he know?* But there was something about that shoot—like the tandem bike thing—it just makes it all worse. All that shit, it was such a comic gag, and it was so fucked up, in hindsight. Because he was so not happy.

TODD LIEBLER: As the elder person on the crew, and maybe the fact that I'm a dad, I definitely felt responsible for the crew. My default was to take care of other people. It's easier, because you don't have to deal with whatever it is inside yourself. I really didn't fucking lose it until I got on the airplane back home.

MICHAEL STEED: I qualify this, knowing there's nothing I could have done, but in retrospect, I wish I had talked to him more. I'm a believer in chaos, so two more seconds with him, and he doesn't decide to walk into a bathroom and do what he did. I wrestle with that.

After his death, this thing kept rolling in my head, where it's like, *I think I killed Tony.* It was always kind of a joke, *Which producer kills Tony?* Or, *Which director kills Tony?* But it's me.[*]

---

[*] *In September 2018, Argento gave an interview to the UK* Daily Mail *in which she disputed the notion that Tony had taken his life because of the photographs in the tabloids in June of that year.*

58

"IT'S HARD TO SEE THINGS AS THEY REALLY ARE"

MICHAEL STEED: Tony was as depressed as anyone with his eyes open. If you travel the world and you see shit, if you're not depressed on some level, you're a fucking sociopath. He was a weird combination of really self-involved but an empath, which is why people fucking loved him.

MORGAN FALLON: It's hard to be around someone of such extraordinary stature, such a high-powered mind, and be able to see things clearly. It's kind of like how a neutron star will bend light; it's hard to see things as they really are.

LYDIA TENAGLIA: I always suspected that we would get a call that Tony died. I didn't think it would be by his own hand. I thought it was going to be an accident, or that he had a heart attack. I did not anticipate "he hung himself." That was hard to understand.

CHRIS COLLINS: We got lulled into what we experienced for two decades; we knew how this thing went down. We understood [his relationship] would end, and there would be a blast zone, and a number of people would be in that blast zone. We would do what we always did: you wipe it off, you pick him up, and you move on. We didn't get the opportunity.

I didn't believe that Tony had the ability to do what he did. I did not see him possessing that kind of facility to end it himself. He just wasn't that guy, and I don't even know who that guy is, but I knew my friend Tony was . . . there was a certain narcissism that would not allow him to do something like that.

LYDIA TENAGLIA: He never liked looking like a rube. I don't know. Who knows? I think he was profoundly hurt, and profoundly disappointed, and profoundly humiliated, and he probably had a moment of epiphany, that he had just fucking leveraged his whole life, his reputation, his words, his family, his money. I think it was just kind of like, *I'm done, I'm exhausted.*

CHRIS COLLINS: It's an inability to break. He did not die of a broken heart. He would still be here if he allowed his heart to be broken, I think. That's what you do, you break and then you mend, and he couldn't break this time.

JARED ANDRUKANIS: He was always a good time. Like, even if it was a bad time and shit was a mess, it's still going to be a good time because he's there. He's going to find some sort of dark humor in the most terrible situation. Crack a joke. Say something. And that made me feel like we were indestructible as a team. Like no matter how bad it got, we were gonna be OK.

But something changed at the end. And I didn't like him as much, as someone who was madly in love. I didn't like seeing how it was changing him and how he interacted with us.

I liked him better when he was just kind of living his best life and looking in the rearview mirror like he stole something. This beautiful life that he had, something people would dream of, and no one else could do it but him. A "slit my wrist" love story is just the shittiest ending to it all.

The wheels flew off. One of the laments, for us, was we were just getting really good. He was just getting really, really good. But I guess the thing he was missing, the work could not provide it for him.

NICK BRIGDEN: He had stepped in quicksand; it was apparent. When he did get sucked down very quickly, and took his own life, it was shocking. It was surreal, because he was such a fucking fighter.

NARI KYE: Honestly, when I first heard about it, I was like, *This is foul play.* I thought someone had murdered him, because it was so unlike him. It was on a shoot, and he was someone who was so perpetually professional. The guy who's an hour early for call time. It was so unlike him, with Eric in the next room and his crew staying at the hotel.

We would always joke that he was like Keith Richards. Someone who's smoked crack and done heroin and traveled three hundred days a year and, you know, eats butter for a living. He felt immortal.

MATT WALSH: I thought he was invincible. He was such a powerful mind, such a strong spirit, I thought he was bulletproof.

DAVID SIMON: When it happened, it made no sense. I'm certainly not of the opinion that anyone is obliged to pursue the logic of any relationship with anybody, based on the idea that somebody's going to take their own life, whether those are the stakes. Those can't be the stakes for anybody in any personal relationship. Nobody's responsible for anyone.

If [his relationship] was ending, or it wasn't on the terms he thought it was, or if something had changed, he was in some hotel room alone, and he feels a level of exhaustion for having committed so deeply and having made choices in life—he'd expressed some pain to me about where it left his daughter and him, and his struggles to work back toward her, to right the ship. He was not oblivious to it. He said, "She's mad at this, and she has a right to be. I have to work with that. It's my job."

ANDERSON COOPER: My brother died by suicide when he was twenty-three and I was twenty-one. I'm aware of the punch-in-the-gut feeling of this information. Very rarely am I surprised by something that somebody does. I think we are all capable of anything.

I know with any suicide, there are people who are just stunned by it and say, well, "This person would never have done that," or, "He was the last person I would think would do that."

That's what people think, but in reality, a few things going wrong in a certain order can result in somebody doing something that most people would never think that he would do. And so, when I heard, I understood. As somebody who's spent a lot of time traveling around the world, with and without camera crews, and spent a lot of time in hotel rooms by myself, in places far away, I understood how that can happen. And it just made me so sad.

JOSH HOMME: When I saw that fucking [tabloid] photo, and I didn't reach out—boy, I really wish I had. I was so mad. Because it was like [*snaps fingers*], "See?!" and not like, "I told you so," but like, "Now you *know*."

BILL BUFORD: When these [paparazzi] pictures appeared, I just thought he would plummet, he would just plummet. *He's publicly exposed. He's publicly vulnerable.* And it hit all kinds of things that I don't understand, but I think I've glimpsed that he kind of—he short-circuits.

DAVE MCMILLAN: Listen: if you're in the best mood, if you're at a great place, and this person you deeply love cheats on you, and you're just a regular person, and only five people know, it's fucking awful.

He not only got cheated on; he got cheated on and ten million people are gonna know tomorrow. The social pressure of that makes it super easy to put a rope on that beam and to jump off that table.

NANCY BOURDAIN: Tony could be very possessive of— He was a control freak. He just—he liked control. That was the only thing I have to say about his suicide that makes sense, the control aspect.

JOEL ROSE: I knew him for so long, and I know that he would want to be in control. And he was in control. But I've always had, since it's happened, I've had this overwhelming feeling that he committed himself to this, the act of taking his own life, and then said, "Oh, fuck, what have I done?"

There was throwaway stuff, he'd make dark jokes, but when Kim called here to say that Tony was gone, it was like, "Tony who?" It seemed so unreal and so foreign to me. I had had an email exchange with him the day before, about the dedication to the book, and he seemed fine. The world is not better off with him not here. It's just not.

JOSH HOMME: I've said so many times, "I wish he'd called me," but it wouldn't have been in character for him to call me in a moment such as that. It wouldn't have been in the white-hotness of that moment. It was always after exiting, like, "I didn't have reception when I was totally depressed. But I got one bar now, and I'm feeling a little better. I'm feeling good enough to say something out loud to your ears." And clearly that was the case for everyone who didn't get a call, which is everyone.

He banded [all] these people, without banding them together. Maybe that's the problem. I didn't meet lots of these people till it was too late. Everyone had this striking similarity, that they felt they could have done something if he— No one was sharing info about him. And so, he had access to us all, we had access to him, but not each other. And so, there was no life raft. He was in a rowboat alone. And I fucking hate that. Because he wasn't alone. He just felt he was alone. He could have weathered that storm if he was on the life raft that he actually built.

ASHA GILL: He would only ever call me out of the blue when things weren't going so OK. The calls would be real Maydays. So I'm kind of fucking mad that, you know, there was no Mayday.

He just never wanted to be a burden on anyone. He was always just— He hid his pain very well. You could see it in the quiet moments. He walked a tightrope between both edges, and that's where his genius and his creativity was. Sometimes he could go a little bit too much into the sort of Edgar Allan Poe side of life, and then he could go in the others. And I'd see him finding the greatest joy in the simplest of things, and the simplest of things kind of catching him.

It was like he was trying to fill himself up with the world, which is one of his most beautiful traits—and I have not seen it in anybody else—just this childlike curiosity about things that hurt, as much as things that are tasty or beautiful or whatever.

And I still find it very hard that he took his own life. He kicked heroin; he went through fucking hell. He's a man of steel inside. Like, the grit to fucking find a way, man's not going to beat me down, I'm gonna find a way and do it myself.

For him to be, without the use of any narcotics or anything, driven to that point, I think that whatever was going on—he would have had to be at such a compromised place, with such massive conflict within him.

SANDY ZWEIG: I just feel like it was an impulsive decision. And Tony could be hyperbolic and sort of overly dramatic. I feel like there was some aspect of that, an impulsive decision that, in another moment, he might not have made.

PHILIPPE LAJAUNIE: When Tony died, it was very surprising, but at the same time, once I learned the background, then I was not surprised at all. Let's put it this way: no one can use drugs the way he was without being scarred deeply; one of the consequences is a lingering depression. Using drugs at that rate, and that kind of drugs [that Tony used] will alter your mental chemical balances, and will generate depression, from time to time.

FRED MORIN: He had just a weird darkness, you know? I don't think he was afraid. I think he had a metaphorical cyanide pill, under his tongue, at the ready, all his life, since he was very young.

DAVE MCMILLAN: When we were in Newfoundland, one of our best friends, John Bil, was in the end stages of cancer. So, of course, Fred wasn't in the best spirits when we were in Newfoundland, because he said, "What if John dies when I'm gone?"

We talked about that with Tony, and Tony was dismissive, completely, about the whole thing. He goes, "Ah, fuck that. I know what I'd do if I'd been given a few days to live: heroin. Give me a terminal diagnosis, and I know where I'm going." It was . . . insensitive.

JOHN LURIE: I wish I could have gotten to know him better, because I could have helped him, I think. I saw a thing that he was hiding, kind of a sadness, a thing—but he wouldn't let you get too close. There was just something behind the eyes, you could feel it, you know. But I would have gotten there. I mean, I'm relentless with that shit. I would have told him to run. At least to take some time [off]. But he almost couldn't go anywhere. I mean, they would know who he was everywhere.

JASON REZAIAN: I always think of Tony as a role model of somebody who started living his best life in middle age. The truth is, that there's a lot of people like that, but we just don't hear about it as much, right? We are so attracted to youth.

I can't pretend to know what led him to take his own life. Like anybody else, I have consumed lots and lots of analysis. I've purposefully not taken part in creating any of that analysis. What I preferred to analyze was the impact that he had on us, but also on Iranians, and other people whose voices he amplified. You get the sense that his life had a lot of chapters, and the chapters that we're associated with, I really hope that when he pondered them in the moment, and in retrospect, he felt really good about them, because he should.

W. KAMAU BELL: The last time we talked was in Nairobi, before we went to the airport [after wrapping the *Parts Unknown* Kenya episode]. We had different flights. He gave me his number and said, "When you're in New York, look me up. We'll go out to eat."

I didn't want to be the guy who's, like, actually taking him up on it. Now I feel I should have been the guy.

KAREN RINALDI: Loneliness kills. And you're thinking, how can you be lonely if you're beloved by all? He managed to cross all boundaries; that's what was amazing about Tony: Black, white, straight, gay, blue, red, anywhere in the world, he was able to cut through all that divisiveness. If you're that person, which would speak to a certain comfort with who you are, how does that person not reconcile with his sense of self and value in the world? And sometimes I wonder if he just had a moment where he's like, you know, fuck everybody. Because Tony also had that . . . just like, "You know what? I'm outta here."

I interviewed him for my book [*(It's Great to) Suck at Something*] in March 2018, just three months before [he died]. I was trying to unwind what it was to be cool. I went to the coolest of cool cats I've ever known, knowing that underneath it, I always thought of Tony as being incredibly nerdy. That's how I thought of him, that's how I felt about him, and my love for him was born from that knowledge of him.

ALISON MOSSHART: He was the coolest motherfucker I ever met.

KAREN RINALDI: The coolness, for me, was awesome to watch, and funny. "You're cool but I kind of know better; but let's talk about that." He got it immediately. My point was that cool is a mask for vulnerability. I talked about some of the research, and some of the theories of that. I remember thinking he understood immediately. It needed no explanation.

I'll put this out there first, since Bourdain was emphatic about one thing above all.

"Simply put?" he said. "I am not cool. I have never been cool."

Admitting to his fair share of recklessness in younger years to compensate for awkwardness, fear, and insecurity, Bourdain admitted that doing the most drugs, drinking the most alcohol, and trying to be badder than everybody else as a strategy for social acceptance was never successful. It didn't really make anyone cool. . . .

"I think cool suggests the absence of caring. . . . It's an almost sociopathic state—the ability to not give a shit about anything. . . . In my experience, people are foolishly attracted to people who know what they want. And when all you want is to play blues better than anyone else—or take heroin . . . that, dismayingly, has an appeal to those of us who struggle with our feelings, needs, and desires every day."

And yet, in spite of all that, we sometimes learn in the most painful way how vulnerability and the veneer of cool we project onto others can hide someone's darkest hour. On June 8, 2018, with the news of Tony having taken his own life, I was reminded that the labels we put onto others have no bearing on someone else's pain. The best we can do is to expose our own pain to daylight and pay attention to the twilight messages we might otherwise miss from our loved ones. [Karen Rinaldi, *(It's Great to) Suck at Something* (New York: Atria, 2019)]

Tony was a complicated guy. He was not an angel. Nobody who is . . . I mean, who the fuck is, right?

The interesting thing about Tony is, you thought he wasn't

paying attention, but he was, and he gave it back in a way that you weren't expecting or didn't understand, or maybe not in the way you wanted it, but he was there.

When I asked him for the interview, for example, for my book, part of me thought, *He's so busy, he's not going to be able to do this*, but it wasn't even a question.

He had this incredible generosity; he was generous and thoughtful and loyal. I felt like saying, "You're giving, but were you able to receive that back? Did you open up that door, too? It can't all be going out this way."

Not to say that he was selfless. I would never do the martyr thing with him; it's not who he was. It was just an interesting flow of loyalty and generosity and awareness. He was hypersensitive to people, which is a tough place to be, and then, could he accept back and feel that love, loyalty, generosity from others? Or was that valve closed? Whatever the wounds were that prevented him from possibly feeling that—it's speculation, who the fuck knows?

MIKE RUFFINO: About a week after he died, everybody was commiserating [in New York] and we all wound up walking by Les Halles, when they were dismantling all those letters and photographs, everything, the impromptu memorial [to Tony]. Just giant pieces of it in the dumpster, and I was standing there, taking it all in, as best I could. It was quite overwhelming. This guy walks by, pushing his shopping cart with everything he owns in it. And he stopped at me, for some reason, and said, "What's this, some kind of cook died? Argh, argh, argh, argh. What the fuck you doing here? What'd he ever do for you?"

SALLY FREEMAN: The thing with Tony was, people went to him for help. He was such a strong force. People used him as a kind of moral compass as to what they thought about things. I remember, when I heard the news that he'd died, I thought, *So many people have lost their anchor.*

DAVE CHANG: After he passed, I was reflective; I think all I wanted was to take from Tony; I never gave to Tony. In our relationship, there were moments when I should have spoken up, and I didn't, because he'd cut you right out of his life, too. That same vengeful Tony who was on your side when protecting you, he would turn it around on you, particularly to those he had known forever.

DANIEL HALPERN: There was always that reserve, and I think I always felt it. I didn't think he was suicidal. I never saw that side of him. I know there was a lot of self-hate, self-doubt, but I didn't think he would leave the world in that way. He should've been around for another thirty years.

You don't meet many people like that in your life, who can do what he was able to do, the ways in which he connected and didn't connect with people. Just being in his presence, as uncomfortable as it often was, was still always very special.

DEAN FERTITA: All I can speculate is, he's not feeling anything anymore. He was so deeply connected to his feelings, and love, and being able to share that with people, that if that was cut off, it was, "What do I do now?"

That idea of searching: maybe he was tired of searching for what to do. But I never felt like he was hinting at it. Maybe he felt alienated. But there was no amount of alienation that couldn't be repaired.

KIMBERLY WITHERSPOON: It would have been so interesting to see him age, instead of the choice that he made. Because, eventually, he would have stopped making so much television, and he might have sat at his desk longer.

And it could have been the meatiest [writing] of all, because he was living the life, right? He was living a big life. Whether he wrote another novel or nonfiction book, he would have had the time. And it would have been brilliant to read, because he could have drawn from everything he lived . . . I can imagine so many things he would have done brilliantly, with time.

ALISON MOSSHART: I don't know if all our detective work is going to figure out exactly what happened. I don't know if we're even allowed to know. Or if it's even our business. I don't know.

59

"HE WAS AN EXTRAORDINARY WITNESS AND VOICE FOR THE WORLD"

SANDY ZWEIG: It never occurred to me that we shouldn't finish the shows, you know? It just felt like we had to. There was so much that was good in those, and so much to put out into the world. We went to CNN, and they were like, "Yeah, sure, you know, if you guys can do it." And then it was figuring out what we do to fill the holes for the shows that never got shot or didn't get completed. And then the struggle, obviously, to do it without Tony's writing.

What was interesting was for the Kenya episode, which is the last one that he had written, he wrote these final thoughts:

Who gets to tell the stories? This is a question asked often.
The answer, in this case, for better or for worse, is, "I do."
At least this time out. I do my best. I look. I listen. But in

the end, I know: it's my story, not Kamau's, not Kenya's, or Kenyans'. Those stories are yet to be heard.

When he wrote that, both Mo [Fallon, the episode's director] and I were like, "Oh my god, we can't use this. It sounds so weird. Like, after this whole show with Kamau, for him to say, 'This is my show' seems so strange."

And then, of course, after he died, it just seemed perfect.

ANDERSON COOPER: It sounds odd to say, but he kind of gave me hope that there was a second and third act in life. I've often felt that I've been doing this job I'm doing, and this kind of work, for close to thirty years now. I'm fifty-three now. What's this gonna look like when I'm sixty-three? And I would look at Tony, and think, *Wow, he's doing the best work of his life.* There are other ways to tell stories. And look how he's doing it, look at the life he's living, and the adventures he's having, and the work he's creating, and the impact he's having. And I always looked at that, and I thought, *OK, that's a path; there is somebody who's doing something really interesting.*

MORGAN FALLON: He was an extraordinary witness and voice for the world. He was an extraordinary television producer. He was a storyteller. He understood the device of film and television better than any of us, and we were lucky that he was powerful enough and willing enough to take risks that we could really push the envelope of what we were doing. For those reasons, and a few others, that will never happen again.

NICK BRIGDEN: There's not a day that goes by, like, even when I'm editing—you can send it out into the world, and get feedback, but there's always that hum underneath: "Is this any good?" And that's always Tony's voice. He's become part of my compass.

NIGELLA LAWSON: I've experienced living through people's illness, and then dying, and it takes you a long time afterward to remember them not ill. And when you remember [them] at last as not ill, you feel something's been given to you. And I find it hard now to think of Tony in a way that isn't really very focused on the end. I feel the shock has slightly taken the other pictures away.

CHRISTIANE AMANPOUR: He must have hidden so much, and the pain of hiding, or being stuck in a situation that even Tony Bourdain felt he couldn't get out of—to me that is a profound tragedy.

His loss is really profound, and it really is meaningful, even in our warp-speed society, in which you can barely process and digest one thing that happens, no matter how profound or how simple, [before] something else comes along to distract you. I think that we can't get over it, and I think we're not over it yet. And I think the world really misses Tony Bourdain, whether it knows it or not, what he provided, and the places he took us every week on CNN, and before that in his other incarnations. It's something that's really missing in our world, particularly if you look at the overwhelming focus, in our media, on just the politics, and on just the person of the president. For many people, it's an exhausting and partisan and often toxic environment. What Tony delivered was the exact antidote, without being overtly political, but just being about humanity and community and people. It was what we needed, and we don't have that now.

JEFF ZUCKER: We haven't been able to, and nor do I think we will be able to, ever replace Tony Bourdain.

AMY ENTELIS: The humanity that he exposed during his storytelling . . . people learn from that and aspire to be as good as he was, which is probably impossible. So many people walk in our door and say—and this was even when he was alive—"I want to be the Tony Bourdain of religion. I want to be the Tony Bourdain of music. I want to be the Tony Bourdain of sports."

And that just tells you that he invented something, and it resonated with people, to the degree that everybody wants to take what they learned from him and apply it to their singular passion. So, we get a lot of that. We roll our eyes a little bit, but in the end, it's really a tribute to him, and how he affected people.

LIZZIE FOX: Once a week, at least, I get a pitch for "The Bourdain of———" Once a fucking week. It was laughable in the beginning, but now I get pissed. You don't have "the Bourdain." It's lightning in a bottle. He created an entire genre of TV that people, for years, have been trying to mimic and capture.

MORGAN FALLON: It's the most ridiculous thing, all the time, I hear people pitching, "It's the Bourdain of this, it's the Bourdain of that." What we did wasn't a method of television producing; it was a method of television producing *with Tony*. And without that element, it will never happen again. Everyone needs to get fucking over it and move on. Don't pitch that shit to me anymore. It's gone.

ALEX LOWRY: Every call I get for showrunning something, they say, "It's the Bourdain of"—insert whatever fucking thing here—but you can't ever have that, because you don't have Bourdain. Sure, I can give you a travel show where it's based around medicine, or drinking, or motorcycles, or art, but unless you have that person, you're just not gonna have "the Bourdain." He was the essence of the whole thing.

DAVE MCMILLAN: When Tony passed away, we figured out that the internet is different, that Twitter is a shittier place. He had a kind of hold over the restaurant [world], the chefdom, you know? And then after, everybody had this fucking self-confidence to mouth off.

There's no interest to be on Twitter after Tony. None. It's useless. It's just a bunch of barking dogs. Tony was always watching, waiting for opportunities to strike like a cobra. Like, when Tony would come out with a good tweet, it would be like, *Agh, bodies everywhere.* It was amazing, you know? He could drop the hammer and make things right.

JOEL ROSE: One of last meals we had together, we went to Papaya King, the three of us, me, Tony, and Ariane. And that kid is—she's impressive. I know he loved her.

HELEN CHO: I think it's important for people to know how much he loved his daughter. She was the world to him. His mistakes, and the terrible choices he made in the last years of his life, do not reflect or equate to the amount of love he had for her. I saw him as a really loving father. I saw him just be really silly, and happily make himself be a fool just for her, just to make her laugh. He'd do anything to make her happy, and was just so proud of her and proud to be her dad. And he'd be so proud of her today.

ARIANE BUSIA-BOURDAIN: I want people to remember my dad as a person who would just open people up to a world outside their apartments, or wherever they're living, and show them that there's another side of the world, they might not even know it. And someone who makes people not afraid to explore and adventure into new things, and do new things, and not to be so scared, but to be very open-minded about everything.

It wasn't until he died that I realized how important he was to some people. I had no clue he was this important or famous or whatever. I didn't know that he really meant something to some people. People who didn't even know him sometimes acted like it was a best friend who died. On TV, he kind of acted like he was your best friend, taking you around the world.

With me, of course, he would always try and show me the world around me, by [helping] me experience new foods and new things, telling me about his trips. That's how I experienced him. And, of course, I would see him on television, and from people's feedback, I could hear that he inspired them a lot, too.

ACKNOWLEDGMENTS

First, my endless gratitude to Tony, who gave me the best opportunities and brought so many people together in love and weirdness and solidarity and tragedy and comedy. I wish that he were still here to bask in all that reflected glory, to borrow one of his favorite turns of phrase.

Thank you to all the people who told me their stories about Tony. And special thanks to Christopher Bourdain, Nancy Bourdain, Ottavia Busia-Bourdain, Helen Lang, and Rennik Soholt for sharing their photos.

Thank you to Kimberly Witherspoon and Jessica Mileo at Ink-Well Management, who keep the world turning forward or, as Kim likes to say, "onward." And thanks to Daniel Halpern for saying yes, and being right.

Thank you to the excellent publishing team at Ecco, especially Helen Atsma, Sonya Cheuse, Meghan Deans, Gabriella Doob, Ashlyn Edwards, Miriam Parker, Allison Saltzman, and Rachel Sargent, for all their hard work that helps turn an idea into a real live book.

Thank you to advance readers Nathan Thornburgh and Alicia Tobin, whose thoughtful feedback made this book better.

And thank you to my parents, my sister, and my son, for their unwavering presence, love, and support.

INDEX OF CONTRIBUTORS

Note: Page numbers in parentheses indicate intermittent references.